THE COMPLETE BOOK OF
FLOAT FISHING

● *A bream safely in the net. Note how the fish is being drawn towards the net with its head just clear of the water*

Allan Haines
THE COMPLETE BOOK OF
FLOAT
FISHING

DAVID & CHARLES
Newton Abbot   London

FIELDSPORTS AND FISHING TITLES FROM DAVID & CHARLES

© Allan Haines 1989

British Library Cataloguing in Publication Data

Haines, Allan
   The complete book of float fishing.
   1. Float fishing
   I. Title
   799.1′2

   ISBN 0-7153-9356-1

First published 1989
Reprinted 1991

Typeset by Typesetters (Birmingham) Limited
Smethwick West Midlands
and printed in Great Britain
by Butler & Tanner Limited Frome and London
for David & Charles
Brunel House Newton Abbot Devon

● *(pp2–3) A peaceful swim and an angler well hidden
from the fish's view by the high bank behind and weed
cover on either side*

Contents

Introduction

There can be few anglers who didn't begin their fishing years by watching a float, usually a fat-bodied and under-shotted specimen, being towed along by some suicidal fish that should have known better. Yet even with such crude tackle the magic of watching a float was then already beginning to work, hooking the angler to a method of fishing which cannot be beaten for the sheer excitement and satisfaction that it provides.

Done well, float fishing is an art. Just watch a top match angler cast a float with great accuracy and then concentrate on the minute tip, striking at a movement barely noticeable by the untrained eye, before playing and landing a catch on fine tackle and a small hook. With patience, thought and practice this skill can be obtained. With it will come the pleasure of knowing you are in total control and able to deceive fish by presenting your bait in a delicate and natural fashion.

Float fishing is a method capable of catching every species of freshwater fish, from mighty carp and tench to tiny gudgeon and bleak. It will tackle farm pond, canal or powerful river with the same effectiveness, and works so well because it is positioned as close as possible to the baited hook and, done correctly, is an extremely sensitive means of bite indication. Floats themselves become part of the angler. They are cherished and cared for, and no matter how many are collected over the years there will always be those old favourites which get first choice. The spin-off, too, is that once well learned, float fishing skills can be applied to other methods. The casting accuracy and understanding of good presentation principles will also make the angler effective with leger or fly rod – in fact there is an old saying among trout anglers that a good coarse fisher usually makes a first-class fly angler.

Although much of this book is concerned with the rigs and floats required to tackle different waters, the need cannot be over-emphasised for the care of and attention to detail regarding rods, reels, tackle and bait. All are of vital importance and play key roles in ensuring that the very best results are obtained under prevailing conditions.

Float fishing, like any skill, takes time to learn well. Use proven methods as the foundation on which to develop your own ideas. Never give up, be prepared to try something new and to listen to the ideas of others. Fishing with a float is a sport in which you never stop learning – perhaps this is what makes it all the more fascinating. For fascinating it is. A float tip registering a bite is something very special and the end product of having mastered the finest angling art of them all – float fishing.

This book will provide most of the answers and hopefully help avoid the many pitfalls but it is you, the angler, who will ultimately decide your own level of success. There are no short cuts.

Allan Haines

1
Tackle

Good presentation is the key to successful float fishing. No matter what float, rod, reel or terminal tackle is used, fish will not respond if a bait is put to them in an unnatural manner. Being able to achieve this most vital of all angling requirements takes skills that can only be gained through experience and practice.

● *A pleasant day for float fishing but a slight ripple on the surface may have helped improve catches*

RODS

Using the right tackle will of course make life a lot easier, and in any type of angling will ensure a higher success rate. Getting everything balanced and in proportion to the job in hand is fairly obvious. In the case of hook size and line strength this should pose few problems to any angler with even limited knowledge. Understanding the need for the right rod is a little more involved.

Development in rod material and design has been rapid since glassfibre became widely used in the late 1950s. Early glassfibre rods still retained the old brass ferrules of the cane rod era and blank diameters were only slightly reduced. Then came the first glass to glass joints and a gradual reduction in both weight and diameter. This was the break-through that has led to the rods we enjoy today. After glass came carbon fibre – again, early models left a lot to be desired when compared with the finely balanced tackle we have today. Rods broke with alarming regularity and some of the actions were poker-stiff and would not allow fine lines to be used with any degree of confidence.

How all these developments have affected the actual look of the rod is easy enough to see. Diameters have been reduced dramatically and this is of tremendous benefit to the float angler since a smaller diameter means there is less wind resistance on both the cast and the strike. The result is, longer casting and a better bite-to-hooking ratio. But don't get carried away with slimness – there are some pretty poor rods around that look perfect. And if your budget is limited don't be afraid to go for a composite rod just because it doesn't look as slim as its more expensive brothers. Generally speaking you get what you pay for when it comes to float rods – there are bad carbons, borons and kevlar jobs, as well as good and in fact some of the composites are excellent value and should not be overlooked.

Perhaps a word here about carbon content would not go amiss. All carbon rods have some fibre glass content, a minimum of about 4 per cent. This is an essential part of the rod's construction and has no

● *Carbon cloth being rolled into rods. Some will have a high proportion of fibre glass and are used to produce composite rods*

adverse effect. However, watch out for very cheap carbons which may be made from a high proportion of much cheaper glass.

Balance is very important, possibly more so than weight, although you must remember you could be holding a rod for five or six hours at a time so if the weight is beyond reasonable limits pass on to another model. Check first of all by fitting your reel so that there is just a couple of inches protruding beyond your elbow when the hand is wrapped around the reel stem and the forearm is laid along the handle – if all is well the rod and reel should feel balanced. If the rod feels tip-heavy and you have to make adjustments by moving the reel nearer the front of the handle, the balance is poor. Having to stick several inches of butt beyond the elbow in order to achieve a balance is just wasting rod length and should not be tolerated. It is possible to compensate for tip-heavy balance by adding some

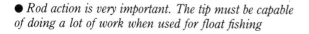

● *Rod action is very important. The tip must be capable of doing a lot of work when used for float fishing*

● *Check the rod handle protrudes about 2 or 3in beyond the elbow when the hand is touching the reel and everything is balanced*

lead to the inside of the butt. However, add too much and you will end up with a rod that is balanced, but heavy and rather difficult to handle on the strike.

If all is well so far, check how your hand feels on the handle. A rod is like a good suit, it must fit properly all round. See that your hand wraps comfortably around the diameter. If the handle is too large or too slim it will make your fingers ache after a few hours' use. Choice of handle material is again a personal one. I prefer natural cork but there is nothing really wrong with sheet cork composite or the EVA type materials, though watch for the EVA that is often used on cheap rods as it does tend to fall apart very quickly.

Actual finish on modern rods is not that important. The fibres are not in need of protection from rotting as were the old cane rods. In fact there was a trend towards not varnishing at all, except for the ring whippings, but this makes for a rather untidy-looking

rod – again a personal thing. Matt finish is a good idea since it cuts down the fish-scaring flash that is so evident from a highly glossed and varnished rod. Check, however, that the whipping has been given a good coating, otherwise you may very soon be faced with rings dropping off.

Ring spacing is vitally important on a float rod if the best is to be had from its action. Too many rings in the tip sections will cause a rod to become sloppy and tip-heavy; too few, and the line will not follow the true contour of the rod when a fish is being played, and it will be difficult to prevent bows forming between the rings thus reducing the efficiency of the strike.

Checking that there are sufficient rings is simple enough: thread a line through them and get someone to pull so as to bring the tip down to form a big bend. Now check that the line follows a close path alongside the rod – if there are any obvious sharp angles the spacing is at fault, and the rings may need to be moved around in order to get everything right. If you think you have found the right rod, there is nothing wrong with altering the ringing if you feel confident enough.

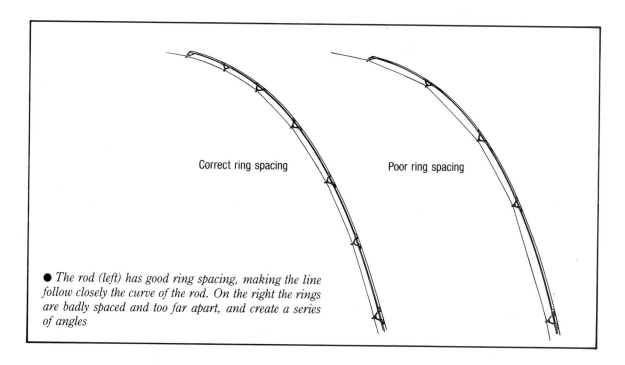

Correct ring spacing   Poor ring spacing

● *The rod (left) has good ring spacing, making the line follow closely the curve of the rod. On the right the rings are badly spaced and too far apart, and create a series of angles*

Check, too, at the butt end that the largest ring is close enough to the reel to keep the line under control; it may be necessary to make some adjustment or addition here, too. The closer the ring is to the reel – assuming you will be using a fixed spool – the larger the ring needs to be in order to allow line to flow freely off the reel and down the rod in a series of spiralling loops.

Choice of ring comes down to a few patterns, and again, like so much in rod selection, is a personal one. Conventional stand-off rings are generally a good choice. Whether or not they are lined does not really matter, and there are arguments for and against. Trend has been towards smaller and smaller rod rings, but too small and the line has a tendency to stick to the rod in wet weather. However, on very fine-tipped rods tiny rings are necessary otherwise the action becomes sloppy. Single-legged patterns are said to have less effect on the action.

If all is fine so far, we must next consider the job our rod will be required to do – it is pointless choosing a rod that is suited to a canal if most fishing is to be done with a waggler on big waters. Length is, of course, one important factor. Here again, modern materials have done much to eliminate the need for short rods. My own favourites are all thirteen-footers, and as a general guide this is the best length to begin with. Anything longer and the action seems to suffer, any shorter and you are imposing an unnecessary handicap on yourself. I would make only one exception to this 13ft rule: if I was likely to be fishing very deep waters on a regular basis I might go up to 14ft.

Rod Care

Caring for your rods is easy. In fact, all that's really needed is a regular check that all the rings are sound and have not become grooved through constant use. Replace any at the first sign of tiny marks forming (of course, this only applies to non-lined types). Ceramic linings need to be watched for chipping.

Keep varnish on the whippings in good order, and freshen up the cork handle by giving it a good scrub with warm water and then when dry a gentle rub over with fine glasspaper.

Ferrules, or more correctly joints, need to be kept clean and free from dirt. Give them a regular wipe over with a soft damp cloth. The rod itself benefits from a regular rub-down with a little furniture polish; this keeps it looking good and also prevents line sticking in the wet.

● *Many rods are made in the Far East but this Taiwanese angler is struggling to keep control over a hooked fish because his rod is too short*

So, having settled for 13ft, the action must be considered. Basically, float fishing calls for two sorts of action: firstly, a very stiff rod with a tip action in the first half of the top section; and secondly, a slightly softer action with less 'tip'. The first rod will be used for close-in work with light floats, in particular stick floats and on running water; the softer rod must not be sloppy, but must have just a slightly more 'through' feel to it. That is to say, the action will come through the top section further than in the first rod; this will be used for fishing wagglers and floats carrying a much greater shot load, usually at long range.

The fastest rod, with the tip action, is likely to have a splice in its first section, giving a fast and positive strike; essential for hitting those fast-biting, running water fish. In general, however, watch out for splices – they have a habit of producing a flat spot in the action which can result in a fish being 'bumped off' on the strike.

The waggler rod needs to be softer in order to prevent breaking when casting long distances, and the strike it produces will be more of a through movement, not a short, sharp and very fast reaction. But when looking for these actions don't expect to find a great deal of difference between the two.

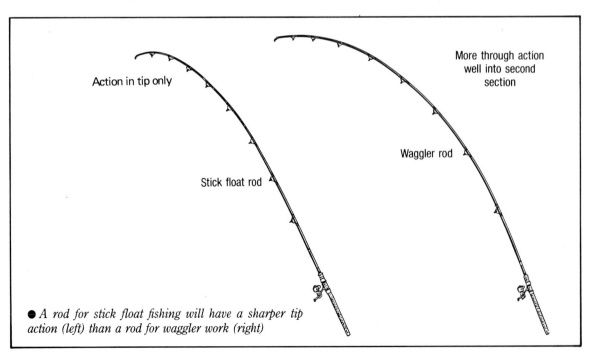

Action in tip only

More through action
well into second
section

Waggler rod

Stick float rod

● *A rod for stick float fishing will have a sharper tip action (left) than a rod for waggler work (right)*

REELS

Just as the wrong rod can make life difficult for the float angler, so can a reel that is either badly designed or maybe just not suited to the job it is being asked to perform. Like rods, reels have undergone a lot of change during recent years. The influence of Japan, Korea and Taiwan has added to the diversification and also contributed a lot towards a gradual improvement; it has certainly widened the choice to a degree where only the best will survive.

Finding the right reel for float fishing is something that should not be hurried. Nor should a purchase be made on the strength of some flashy piece of engineering that will probably turn out to be nothing more than a hindrance later on – the best reel is often the simplest. It will have smooth lines, with no protruding knobs, screws or buttons that will, sooner or later, catch on the line.

Body material can be either metal or a fibre such as carbon – the difference will be in weight and price. Both materials work equally well in terms of fishing ability, with carbon having the edge on weight reduction. But don't be led into the trap of buying a small model just to save on weight. The miniature reels now available have very limited use, and it is far better to keep to the more standard sizes.

First choice must be a fixed spool reel, for this type will cope with just about any float fishing situation, although centre pins and closed-face models do have their uses. Spare spools must be available, and ideally in a shallow form that will take no more than a 100 metres of, say, 2½lb line. Any deeper, and you will need to back them up for general purpose float work. And while you are looking at the spools, check that the release system does not demand a protruding button on the front face. Such a button was a feature of the old-style Mitchell reel and always led to line picking up around it and tangling into a great ball. I cured mine by grinding down the buttons until they were flush with the front face. Mitchell later modified the fault and all is now well with its design.

A push-button or snap-off spool is far better than one that has to be removed by means of any form of screw. Taking things off on the bank usually results in the loose bit falling into the water. Spool width should also be generous. A wide spool will give

● *The reel spool on the right is correctly loaded with line and has a smooth front profile free of protrusions which could cause line to snag. The one on the left is both underloaded and has a protruding button on the face*

smoother line flow during casting, a vital factor if float fishing is to be efficient.

Actual design can be either with a normal spool, which locates inside the revolving bale arm carrier; or the skirted variety which sits over the carrier and reduces the chances of line blowing inside and behind the spool. Most of the latest designs are of this skirted type, and I must admit to having a personal liking for them.

While looking at the front end of the reel it will pay to consider the actual bale arm. This part of the reel will be heavily stressed over the seasons; it will carry mile after mile of line back onto the spool and will be subjected to enormous wear and tear. A roller will reduce this wear, and the damage that can be caused through friction to fine line – though do check it to make sure it does actually roll. There are a few around that fail miserably. Although the roller must be free-running, it must not have end float between which line could become trapped; again, take time to check.

Open and close the pick-up a few times, too – it should respond smartly, but not snap shut like a rat trap. It is worth asking the dealer if he stocks spares such as springs. Some of the best manufacturers include them with a new reel, which is even better.

Arguments rage about the values of manual or automatic bale arms. I have used both, and at one time would entertain nothing but an automatic for float fishing, but it is very much a matter of personal choice. The auto system is possibly faster and of

● *This type of 'T' handle is best on larger versions of reel*

One development that has not always worked well concerns the ever-increasing speed of reels. At one time a reel with a gear ratio of 3 to 1 was considered fast, but gearing has constantly risen to produce really high-speed versions; this results in a reel that feels stiff since it has to be turned through steep gearing much like riding a cycle in top gear. Fast reels cause other problems, too, and are prone to causing the hook or bait to spin through the water on the retrieve. This results in the line twisting and ending up in an annoying tangle. A ratio of up to about 6 to 1 is possibly the fastest I would want, and even then it takes a little self-control not to crank the handle round too fast.

And talking of handles, many new reels come with the 'T' style, once reserved for the larger models as used for carp and pike. These are fine, although sometimes they feel rather cumbersome; I prefer the simple round or flat-ended type for float work. After all, the handle needs to be just large enough to be held by finger and thumb.

It goes without saying that a handle that folds down neatly is less likely to get damaged when dumped into a tackle box – and let's confess, we all get a bit careless or untidy at some time or another. The important thing with folding handles is to get the sort that snap back into place firmly and cannot disengage themselves just at the vital moment.

Reel designers seem to have spent a lot of time developing drag systems that allow the angler to make an accurate setting at which line will be pulled off the spool with the bale arm closed. In fact, such a facility merely takes the responsibility off the angler when playing a fish. Drag and clutches are fine for the big fish boys, but really the float angler can get along fine without them. Usually mine are screwed down hard since I prefer to play fish off the handle, believing a well-looked-after reel and a sensitive

greatest interest to match anglers. Most work by a 'finger dab' principle, which means the bale is pressed down slightly with the forefinger to release it from its location. The finger releases the bale, allowing it to open as the cast is made. The idea works well, but choice is still limited to just a small number of models.

The important thing is to find a reel that has a sound bale arm which works smartly and efficiently every time. It need not be fancy, and like other parts of the reel's profile should be designed so as not to cause snagging – if you can find an edge or screw that looks as if it might catch, the chances are it will.

Much has been said about the direction in which a bale arm should rotate, and there is certainly some merit in one that carries line towards, rather than away from the forefinger as it rests across the leading edge of the spool. If it rotates to bring line towards the finger it will be easier to fish with the bale open while running line off under finger control, as may need to be done on running water.

● *Plenty of choice, but appearance is no guide to what will prove to be the best float (Chapter 2)*
● *(below right) A nice set of canal darts. The base is partly loaded to give good casting qualities and a fine tip gives good bite registration (Chapter 6)*
● *(far right) A fine range of conventional stick floats. The stems are made from heavy woods such as cane or lignum to balance the light balsa of the upper body section (Chapter 6)*

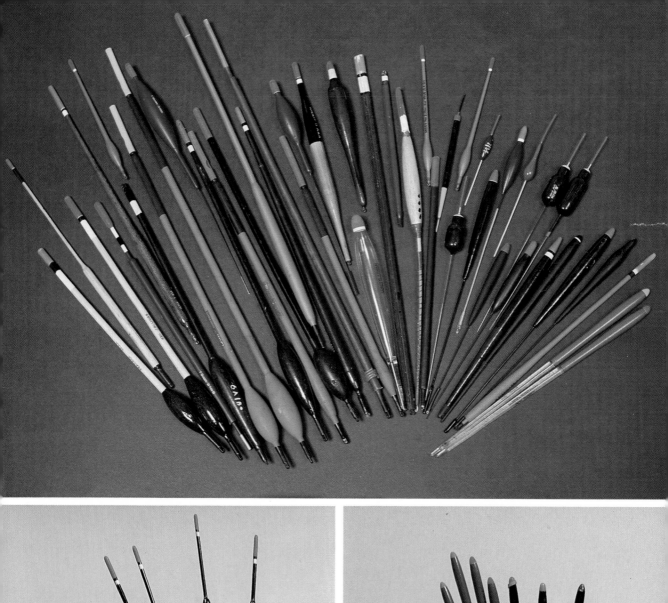

hand will out-perform even the best clutch every time.

Clutches and drags do, however, come in handy if you are fishing at long range with heavy float tackle and have to strike really hard to take up line stretch and any slight bow that may have formed. In such cases a setting that will prevent a break is a bonus. My only advice is – don't get too dependent on them.

To check a drag in the shop, screw it down fairly hard and then unscrew it one setting at a time, turning the spool rim with your fingers after each adjustment. If the drag is coming off correctly and in small stages, each turn of the spool will get a little easier. If it comes off in big leaps, the clutch is of poor quality.

Location of the drag setting knob can vary a lot from reel to reel. The first types were on the front face of the spool and worked through a series of clutch washers built into the spool. These worked well enough, but making adjustments meant you had to fiddle around at the front of the reel – not a good idea if you were playing a fish at the time. Side location, usually as an integral part of the handle spindle, is another possibility. Positioning is reasonable enough, but some of this type can be a little difficult to set accurately.

Possibly the version that has made most friends is the rear drag. With this set-up the adjustment knob is right at the back of the reel body and works through the main spindle which carries the gearing. They can, if well made, be adjusted with considerable accuracy and are easy to re-set while playing a fish.

Closed-face reels

Before we leave fixed spool reels it is worth looking at 'closed-face' varieties, where the spool is completely surrounded by a housing inside which is another similar-shaped piece carrying a pin. This is the line pick-up pin which acts in the same manner as a bale arm; its sole function is to engage the line and carry it around the spool. The pin is released by pressing the forefinger against a circular catch on the front of the reel.

● *Ray Mumford with a fine catch, proving that his style of camouflaged floats does work (Chapter 2)*

● *A well-designed rear drag knob is the easiest means of tension adjustment*

● *A closed-face reel has many advantages over a conventional fixed spool and also a number of design characteristics which sometimes work against the float angler*

Tackle

First thing to check with a closed-face is that you can actually reach the release button when the reel is on a rod handle and you are holding it normally. If you can't perform this operation without having to stretch, the reel is not for you.

One advantage of a closed-face over a conventional fixed spool is that the line is buried away inside the housing where it is less affected by wind – a big advantage when fishing against a headwind. And because there is no bale arm to snap over, a closed-face can be fished well on running water – in this situation the pick-up pin is left disengaged and line

● *The release button of a closed-face must be easy to reach when the hand is wrapped around the handle*

● *Two excellent centre pin reels. Note how line on the darkest one is loaded to one side*

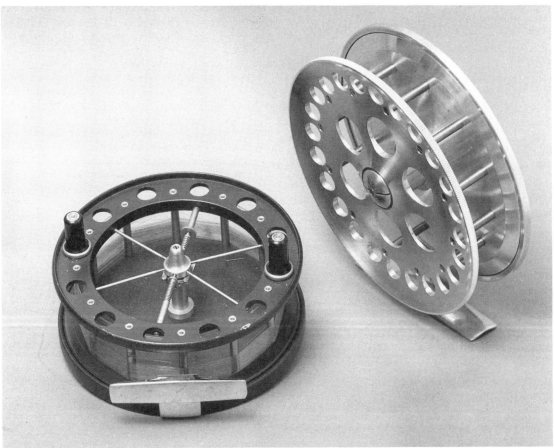

allowed to run off under finger control. Once a bite is seen the finger traps the line and the handle is turned to locate the pin. It is even possible to strike directly against the pin just by turning the reel handle.

Sounds fine so far, and without doubt a closed-face is a vital part of a good all-round float angler's kit, but they also have a few drawbacks. For a start the spools are usually narrow, so line does tend to 'bed in' if too much is loaded on. This is especially evident when you have been fishing for some time and maybe a few big fish have put pressure on. The result is, line sticks as the cast is made and distance is lost.

Some anglers have been using closed-face reels for years without trouble while others have cursed them from their first outing. Perhaps it is fair to say that they are fine under the right conditions, but the very nature of their design has some inbuilt limitations. As a rule, consider them best for close-in float fishing on running water or on those days when wind conditions are really bad.

The centre pin

Finally, the centre pin: the father of all reels and one that still has its uses. When it comes to sensitivity and angling pleasure you will find one hard to beat. It is, however, a fact that mastering one so that fishing is not handicapped is an art. Unfortunately the advent of the fixed spool has meant that much of this skill has been lost in a generation that was never obliged to use anything else.

For trotting and close work the centre pin is master. It allows the angler to control tackle perfectly, inching it delicately through a swim. There are no bale arms or pick-up pins to worry about, you are in direct control at all times. Limitations begin when distance is the order. Only a very good centre pin angler can hope to perform anywhere near as well as even an average fixed spool user. If you can find a really good 'pin' it is worth having one in your box for those odd occasions when you need something just a bit more refined, or maybe just fancy a change. After all, fishing is about pleasure, and being able to master a centre pin and enjoy the superb presentation it can achieve is pleasure enough.

Reel Care

Like any piece of precision equipment, reels will work best if cared for properly. Leave them caked in groundbait or dump them wet into your box and forget about them until the next weekend and they will, sooner or later, let you down. Corrosion is the biggest enemy, and while modern materials have done much to make our life easier, a few moment's work will pay dividends in the long term.

Manufacturers of reels try to make them 'idiot proof' before they leave the factory. This usually includes packing them with grease in the hope that even if totally neglected they will continue to work with some degree of efficiency. That's fine if you are an 'idiot', but as a float angler you don't want all that built-in stiffness. So begin by stripping down the works and washing out all that grease with paraffin. Next, lubricate everything with a fine oil – sewing machine oil or fine cycle oil is ideal. There is also a non-spreading oil available which is specially for reels, but I have never bothered to use it and don't feel I've suffered as a result.

Oil everything that moves, but try not to splash it about so that it can find its way onto the line or over areas where your hands will go. Fish will not appreciate an oil-tainted bait. Having stripped off all that grease, you have made yourself more work, since you will now have to clean and re-oil everything regularly to keep gears and springs in good order.

Take time to wipe over the reel's body – a damp cloth is all that's needed. Pay attention to the bale arm, wiping off all traces of dirt and caked-on groundbait; take off the spool and wipe inside the bale arm carrier. Keep an eye on the return springs of the bale arm mechanism. If they appear to be weakening it's time to change for new ones before they pack up altogether – usually just as you're starting to catch fast.

Servicing is also carried out by most of the major manufacturers and it is well worthwhile sending yours back at the end of every season for a complete overhaul. The cost is minimal and the long-term saving makes the effort a good investment.

Keep your reels either in a proper pouch or at least wrapped in a clean cloth. Leaving them to roll around unprotected in the bottom of a tackle box is a sure way of shortening their life.

LINE

Line is just as important as the rod and reel – a poor quality one, or one that does not perform well, will ruin any chance of good presentation. And there is a lot more to selecting the right one than just deciding on the correct breaking strain. Monofilament lines come in many colours and under a whole host of fancy names. In fact they are all produced by just a handful of manufacturers, but are finished off to the demands of their customers, namely the tackle companies who each want a line with their own brand name emblazoned across it. Line is usually supplied in bulk from the factory and then spooled into 100-metre lengths by the tackle firm or distributor. Unfortunately this is often where the trouble starts, because a badly designed spool can ruin an otherwise good line. Small diameter spools upset the line by causing it to remain in tight coils when wound onto the reel. Line spooled too tightly will have the same fault and will be difficult to manage. So lines that are identical at the production stage end up with totally different characteristics under fishing conditions. Thankfully we can take a few precautions when we load it on a reel to ensure that the best possible results are achieved.

A spool that has been subjected to direct sunlight will be much weaker than a similar one that has been kept in a cool dark place. The ultra violet rays of the sun are deadly to nylon lines, so if the local dealer displays his lines in the shop window, buy yours elsewhere.

All nylon line is not the same: some has no stretch, some has a little and a third type stretches considerably. These characteristics can work either for or against the float angler depending on the style of fishing the lines are used for.

The non-stretch line has usually been stretched during production, giving it a thinner diameter in relation to breaking strain of other, more stretchy varieties. While this finer diameter can mean better casting qualities and more supple hook lengths, the line will have lost much of its ability to absorb shock, such as on the strike or from a fish that takes off suddenly for the nearest tree root.

A line that is too stretchy will result in bites being missed or the hook not being set properly – in this case the line has taken up too much of the strike force before it can reach the hook. So while line

● *Line comes on an assortment of spools — some of which can ruin nylon before it gets as far as being loaded on a reel*

diameter to breaking strain ratio is very important, the angler should be aware of the price he will have to pay, viz other qualities lost. In higher strains, non-stretch line is fine, but beware of it in anything less than, say, 3lb to 3½lb. As hook length it is fine because the main line will absorb much of the shock – that is, assuming it has some stretch of its own – but even so, use at least a couple of feet. Tied up in shorter lengths it does tend to break off very easily.

For most of my float fishing I use a line that has not been pre-stretched – you can usually find a suitable one by checking the prices and diameters. The more expensive and thinner ones are usually the pre-stretched variety. If in doubt, consult the dealer at the time of purchase. Among my own favourites are Bayer, Maxima and the old-established Racine Tortue. Even these have different characteristics which we will look at later.

Lines also fall into two other classes: those that float and those that sink. A floating line can be a real problem if you are trying to fish at long range with a waggler and there is any hint of wind or surface skim. Under such conditions you will need a line that sinks – or at least one that can be made to.

Maxima falls into this sinking category, and has a dull surface appearance; Bayer also sinks, but not as quickly as Maxima because the surface finish is left a little bit shinier. You may find others that are much shinier, often among the very cheapest brands.

● *Conditions like these demand a line that can be sunk beneath the surface quickly before it is blown into a bow by the wind*

How to Load a Reel

Having decided on the right line for our fishing we must next load it on a reel. This is where even more faults can be built in if extra care is not taken.

For a start, the correct knot will make sure it stays on the spool (see illustration). Try to position the knot to the rear of the spool and cut off the loose end of nylon to leave about a full spool width. This will ensure it is supple enough to be laid down under the coils and will not stand up stiffly to snag line as it runs off during casting.

When loading a fixed spool it is common practice to stick a pencil through the line spool's central hole and wind line onto the reel. This is fine and will usually cause little trouble later on. A better method, however is to get someone to hold the spool facing the reel and then allow line to spiral off the side in much the same manner as it will come off the reel during casting. What is essential is that line spirals off the spool and onto the reel in the same direction of rotation (see illustration). Do this and you will take out any twists that were wound in during initial loading after manufacture.

Load while keeping a little tension on the line, just enough to keep everything neat but not so tight as to force the line to cut into itself as it is laid on the spool.

Properly loaded, the reel spool should be filled to within a couple of millimetres of the lip. Overfill, and line will spill off in an uncontrollable fashion; underload, and the line will have to climb the lip and will not cast smoothly.

With closed-face reels the same rules apply, except that overloading will quickly cause tangles inside the housing. And if you should suffer from line bedding into

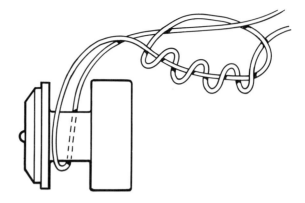

● *A simple knot to tie and one which works well for tying line to reel spool*

itself after catching a few good fish, it may be because the spool is carrying too much. Reduce the amount considerably and see what happens. My ABU 506 shallow spool needs no more than about 50yd of 2½lb line to work best.

Although manufacturers frequently suggest the amount of line their reels should take they are often way off the mark. Use them as a guide and nothing more.

Centre pins can be loaded by just winding line off the spool using the pencil method. But again, don't overload – you need surprisingly little line on a centre pin, and 30yd is usually more than enough. It helps if the bulk of line can be loaded towards one side of the reel, leaving the other side free to take just the amount

● *A popular means of loading a reel with line is to push a pencil through the plastic spool on which the line is supplied, keeping some tension on the spool to ensure even loading*

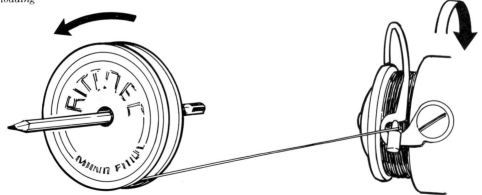

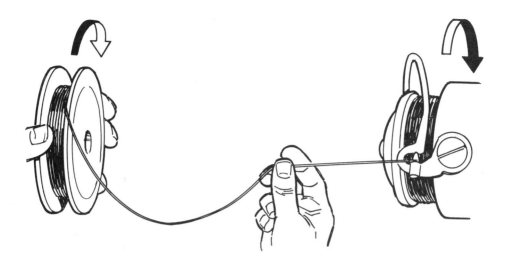

● *The best method of winding line onto a reel is to allow it to spiral over the edge of the plastic spool, spilling off in the same direction as it is being wound onto the reel*

of line needed for the fishing to be done. By keeping only a few yards on one side a better flow can be achieved because there will be no tendency to bed in or stick.

Actual direction of loading a centre pin is something you will need to decide yourself. Some prefer to run the line so that it comes off the bottom of the reel and goes up at an angle towards the first ring. Done this way, the reel is wound in the usual direction but because of the angle formed by the line to the butt ring,

● *Spools should be filled with line to within 2mm of the lip (left). Underfilled line (centre) will not flow off correctly and casting will be difficult. The spool (right) is overfilled and will result in line spilling off*

there is a danger of it being affected by wind and blown into a bow. There is also a small amount of friction over the ring. By loading line in the opposite direction it will run off from the top of the reel and stay parallel to the rod at all times. Both methods are correct, the choice is yours to make.

Check line regularly for weakening and for damage. If you have been unfortunate enough to tangle a few times around the back of the reel spool, damage may have occurred and a new line is a must. If you have a habit of moving shot around, the first few yards should be cut off regularly and destroyed. Line is cheap by comparison with other tackle and should not be expected to last forever.

One final plea, however: change line regularly and discard it carefully – the best idea is to cut it into small lengths and burn it. Monofilament is a potential killer of birds and wildlife if left lying around. We have already lost the right to use certain sizes of lead shot, so don't let the same thing happen to line.

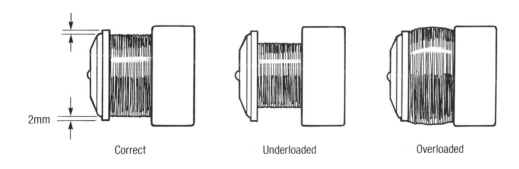

2mm   Correct   Underloaded   Overloaded

Generally speaking, I find that one of the three already mentioned suits my needs no matter which method of float fishing I am using. But there are many other good brands and maybe you will take to one of these more readily – like so much in fishing, it is all a matter of personal choice. Lines to an angler are like washing powders to the housewife and one works much better than the other . . . or so they claim. Chances are they are chemically identical.

Stick float fishing, or for that matter most fast water methods – certainly those that demand using a float 'double rubber' – will call for a floating line, or at least one that stays fairly high up in the water. The one exception is probably when you are struggling to fish a stick float in a bad downstream wind – when you have probably picked an unsuitable method.

Lines, no matter which you choose, will sooner or later decide to float when you want them to sink. No real problem, provided you know the tricks. Line usually floats because it has become greasy and cannot be sunk through the surface tension of the water (this is the film that supports insects that seem to be able to walk on water). Surface tension can be broken by the use of washing-up liquid rubbed along the line. The easiest way is to soak a piece of clean, soft rag in the liquid and run the line through it a couple of times – you can actually do this by casting and winding line back through the rag. If you find yourself on the bankside without washing-up liquid, try rubbing the line down with some mud.

Another good tip is one you can take from fly fishermen, who de-grease nylon leaders with a mixture of washing-up liquid and Fuller's Earth powder. Buy Fuller's Earth from a chemist and mix it up with the liquid to form a stiff paste. It will eventually dry to the consistency of hard plasticine and can be used many times. Certainly worth keeping a ball in your box.

Some anglers beat the floating line problem by keeping a spool specially treated. They do this by having a loaded reel spool permanently submerged in a container filled with washing-up liquid. Personally I find the line gets tacky and does not flow smoothly off during casting.

Making a line float is a simple task – just rub it with a little Vaseline or a smear of Mucilin fly line grease. The slightest amount is all that is needed.

Next stage in line selection must be to consider which breaking strain is best suited to float fishing

needs. For this exercise I will assume that you are using a fairly conventional 'float rod', one that would perhaps be best described as a match rod rather than a 'whopper stopper'. It goes without saying that the more powerful the rod, the stronger the line must be in order to cope.

Float fishing will demand lines from around 1½lb for close-in work with a delicate stick float, up to maybe 3½lb and even 4lb for really long-range work with very heavy wagglers and big, bulky Avon and balsa floats. For general purpose fishing on waters where I might expect to catch anything from small roach up to bream and sizeable chub, a good 2½lb is all I would need, bearing in mind I am likely to be using a 13ft match rod most of the time.

There is much argument as to the advantages of fine lines, and many anglers will claim a fine one is less affected by wind than a thicker one. While this may appear, at least at first, to be correct it is in fact not so. By doubling a line's diameter you also increase its total volume by around four times and therefore the weight by the same ratio. The mathematicians among us can of course work out the exact weight-to-diameter ratio by calculating the area of a line section against its diameter. There is, of course, a limitation as to how far this theory can be taken in practice – a small stick float would be most inappropriate to use with a 5lb line.

As a rough guide the following is a typical diameter to breaking strain comparison:

½lb	003in (.08mm)	2.6lb	006in (.15mm)
1.1lb	004in (.10mm)	3.2lb	007in (.175mm)
1.7lb	005in (.125mm)	4.4lb	008in (.20mm)

The Imperial to metric conversions are all approximate but are within an acceptable accuracy for angling needs. The examples used are for Bayer, and are typical of a good, general purpose line.

In addition to being of an acceptable diameter and stretch, line must also be supple. If it is springy it will tend to tangle and be generally unmanageable; a good line lacks what is known as 'memory', that is to say it does not try to return to the coils in which it has been wound. Surface finish should feel smooth to the touch and not have any obvious rough or flat areas – on a really bad example you may be able to see tiny flats along its length. This is a serious fault and one that will lead to all sorts of breakage problems very quickly.

2
Float Design and Accessories

A few years back not many top-class anglers used shop-bought floats, preferring instead to spend many hours making their own. Some were works of art, others looked rough, poorly painted and were generally rather dull. Picking the good from the bad, however, was not as easy as it may have seemed.

The reason for all this homework was you just couldn't trust a shop-bought product, where the selection was often little more than some natural quills, cork or balsa bodies and a complete lack of load marking. The home float-maker could pick the materials that worked best in order to produce a float tailor-made to the needs of a specific water; these pioneers were in fact responsible for models such as the zoomer, missile, ducker and even the stick float. The best the early professional manufacturers could do was churn out more and more porcupine quills with too much paint on the top, and bottom rings that fell off very quickly.

Thankfully, bought tackle has come a long way since then and the modern angler stands a pretty good chance of purchasing floats of at least a reasonable standard. Even so, a good working knowledge of the materials and designs involved will be an advantage.

TYPES OF FLOAT

The first thing to consider is the purpose of a float. It is there to register a bite, support the bait in the water and enable the correct presentation in the place required. A float you can't see is totally useless. If you don't believe me, try fishing a bristle-tipped waggler 30yd away with the sun on your face. Equally useless is a thick-topped chunk of peacock quill with 2in sticking out of the water if you are fishing for tiny, shy-biting canal roach.

Both these examples may seem obvious enough, but remember they must both also support the bait in the right place – try holding that bristle tip back hard against a flowing river and it would fail miserably, although the thick quill could be made to work to a degree, as will be described later on. A float that is too small for the job is also a big handicap. Getting the distance required will be difficult and if conditions are anything but perfect it will be a major struggle to maintain correct presentation. I would always advise a beginner to opt for a float that does the job easily rather than just do it. A few bites may be missed as a result but the overall performance is sure to be better in the long run.

The real secret of buying floats is not to be impulsive. If you don't know exactly what a certain float is designed for, leave it alone. Chances are the makers hadn't much idea either. Simple patterns are often the best, and if I had to choose just one pattern with which to fish for the rest of my days it would be for straight pieces of peacock quill in a variety of lengths and thicknesses.

So why all the fancy pattern? The answer is simple: 'floats catch more anglers than fish', and anglers just can't resist 'em. I have hundreds, both home-made and shop-bought, but even now I still spend money adding even more . . . just in case they might come in handy. Presumably you know the waters you are buying floats for, or at least the general conditions likely to be encountered, and you can check the type you will need by referring to chapters 6 and 7.

What must be appreciated in order to get the right float from a range of a certain pattern is the quality of the materials used, and how this can be ruined by a few simple mistakes at the manufacturing stage.

Unfortunately manufacturers seem to feel they have to construct floats that are 'idiot proof', and the result is thick paint, gaudy tips and shiny varnish, which actually spoils what may otherwise have been a good design.

Floats must be sealed. One that takes in water will very soon begin to sink, and you will need to remove more and more shot until finally the whole thing is totally waterlogged and useless. Sealed, but not overdone is the sort of coating you must find. Applied correctly, a coat of paint or varnish will be as thin as possible, and the thinner the better provided it still does its job of sealing out water.

If you can still see the grain of the balsa wood beneath this skin it is a good sign, and this float will be able to carry the maximum amount of shot for its size and be as light as possible, giving good casting qualities. A float that is heavy because it is loaded with half-a-dozen thick coats of paint will take less shot, and because the overall weight is greater, will fly badly.

Varnish on commercial floats is still commonly gloss finish, and this will cause fish-scaring flash as it zooms overhead. Far better to have a matt finish. Colour of the float – apart from the tip – doesn't matter that much. In fact it can help, if you make your own, to paint them in a variety of colours to aid identification in a crowded box.

Even on this subject there are widely differing opinions. Black was always the 'in' colour, and those really 'in the know' would use nothing but matt black, for the reason just discussed. Others, and matchman Ray Mumford in particular, always painted floats in a camouflage style, believing the mixture of colours helped to break up the float's outline (see colour photograph on p. 18). Green came and went, too, the theory being that a green float looked, to a fish, like a natural twig. Next it was the turn of grey to be 'in fashion'; it was a favourite on canals but why, no one seemed to know.

This was all until professional float-maker Peter Drennan gave the matter some thought: the result was a totally clear plastic float called the 'Crystal'. Until the clear float we were miles away from solving the mystery of optimum float colour. However, the principle is easy to understand – try a little experiment for yourself. Turn on the living-room light and hold your hand up towards it – your fingers will appear very dark. Try the same thing with black,

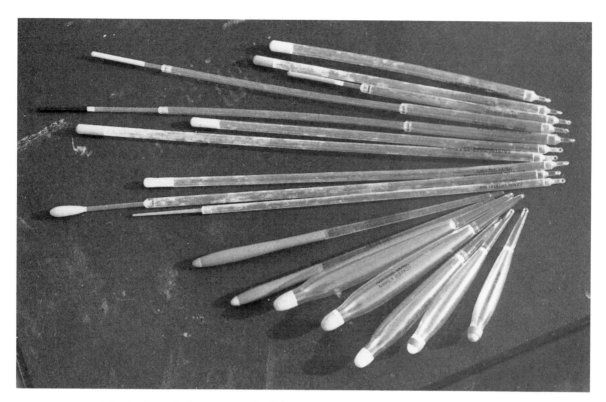

grey or even white floats and they, too, will all be dark. This is exactly what a fish sees as it looks upwards, since the brightness of the sky makes everything above appear as a dark outline. Clear floats are the only ones that do not cast a solid shadow, Well, that's the theory – I've used the lot, and am still not convinced about anything except the necessity of a non-flash finish.

What is important is the tip colour. If you can't see it, the best float in the world is useless. Favourites are reds and flame orange; yet one of the most versatile is black, and a black tip cannot be beaten firstly on light water such as is found on wide rivers and big stillwaters, and in a facing sun. Orange and red are fine when faced with dark water, such as when fishing tight to the far bank or where there are overhanging trees.

No matter which colour is selected it should have a contrasting band of black or white beneath it, about half an inch from the tip – that way, lift bites will be much easier to spot. Commercial makers often get this band wrong, too. A thin line is no good since this must all be visible at range – mine are painted with a line of at least 3mm.

● *Clear plastic floats, invented by Peter Drennan to combat the problem of shadows scaring fish in shallow water*

Getting really bright tip colours on your floats is not difficult. The fluorescent paints used need a matt white base to enhance their effect, so give your tips a thin coat of white and then a coat or two of the chosen colour, remembering not to overdo it either in thickness or length applied – 15mm is about right for all but very special floats.

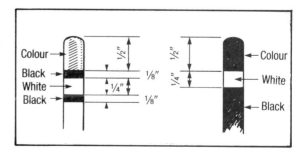

● *Contrasting black or white bands added to float tip colours will make lift bites easier to spot*

Materials need some thought, too. Because we are looking for a float that carries weight in the form of shot, it must be made from a buoyant material such as balsa wood. Woods that are denser do have their uses, but not as the main part of a float. Many woods and synthetic materials have been used in float making, some with a reasonable degree of success, but my own personal favourites are, without doubt, balsa and peacock quill. Both have the qualities already described.

There are alternatives to peacock, the main one being a dried Indian reed called 'sarkandas'. It is straight, stronger than peacock and looks perfect for the job, but the resulting float will not perform anywhere near as well as an identical one of peacock. The reed is just a little denser than quill and therefore casts relatively poorly. Painting reed is also a problem. The shiny skin needs a lot of sanding work to provide a key, and even then flaking seems to be common.

The density of material must also be considered when buying or making floats that have an insert of thinner material in the tip. For example, a straight peacock quill with a thin tip of relatively dense cane will tend to be tip-heavy in flight and fall badly during casting – far better, although harder to produce, is a tip of peacock. Density has nothing to do with bite detection: a light peacock insert of, say, 2mm diameter will take exactly the same effort for a fish to pull under as an insert of similar proportions made from cane. It's all a matter of basic physics and Archimedes' principle.

Plastics continue to improve and we shall see them used more and more in float manufacture – already they have shown that it is possible to produce an endless number of identical floats, something that is not possible with quills or woods since every piece has a different density. Polystyrene is another good synthetic for float bodies. It takes a lot of work to form it well and it cannot be varnished or painted with cellulose substances, but it is extremely buoyant.

Wagglers

Buoyancy and balance are without doubt the two qualities that will have the greatest bearing on the way a float performs. A heavy material used for the main stem of a waggler will reduce its casting capabilities considerably; also, dense materials take insufficient shot loading and will not ride the water well.

The actual shape of a float is also important, although few anglers will agree on all points in this department. At one time nearly all wagglers had bodies, either of balsa or cork, to give them the large shot-carrying capability needed for distance fishing. But as rods and techniques have improved so the need for this bulk has been somewhat reduced. Three body shapes are most common: with the bulk towards the top, towards the bottom, or one that tapers equally both ways.

A body with bulk towards the base of the float (A) will cast best because the weight is nearest the leading end during flight. It's a bit like a model aeroplane needing a lump of lead in the nose to make it fly well.

A body with a thicker section towards the top (B) is a little more stable once in the water and will have more resistance to currents. But really the difference is minimal. An evenly tapering body (C) is something of a compromise and certainly casts and rides well enough. The sleeker lines of this type also make entry into the water quieter.

So, bodies add to the shot-carrying capacity and provide a little extra stability to a waggler. I

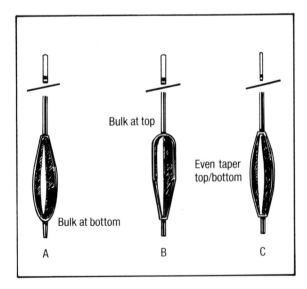

● *Common body shapes for wagglers; each will behave differently both in flight and in the water*

particularly like a peacock quill with a slender body of balsa, so slender as to be hardly noticeable, nothing more than a slight swelling towards the base.

On a waggler the length of stem is critical if it is to do a proper job. The float must be long enough to cope with wind and drift – the angler uses the float's length to bury as much line as possible beneath the surface. It might therefore be reasonable to suppose that the longest waggler would be the most stable under a given set of conditions. I, too, believed that for a long time, and even went to the degree of making peacock floats so long they had to be carried in the rod holdall. All I achieved was to possess a set of floats so long they were almost impossible to use. They cast poorly, made striking difficult and were only partially successful at beating the strong downstream winds that have a habit of blowing down my home Fen waters.

But my experiments taught me a lot about float design, and I've now settled to a range of up to about 12in as the optimum length. With these it is possible to get a lot of line beneath the surface, but not to such a degree that too great an angle is formed which might threaten the strike effect.

Stick floats

Stick floats are one pattern where a very dense material can be to your advantage (see colour photograph on p. 17). This is easy to understand if we first consider the role of the stick float.

Originally designed for fishing a running water where the bait must be held back against the flow, the idea was to build a float where the balance of buoyant and dense materials worked in relation to each other. The buoyancy was contained in the balsa upper third of the float, and the dense section the remaining two-thirds which was the tapered stem: properly balanced, the balsa rides the current well, but when held back against it the dense bottom material prevents the float riding up, out of the water.

The traditional pattern was a balsa top and heavy cane for the stem, but plastic, glassfibre lignum and even carbon have found their way alongside wire. Cheap stick floats may look just like the real thing, but they are likely to have stems made from a lighter and softer wood than cane and will not work as efficiently. A really good stick float will try to cock

slightly without any shot. It may pay to go for the stick floats with unpainted stems – the clear varnish used instead will at least allow you to see what material has been used.

Top shape is another consideration to make when choosing the right stick float. A tapered, slightly pointed top (A) is the normal profile, and this will work fine on waters of a fairly even pace and without too much turbulence. As pace and undercurrents increase so the tip should be more bulky. A dome shape (B) is a good one and has the advantage of being very buoyant and also easy to see at considerable range. Third choice is a flat top (C). This profile can be dotted right down almost flush with the surface and will register bites well, yet still holds up against the current.

Rings are not needed on the stem of a stick float and can even be a hindrance. Go instead for a good plain stem, although on wire patterns there may be some need for a short length of whipping to be added in order to give the rubber attachment sleeve something to grip to.

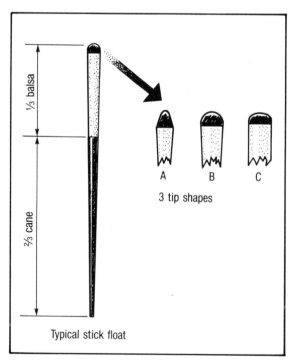

⅓ balsa

⅔ cane

A   B   C

3 tip shapes

Typical stick float

● *A good balance of balsa and stem material is vital if a stick float is to work correctly. The tip profile will also vary according to the task the float is to perform*

FLOAT MAKING

Making your own floats is not so much a course of action intended to save money, but rather one to provide the types and special patterns not usually supplied by normal commercial sources. Producing your own also has the advantage that you know exactly what materials have been used and can therefore ensure that a certain pattern will behave as it should – for example, a stick float needs a dense stem to counter-balance the upper, balsa section of the body.

Buying these materials is not difficult. Most tackle shops sell reasonable selections of peacock quills, balsa, paints and varnishes. Some even provide ready-shaped balsa bodies and stick float stems. If you can track down well-shaped stick float stems you will save a good deal of time and effort, but be sure they are actually made from a heavy cane or lignum.

Paints and varnishes need to be compatible, that is enamel paint cannot be varnished or painted over with a cellulose product. They work fine in reverse, but get it wrong and you will end up with a nasty reaction that results in bubbles. In any case, a slower-drying enamel seems to provide a more flexible finish and one that is less prone to flaking.

As float making becomes very much a part of your angling interest so the assortment of woods, quills and paints will grow. Start with some basic requirements and see how things progress, building a number of one pattern of float before tackling another. Only by making, say, six of a type at each sitting will it be worth the time and trouble. And in any case, it is always a good idea to have all your floats as matched pairs just in case you lose or break one – the remaining one can be used as a replacement for the rest of the session and then used as a pattern for copying others.

A very sharp cutting instrument is essential. Use one of the special modelling knives or a razor blade, but in the case of a razor blade watch your fingers. A good, flat, cutting-board is also a sound investment and will certainly prevent many a domestic upset – the sort that seem to develop over little things like cuts in the dining-room table-top.

Glasspaper is going to be required in several grades from a medium/coarse down to the smoothest 'flour' grade for finishing. Add a reel of fine whipping thread, some fine wire for making eyes and a tube of strong glue such as Araldite. This type of epoxy glue is better than the 'super glues' for float making because it dries more slowly and allows you a little more time to ensure everything is set up correctly before setting actually begins.

Drill a piece of 3cm wood with a series of holes varying from 3mm to 4mm in diameter – this is going to serve as a drying stand into which the floats can be placed after painting. A good alternative is a square of thick expanded foam packing material, into which floats can be pushed after making a few holes with a scrap piece of 3mm cane. Brushes, paints and varnishes will all be needed, but otherwise there is little that cannot be found around most households.

The only luxuries that can be a great help are a small jig and an electric drill. The drill is for boring holes in balsa bodies and also for using as a lathe to speed up shaping; the jig is a simple affair that can be made in a matter of minutes by anyone who has access to a lathe. The purpose of this jig is to ensure holes are drilled centrally in balsa dowel that is later to be formed into bodies. It is a piece of steel bar into which a hole of, say, 3mm has been drilled at one end and then the opposite end bored out to take a particular diameter of balsa dowel – 12mm is a good size.

Having produced this jig, a piece of balsa can now be pushed into the jig's bore and then drilled by using the 3mm hole as a guide bush. Never force a drill through soft balsa as this will cause it to 'run' at an

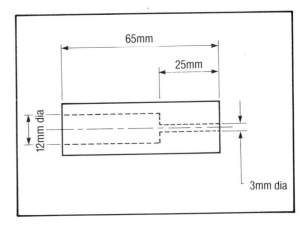

● *A simple drill jig that will hold a length of 12mm balsa and ensure a concentric hole is produced*

Drinking Straws

Plastic drinking straws are excellent for making up some simple floats. They are reasonably tough, carry a fair amount of shot for their size and because they are light, they cast very well. A selection of different diameters will enable stepped patterns to be created, too. They have the advantage over other materials in that every one of a packet will be identical in size, so repeating floats with the same shot-loading capacity is simple.

Start by cutting a straw to the length required – this is where a knife must be especially sharp, and some care is needed not to crush the straw. If possible, use a piece of small diameter scrap balsa inside the straw as a support for the thin walls. Some form of bottom stem is also going to be required. For this there is nothing better than a short piece of the correct diameter cane. Before glueing in place, complete any tapering that may be required to give it a nice appearance and also balance.

If an eye is needed, this can also be added either before or after glueing the cane to the stem. When glueing is carried out, be sure there is enough to go all around the stem and to form a good seal. A neat finish can be made by smearing everything down with a finger-tip.

Final step of this simple construction is to add a top to the straw. This should be a balsa plug, sanded down to form a neat push-fit inside the straw. Glue it in place and then shape the top to a neat dome. Alternatively, a smaller diameter straw or a piece of peacock can be glued in to form an insert tip.

By using a variety of different makes of straw it is possible to produce some very interesting floats, even adding bodies of balsa if required.

Painting, other than that needed to seal the balsa tops, can be just a thin coating. The straw itself will be waterproof so any paint or varnish is only acting as a strengthener.

---

angle and produce a hole that is not concentric to the outer diameter. Take your time and ease the drill through using only the minimum amount of pressure With long bodies it often pays to drill in from both ends to reduce any wandering effects.

If you intend making lots of varying sizes, the simple jig described can be repeated in any combination of bore and drill size required.

Quills

Preparing quills for float production is not difficult, but get it wrong and a very good piece of material can be ruined completely. First select the best quills from a batch. These will be the ones which are as straight as possible and free from crush marks or any sign of having been bent – look for tiny creases running across the quill.

First stage is to strip off the feather fibres or herl. Be careful – if this is simply pulled off the quill, there is a danger that the quill's skin will be damaged and made useless. A far better plan is to cut it away with a razor blade, working the blade with a sawing motion from the thick end of the quill towards the thinnest end. By cutting in this direction the blade

will tend to move away from the quill, being directed by the slight angle the herl makes at its roots. If you work from the other direction, it is very easy to make cuts into the quill.

Having reduced the herl to a very short stubble it can be smoothed with fine glasspaper to finish. And while doing this it is a good idea to give the smooth, slightly shiny side of the quill a gentle rub down with a fine grade, too. Don't overdo this operation – all it needs is enough to take off the greasy surface.

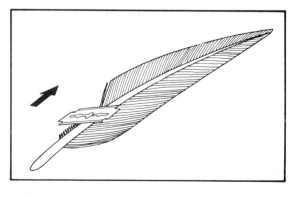

● *When removing herl from a quill always work with a sharp blade and begin from the thickest end*

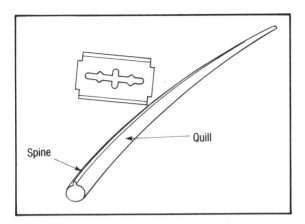

● *When quill has to be cut start from the spine side to reduce the chances of crushing*

On one side of the quill you will notice a sort of spine running between two slight depressions in the otherwise round quill. This spine gives strength, and it should not be sanded off beyond what is required to smooth it enough for painting. Cut the quill to length with a sharp blade, starting on the spine rather than the oval side. By cutting from this slight edge there is less chance of any crushing.

Slightly bent quills can be straightened by carefully working them through the fingers while applying gentle pressure against the bend. Don't try to rush it, but work along the quill allowing the pressure to ease it straight – sometimes a little gentle heat from a low gas ring or a candle will help while you do this.

Inside a quill, say, from a peacock, there is a soft pithy substance into which a base stem or tip insert will need to be glued. In the case of large quills a thin cane stem can be simply sharpened to a flat point and pushed some way inside without causing damage. But great care must be taken not to compress the pith too much, otherwise there is a danger of the quill splitting. A safer system is to open up a hole, firstly with a darning needle and then with a sharp drill, turning it carefully between finger and thumb.

After glueing in the base stem, the top end of the quill will need to be sealed. In the case of a float with an insert, the glue used for fixing the two pieces together will do the job well, but in the case of a plain top try either a blob of varnish or form a small dome of Araldite on the top of the pith.

Once everything is dry the quill can be given a

final rub over with a very fine grade glasspaper prior to painting.

Collecting other quills such as crow or pheasant is something that can be done every time you visit a fishery. Best quills are those that are moulted naturally; plucking them from a dead bird often results in the thick part having a soft, blood-filled end which is useless unless completely removed. Best thing to do with such quills is cut them up and use as inserts.

Painting

Painting or varnishing any float, including quills, needs to be done as lightly as possible, the idea being to lay on just enough to create a seal without taking away any of the buoyancy.

Start with the tip, which will need a coat of matt white paint to bring out the brightest shade when a fluorescent colour is added later. Don't rush the job, and allow plenty of time for the paint to dry completely. Once dry, give it a gentle rub over with some 'flour' glasspaper and add another thin coat. Two thin coats should be sufficient and will be far superior to one thicker skin.

Once the body and stem have been painted and the undercoat white tip is completely dry, the final tip colour can be applied. This fluorescent paint is slightly transparent and the white base will make the finished colour very bright. In order to get the best from this effect, keep the final colour as thin as possible, applying just enough to obtain the required shade.

After painting, push the float into the drying base and leave overnight, after which the shot loading can be checked and painted on the base. Special stick-on transfers are available for this purpose but painting is usually both quicker and more permanent.

Many float-makers find the best method of applying paint and varnish is with the finger-tip. This method allows the paint to be worked well into the wood and also ensures a nice even coat. Alternatively, a good quality brush containing bristles which do not become loose. It helps, too, to paint or varnish in a warm, dust-free room.

● *A nice catch of small carp. Fish like these will stay close to the bottom if a firm groundbait mix is used (Chapter 4)*

Balsa

It will pay to seal any balsa wood prior to painting, whether bodies or stems. Dope is as good for this as anything and can be purchased from any model shop; it has the added advantage of drying very quickly so that two coats can be applied within a matter of fifteen minutes or so. But again, use only enough to do the job, otherwise shot load will be reduced.

Prior to sealing the wood should of course be smoothed by rubbing down with fine grades of glasspaper. Once correctly painted the wood grain should still be just visible.

Balsa comes in a variety of grades from very hard to ultra-soft. The harder it is, the lower its shot-carrying capabilities – but a wood that is too soft is more difficult to finish and seal, so in reality there is not much difference overall. A good choice is a medium grade for bodies and a slightly harder wood for stems. The harder balsa will be stronger than the soft when required for making into a thin stem.

Sarkandas

Although not one of my favourite float materials, this Indian reed is common and cheap. It is, however, difficult to paint and unless a great deal of careful rubbing down is done it will not take a coat of any description. Rub glass paper around the reed rather than along it, and don't be afraid to leave some visible scratch marks. It is worth trying a mixture of paint and varnish, too, making up the preparation with equal quantities of each.

Foam

Expanded foam is very buoyant and can be used to make up float bodies which take a lot of shot. The only problem is in the finishing because it is a difficult substance to sand and the resulting paint job will not look good. Having said that, it is a material that casts extremely well and is one to use if performance is preferable to appearance.

On no account use any cellulose substance, either glue or finish coating, as it reacts violently and reduces a nicely formed body to an unsightly lump.

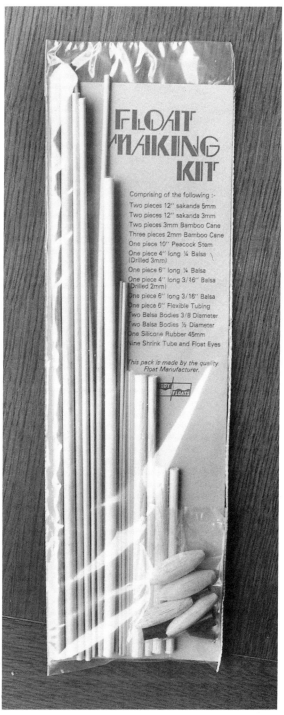

● *Former world champion Dave Thomas braved a cold morning to catch these nice roach and chub. Not the sort of day to use a lot of feed (Chapter 4)*

● *A ready-packed kit of balsa stems, bodies, cane and accessories for making a whole range of floats*

Eyes

Wire eyes for stems can be purchased, and there are some very good ones available made from stainless steel wire. Short plastic stems with eyes are also made now and these are excellent for making wagglers. Making your own is simple, quick and almost cost-free. A length of household electrical wire will provide a good source of material – just strip off the outer plastic casing to reveal the wire beneath. This can then be wound around a suitable piece of wire such as a large pin, small nail or even the stem of a wire-stemmed stick float.

Form the eye by winding the wire completely around the pin so that it forms a full loop. The two 'legs' that will be used to whip it to the float need to be about a centimetre long. If you want to produce a large number of eyes, make up a little jig by pushing two headless pins or short lengths of stiff wire into a block of wood about 25mm apart. If pins are used, snip off the heads with wire cutters.

Wire can now be wound around one wire, across to the other, round it and back to the beginning, repeating the operation until a number of eyes are produced as a single string. Separate them by cutting through the wires midway between the two pins.

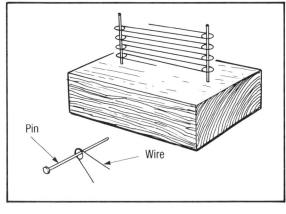

● *Two methods of making wire eyes. Single eyes can be formed around a pin or length of wire. For mass production make up a small wood block with two headless pins around which wire can be wound*

Stick float stems

Stick float stems must be of a dense material, and the usual cane or lignum takes a lot of shaping. Try to form a nice taper on the stem firstly by shaving it down with a sharp but strong blade such as a craft knife. Razors are not up to this job and will blunt very quickly.

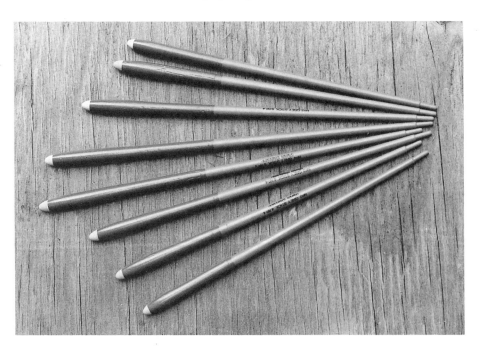

● *A set of well-made stick floats. The stems have a nice taper and blend neatly into the balsa upper section*

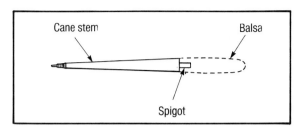

● *A good method of joining a stick float's cane stem to a balsa body is via a spigot formed on the cane*

Where a stem enters the upper balsa section of the float, some form of spigot will be needed to ensure there is enough of the softer wood left to provide strength. Form this spigot – which needs to be about 15mm long – by making a shallow cut around the stem and then carefully cutting down from the thick end to the cut, taking off a sliver at a time before finally sanding the spigot round. Try to keep the shoulder formed by the spigot as neat, sharp and square as possible.

Once glued in place, the balsa is easy to shape to the same gradual taper. Sanding the cane and lignum takes a lot of time and quickly takes the edge off glasspaper, and this process can be speeded up by sanding with an electric drill. Use only a low speed and even then take care, as friction will generate a lot of heat.

Whenever a stem, body or bottom stem are to be glued together, check that the best possible position has been found. By turning a body or perhaps the stem before the glue has set, it may be possible to correct any slight eccentricity or curve in the finished float.

Cork

Cork is very buoyant, but it is not the easiest body material to shape or to seal afterwards. Start shaping with a razor blade by slicing off thin pieces, and finishing off with reducing grades of glasspaper. Varnish is best for sealing cork and a slightly thicker-than-usual one is ideal. Old varnish that is beginning to dry out and thicken is very good. Cork's natural surface is open and porous; it can be filled with a conventional wood filler but a far better, and cheaper, idea is to use some of the cork dust made by the sanding, mixing it with a small amount of varnish or glue and then smearing it into the holes. Allow plenty of drying time before smoothing off.

Pith

Elder pith – the soft inside of elder branches and twigs – is another cheap body material and one which is ideal for big floats such as the crow-quill Avon. Use pith from dead wood rather than the sap-filled inside of new wood; handle it carefully, and don't rush the drilling – which is difficult in any case. Shave it with a razor blade and sand gently. Seal with a quick-drying, but thin, varnish and be sure to protect this delicate material by giving floats made from it a secure place in the box. If left to bounce around, they will soon be damaged.

Wire stems

Wire for stick or pole float stems needs to be very stiff but as thin as possible. Finding the right stuff is not always easy, but a visit to the local model shop will usually produce something suitable. Fixing wire into balsa is not too difficult in the case of fairly long-bodied floats – it is just a case of pushing it home after smearing with glue. For shorter floats, the wire may need to be roughened slightly in order to give a better grip – rubbing a file over it is enough to produce the required surface. Be sure, too, that all traces of grease are removed before glueing.

Whipping

Delicate quills and thin balsa stems can be given some extra strength by whipping the ends with fine thread. Use the thinnest you can find and don't overdo the amount; 3 or 4mm should be enough in most cases. Whipping must be neat and firmly wrapped to do its job properly, but take care not to bind it too tightly otherwise it will cut into soft woods such as balsa, and cause distortion.

Spiral whipping around the stem of a fine quill is supposed to give extra strength, but just how much is something open to argument. Also, the extra varnish needed to hold the thread in place will have some effect on the load-carrying capacity. Good places to add whipping would be at the end of a balsa body and at high stress areas such as near the base of a quill where the stem enters.

The Float Box

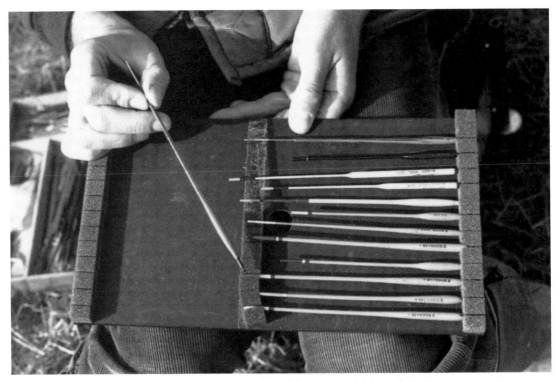

● *Ready-slotted strips of foam are sold by tackle shops and can be glued to any float box*

All these accessories are going to need careful storing in a float box. A good one has trays that can be lifted out to give easy access to several layers of floats.

Avoid those in which the contents can end up as one big jumble, and go for a model that allows each float to be stored in its own slot, or which at least permits each group of similar type to be housed together. A compartment for stick floats, another for short wagglers, one for self-cockers, wire stems, Avons etc is fine, but it will be up to you to keep it neat and tidy.

It is possible to kit out a box yourself by glueing in foam strips. Make them up or buy ready slotted strips from a tackle shop – and don't forget to keep those shots, scissors and other heavy or hard objects from getting in with the floats.

I don't much like wooden boxes with sliding lids. They are fine until they warp, at which stage they can be almost impossible to open. Go instead for hinged lids

with good catches and select a box that is as big as possible. A good investment is one that sits just inside your tackle box, and which will have enough room for the selection of floats that is sure to follow. Plastic float boxes are fine and there are some very good ones about that are designed specially to fit into certain tackle boxes. But watch out for the cheaper varieties that are of hard material and crack easily in cold weather.

A float box should be a work of art, and it is certainly the most valuable piece of kit you will ever own once it is fully kitted out. Treasure it and keep it tidy. Break a rod and it can be replaced with no more problem than finding the cash – lose a float box and it may mean years of work lost, too. Your floats will become very personal items of tackle. Those old pieces of peacock will be familiar to you and no matter how hard you try, the replacements will never perform in the same way.

● *A lifetime's collection of floats like this needs treating with care. Each one is slotted into its own place between strips of foam*

ACCESSORIES

Stocking up a well-equipped float box involves far more than just packing it with floats. There is a whole host of bits and pieces that are needed in order to be ready to tackle any type of water or prevailing weather condition.

The best floats can be ruined performance-wise if they are attached badly to the line. I've seen line passed several times through the bottom ring of a waggler as a means of attachment. It works, that's true, because you can move the float around, but it also puts a weakness into the tackle by causing kinking of the line, and sooner or later a break will occur. Not a method I would advise . . . ever!

One or two bits of rubber tubing comprise another way that is popular for waggler attachment. Again, this is wrong; the line is held too close to the stem, causing the float to be rigid and not hang freely. Constant casting will cut through even the best rubber or silicone. Threading a waggler straight onto line via the bottom ring and then locking it in place with shot poses little difficulty – that is, until a float change is needed, when the whole tackle would need to be stripped down before the change could be made.

Answer to all these problems is to use a float adaptor. There are many patterns available – some are small and difficult to use when fingers are cold, others demand that every float is fitted with a base ring, something you may not want as your float

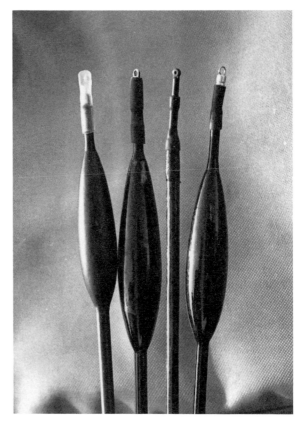

● *Float adaptors can save time and trouble when it comes to changing patterns but choose them with care*

● *Three ways a waggler can be attached to the line. Only the one on the right, using a good quality adaptor, is ideal*

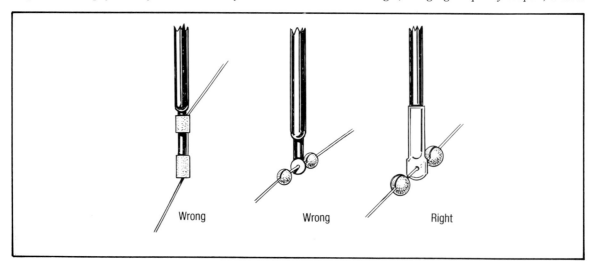

Wrong   Wrong   Right

collection grows. My own favourite commercial pattern is a simple silicone push-on type that can go over a bottom ring or straight onto the stem. Wet one before pushing it home and it will stay put all day. In fact I can't even remember ever losing a float because of one of these adaptors coming off. The adaptor has a hole in the bottom through which line is threaded and should a float need to be changed it is simply pulled out of the adaptor and a fresh one inserted. This style of adaptor also has the advantage of being cheap, so you can have a good supply to hand.

Stick floats don't need adaptors. In fact to use one will cause an angle to form in the line and the float to perform badly. For this style of fishing, or for any float that is to be attached 'top and bottom', a supply of silicone tubing is needed. Use pieces about 1 to 1.5cm long for the base and a narrower piece at the top – about 3mm is ideal for most. Silicone, although more expensive than valve rubber, is stronger and less likely to be cut through by the line. Buy a good selection of diameters, too, for there is nothing worse than a piece of tubing that keeps slipping or is so tight that adjustment is difficult. But no matter what tubing you use, always wet it, or the float, before fitting – that way there will be less risk of friction damage when adjustments are made.

It pays to take tubing off floats after use. Leaving it on may damage paint or varnish and will weaken the tubing, too. A few strips of tubing in white, black and if you can find some, bright orange, will be handy for making temporary colour changes to float tops. I have found that under certain conditions a short piece of, say black, tubing fitted near the tip colour gives a bit of extra contrast to watch. This works well on those swims where part of the water is dark and other areas light.

For pole floats and some plastic wagglers it is possible to buy interchangeable tips. If your floats allow this it is a good way of increasing scope without adding pounds to the initial outlay.

Add to your box a pair of scissors for cutting up tubing; a small knife for opening difficult shot; at least two disgorgers – you'll drop them in the water with amazing regularity; a selection of felt-tipped marker pens, and a bottle of typists' 'Tipp-Ex'. The last two rather strange additions can be used to make quick alterations to tip colours – by painting on a covering of white Tipp-Ex and then a coat of the

required tip colour, a very effective change can be made in a matter of seconds. If you want to get back to the original colour you'll need to remove the bankside artistry with a soft cloth that has been dipped in surgical spirit.

Shots

Your box will also need to contain a good supply of shots. It is vital, however, that these are never permitted to roll around with your floats – if they do, you will very quickly end up with a lot of chipped, broken and generally ruined ones. Therefore always keep shot in a proper dispenser or in spill-proof containers of individual sizes. If you use a dispenser, each section must be marked clearly with the size of the shots it contains.

Most sizes of lead shot have been banned, and there have been many developments in alternatives. They are more expensive than lead and much harder. Some must not be moved on the line without first opening them slightly – using your teeth to attach shot was never a good idea but with the harder non-lead ones it is deadly and unnecessary. Instead, pinch them on with your fingers. The larger ones work best if a very small bore length of silicone tubing is threaded on the line first and shots pinched over it. This idea prevents slipping and possible line damage that might otherwise be caused by the hardness of the shot.

Lead shot of size 8 and smaller are still permitted and it is well worthwhile keeping some handy in sizes 8, 10 and 12. Size 13 is about the smallest you will have any need for and even then only on canals or when pole fishing. The best shots, whether lead or alternatives, should be perfectly round and their split must be central and even in every way. A badly formed shot, oval or cut offset, will spin in the water and lead to tangles and kinking of the line after a few retrieves.

For both lead and alternatives a good shot is the softest available. The shiny black lead ones are usually hard, difficult to close and tend to slide about on the line. Always check what you are buying and accept only the best, even if it is a little more expensive. The cost will be well worthwhile in avoiding lost fishing time.

Tubing made from tungsten is another good means of adding weight to a rig. This flexible tubing

● *Shots left to roll around in a float box will cause untold damage. Always use a well-designed dispenser to hold each size in its own compartment*

● *A fine diameter length of silicone tubing onto which large shots can be pinched will prevent slipping and line damage*

is available from tackle shops and can be used in a number of ways for shotting tackle. It works very well as a replacement for strings of shot as would be used with some Avon rigs.

Other accessories

Most anglers want to use a rod rest at some time during a session, and for the float angler the right choice of pattern can save a lot of time and trouble. The best types are those which have no odd corners on which line can become trapped and with a wide head – at least 12in and better still 15in. The narrow 'vee' type are not suitable for most float fishing.

With float fishing you need to be able to drop the rod onto the rest quickly and without having to search for it. A shallow plastic top is best – the

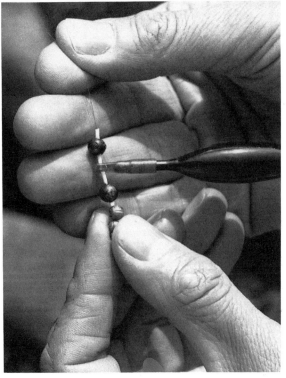

plastic will not damage the rod's varnish, and by bending the alloy arms the 'vee' can be adjusted slightly if required. Rests that are adjustable for angle by means of screws or wing nuts are usually more trouble than they are worth. They either slide about, turn on the bank-stick or just provide another protrusion on which line will get caught. An alternative to a rest is to use the keepnet top, which can be bent into a concave shape – a reasonable enough idea but it does mean you must use a net every time.

Buy two rests so that you have a spare which can be used as a support for the rod butt if you are forced to stand in the water, well out from the bank. Bank-sticks that are to be used for wide rests must be rigid. Go for ones of reasonable diameter rather than very thin models and if possible made from alloy to keep weight to a minimum. The points are best if flattened to provide some resistance against turning in the bank.

● *A rod rest is an essential piece of equipment, but choose a wide one like this rather than the steep 'vee' type*

Nets

Keepnets and landing nets also need selecting with care, especially if you intend to venture into the world of match fishing. It goes without saying that landing nets need to be large enough to cope with the sort of fish you are expecting to catch. But a net that is oversize is going to be hard to handle and will get in the way.

Shape is not too important, although I prefer triangular types. The net itself must be deep enough to prevent fish escaping – something to watch out for when fishing from a high bank. If you get a net that is too deep, tie a piece of string around the bottom so that it is just deep enough for the swim in question and the sort of fish you're likely to catch. A shallow net will also save a lot of time and tangles in the heat of match battle.

A telescopic handle is a must and one of at least 10ft is a good idea. But don't try lifting a heavy fish with one of these long poles or the result will be an expensive break and a fish lost. Instead, pull the net

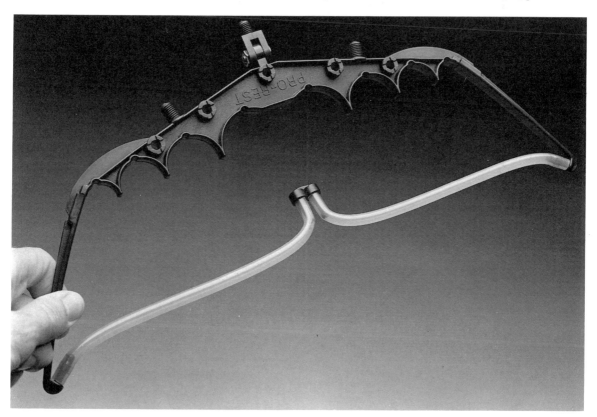

● *A landing net made from micro-mesh will be difficult to handle in fast water. A better design has just the bottom made of this fine netting and the sides made of a coarser grade*

backwards across the water until the hand can take the strain much higher up the handle, and then lift it clear.

Fine-meshed nets are good in that they do not permit shots to fall through and tangle, although a micro-mesh net is almost impossible to control in fast water. A good pattern is one with the sides made from a fine, but not too fine, mesh, and a bottom of micro-mesh. Try also to find a lightweight frame of fibre glass or alloy with a cord front edge.

The keepnet needs a large top ring and should be as long and as wide as practical. Knotless mesh is very kind to fish and is preferable at all times, even on waters where knotted types are still permitted. At the bottom of the net a ring of some description should be fitted, through which a bank-stick can be passed to peg the net out in shallow water.

3
Tackle Layout, Shotting Principles and Casting

Understanding the basic principles of shotting will help ensure a reasonable level of success. Good shotting governs presentation of the bait, prevents tangles and aids casting accuracy and range.

Being well organised on the bankside will make it easier to concentrate, cast correctly and fish more efficiently. This chapter deals with how to get set up and begin fishing in a manner that will keep everything running smoothly.

TACKLE LAYOUT

Successful float fishing demands organisation at all times, and an efficient and comfortable layout of tackle is essential in order to save time and prevent problems as the day's sport progresses.

If a tackle box is to be employed as a seat, it should be level and firmly positioned. You will not fish effectively if forced to balance on a box that leans at a crazy angle and threatens to tip you headlong into the water at any moment. Fit adjustable legs to your box – usually just two on the front corners is sufficient, but four will give even more range and can be extremely useful when fishing from a standing position in the water. Set the box to your liking – this may call for a bit of bank digging or building up with driftwood or stones. If you are forced to dig out a spot, be sure to check first that it is allowed by the club whose water you are fishing; in any case, keep it to a minimum.

On arrival at my swim I usually empty all the contents of my box onto the bank, position the box and then set about assembling everything in a set order. The first mistake many anglers make is to begin setting up a rod in haste. Far better to sit on your box for a few moments and recover from the walk. Spend time looking at the water and surrounding bankside, it will be worthwhile later. You may spot something worth thinking about such as a weed bed or overhanging tree, or perhaps a few signs of big fish feeding close under the far bank.

Fully recovered and composed, the next stage is to put together some tackle – this should begin with the landing net. Once assembled, it is there just in case something is accidentally knocked into the water during the next few minutes. Screw a bankstick to the keepnet and get it in place. It needs to go as close as possible to the front of your box and slightly to the right or left, according to personal preference – I hold fish in my right hand when unhooking, so in theory the net would go to that side. In practice I tend to put it to my left, because I usually swing fish in from the left, so any that drop off have a reasonable chance of landing in the net – a vital consideration in matches and one that has won me more than a few close-fought battles.

Keep the rim of the net low and as flat as possible to give the maximum area into which a fish can fall.

The net also needs to be put into as much depth as possible for the comfort of the catch. Stake out the end, too, to prevent it all collapsing when the first boat passes or a gust of wind catches on the exposed portion.

Next, lay the landing net alongside the keepnet and also slightly over the bank edge. This is another catcher for dropped fish. It goes without saying that this net is always on the left of a right-handed angler and is never out of reach. You must be able to grasp the handle by instinct and without having to look at what you are doing.

Nets in place, now the rod rest, if one is to be used. Position it so that the rod tip is just above the surface and well out of the way of a strike. Again, it needs to be placed so that the rod can be dropped and will land on it without the angler needing to look for it. Watch out also that the rest's stick does not obstruct the way into the keepnet.

Next: a towel to the right and front of the box for wiping hands (not for holding fish). The float box and accessories box go either to the left or behind the tackle box. Hook wallet needs to be immediately to hand, too. Disgorger, plummet and shot box are best placed in some form of container, either in the corner of the groundbait bowl or in one of the side-trays that are fitted to many modern boxes.

Bait tray goes to the right, very close to hand again. Ideally you should be able to select the right bait without having to bend, so organise the tray or stand so that the bait boxes are at the same height as the seat box. Depending on the bank terrain, the groundbait bowl goes just behind or in front of the stand. If it is in front, be sure you can actually reach it without knocking an elbow on the bait boxes.

Umbrella should be handy at the rear, along with the holdall and any other bits and pieces such as spare groundbait, bait and your vacuum flask. Catapult goes in the groundbait bowl or across the bait boxes. It pays to have a spare or two handy, just in case of breakage.

Having got this far, start assembling rods – but remember to keep off the skyline. If you can manage it, carry out the operation sitting in the

● *Getting your box firm and level is very important. Driftwood and rocks will help, but take special care to do a good job so that you are both safe and comfortable*

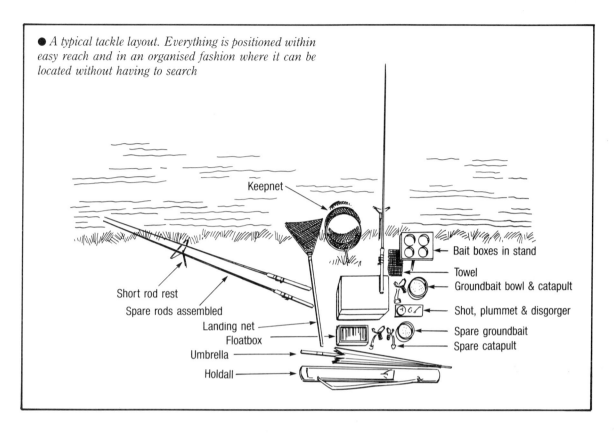

● *A typical tackle layout. Everything is positioned within easy reach and in an organised fashion where it can be located without having to search*

Keepnet

Bait boxes in stand

Towel

Groundbait bowl & catapult

Shot, plummet & disgorger

Short rod rest

Spare rods assembled

Landing net

Floatbox

Spare groundbait

Spare catapult

Umbrella

Holdall

fishing position. Try fitting the reel to the butt and assembling each section of the rod after threading the line. By threading up this way and then fitting tip to middle, and finally middle to butt it is possible to do the whole job without even stretching out an arm.

If a second rod is required, set that up, too, before fishing starts. Be sure to place it well out of the way of onlookers and clumsy feet and also well out of the way of your casting and fish swinging. Whenever possible, mine go along the bank to my left and facing slightly towards the water. Use a short rest, or perhaps your net bag, to lift the tips clear of the ground so they can be seen more easily.

By now you are about ready to start fishing, but before you begin, just cast your eyes around you for a last check that everything is in place and nothing has been left lying around just waiting to be blown into the water. Can you reach every item of tackle?

● *England international Bob Nudd in action. Note how the keepnet is close to hand and positioned so as to catch any fish which may fall off as they are swung in*

Are all the bait boxes level and safe? When you sit on the box is your rod still just off the water surface? Answer 'yes' to all these questions and you are ready to begin.

Unfortunately all swims do not have 'armchair' facilities, and you may be forced to actually stand down in the water. Don't let this worry you, in fact it can be a very pleasant and efficient position from which to float fish . . . assuming, of course, your waders don't leak. If a bank is really bad, or is very high so that you would be perched way above the water, then it may be better to get into the water. Both cases will mean a different set-up of tackle to a 'sit-down' swim.

Assemble things in the same order, but position the seat box so that it can be used as a platform either to the side or in front of your fishing position. Take care when setting up, and be sure you are going to be safe. Mud has a habit of claiming boots when you try to move about, and watch out for dangerous ledges that could deposit you a lot closer to the fish than would be good for your health.

A rear rest may be required to support the extreme end of the rod while adjustments are being made to the tackle. Use a wide one and get it in the right position so the rod is easy to reach without stooping. The landing net will need some support in the form of rests, too, otherwise the net end will sink and be difficult to lift when required to land a fish.

A bait apron will make life easier when fishing from a standing position – it can take not only bait but spare hooks, disgorger, catapult, shot box and maybe a few possible float alternatives that may be needed should conditions change suddenly. The seat box can take extra bait or groundbait bowl, both of which tend to float away if left to their own devices. Get everything out that is going to be needed and then stow the rest away safely on the bank behind but still within reach.

Once you start fishing try to remain as still as possible in the water. Constantly moving your feet around will send shock waves through the water and eventually drive fish further away from you, and in the case of a match even into the next peg.

If you know you will be fishing a swim where standing in the water is a possibility, it may be worth taking along a platform. I call mine the 'oil rig'; they are usually of alloy consisting of a frame and legs onto which the seat box fits. The best also have bank-sticks and rod-rest stick-holders. With a platform the standing swim can often be converted into a sit-down one. A platform may also come in handy on fast-flowing rivers which tend to push a seat box over – without one, a conventional box would have to be filled with water and a few rocks in order to keep it in one place.

Other tackle, such as the keepnet, needs to be positioned with perhaps even more care than when being used from the bank. Keep it low and flat and in the best place to catch those dropped fish.

Warning

When setting up in the water, take into account what will happen should a lock gate be opened suddenly or a boat pass by. Commercial barges can be a real problem and many an angler gets very wet from the bow wave sneaking round behind his pitch.

● *A platform for the tackle box will make those difficult banks so much easier and more comfortable. The adjustable legs ensure a level seat from which to work and reduce the danger of falling in*

At the end of a session begin the packing-up operation with the same precision as the assembly. Unless you are in a match it will pay to return your catch first of all and then stake the net out on the bank to dry. It's surprising how much a wet net will weigh by the time you have walked a couple of fields. A dry net also tends to smell a bit sweeter than a wet one that is to spend the next half-an-hour fermenting in the car boot.

Fit lids on bait boxes next, and put them up the bank out of harm's way. Take down the bait tray, and tip left-over groundbait on the bank for the birds. If you feel comfortable there is nothing wrong with breaking down rod and tackle from your sitting position – after all, you will be able to reach everything from there and can pack up without picking your way across a maze of equipment. Once the rods are taken apart I like to put them in their bags and into the holdall, well away from danger.

Check that shot boxes are closed and all floats are in place in their box. Pack up neatly and dry off as much as possible to save time later. The very last thing to come down is the landing net – exactly the reverse to when you started. But there is just one more thing to do before leaving, and it is as important as anything you will ever do on the bankside. Pick up any litter that is around . . . yes, yours *and* anyone else's that may have been there when you arrived.

SHOTTING PRINCIPLES

Shotting is the most important part of float fishing technique. Get it wrong and presentation will suffer, tangles will be frequent and casting will be impeded. The art of shotting is perhaps the most vital of all angling skills and must be learned well – but without allowing it to become too complicated. I well remember one of my Peterborough DAA National team colleagues telling me that it was not how much or how little shot you used that mattered, it was where you put it that was the real secret. That was a lesson I never forgot, and it is one that perhaps should become the basis of all your shotting principles.

This particular angler was known for his habit of fishing with a lot of weight and larger than normal floats. His rather crude-looking tackle still caught him more than his share, even on waters where catches were mainly of tiny fish.

Shotting needs to be balanced, otherwise even a large amount of weight will not give good casting range. As a general rule for waggler work at least two-thirds of the total weight will need to be located around the float, usually in the form of locking shot, with the remaining third broken down and spaced down the line.

You can try a few little tests to get the feel of different rigs. Select a float of, say, four AAA shot load and lock it at 8ft with two of these shots. Place the other two together about 15in from the hook and try casting. The result will be a terrible, splashy and very short-range cast because the two loads will be working against each other. Now put three AAAs at the float and the fourth at 15in from the hook; this will cast much better but still not perfectly.

Remove the single shot and break it down into a selection ranging from a BB down to a no 8, spreading them down the line evenly from a foot below the float. The cast will now be smoother and the tackle will fly much better, laying the line out straighter.

However, even with this simple rig all is not right, and unless used with a lot of care will cause the hook to fly back during flight so that it catches on either the float or one of the shots. In order to prevent this, apply the 'half-depth rule': this involves setting the tackle at the desired depth, locking the float with

shots and then spacing all the others from just below half depth down to the hook. There are some exceptions to this rule, for example, when fishing 'on the drop' for fish feeding high in the water, but for 99 per cent of waggler fishing it is an idea that will serve you well.

Locking shots apart, the smallest will always go nearest to the hook, gradually increasing in size nearer the float. This principle applies also to stick float fishing, except in a few situations.

Bulk shotting is a term used to describe a rig that has a number of shots bunched together down the line. This rig will be used to beat surface-feeding fish such as bleak that may otherwise intercept a bait meant for better quality fish feeding beneath. It will also be called for to tackle deep waters, and ones where there is a strong flow and a need to get a bait down and controlled quickly.

Several small shots, say four BBs, are better than the equivalent two AAA or a single swan shot. They seem to hang on the line better, are less likely to slide about and, of course, permit you to move some weight around easily. And never be afraid to move shotting around. It often happens that a text-book rig will not be as effective as something a little unconventional. Moving the bottom 'tell-tale' a few inches closer or further away from the hook may bring an instant response. But think about what you are doing and why – that way you will understand what effect a certain shot is having on the tackle.

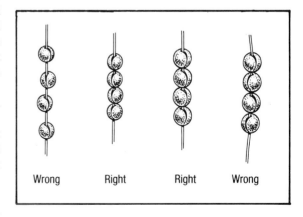

● *Bulk shots need to be attached with care. Leaving small spaces between each shot will cause tangles. Try to get all the shots with their slits facing the same way and central on the line*

Plumbing the Depth

The very best of shotting patterns and a faultless cast will all come to little in the way of bites if the depth at which the tackle is set is wrong. With a few notable exceptions (such as rudd, chub, dace and bleak) coarse fish usually feed on, or very close to, the bottom and it is there that our bait is going to attract most attention. With this in mind, one of the last things to do before starting to fish – before even baiting a swim – is to plumb the depth accurately.

I know a fair number of very good match anglers who never carry a plummet of any description. They rely on knowledge and the ability to very quickly work out an exact depth by altering their tackle and reading the signs that register on their float. For a start, however, we will look at the rights and wrongs of finding the depth with a plummet in the traditional manner.

A plummet is a weight, usually between ¼oz and 1oz, that can be attached to the hook or bottom shot. The oldest pattern is pear-shaped and has a small cork pad let into the base and an eye at the top. Line and hook are passed through the eye and the hook embedded in the cork.

● *Two types of plummet. The round type is a favourite of continental anglers, while the conical shape is a more traditional British pattern*

Continental patterns are usually spherical in shape, split in half and held together by means of a spring. When two small protrusions at the spring are pressed together, the plummet opens to reveal a hollow inside. The hook or bottom shot can be trapped inside this hollow, and once the spring is released the plummet remains in place. Alternatively you can use a lump of one of the putty-like lead shot substitutes, but be sure to remove all traces of it after the job is finished

otherwise shotting will be upset by the extra load.

To plumb the depth accurately, first of all set up the tackle rig in the usual manner, float, shots and hook. Be sure the shotting is correct and the float set to the estimated depth. Open the bale arm of the reel and gently swing the tackle out with an underarm action, raising the rod tip to give the required distance. (If the fishing range is much beyond five rod lengths then it may be better to employ the method on p. 55.)

For example (A), let us assume the float has been pulled under by the plummet on this first check. If so, lift the rod tip gently and try to feel the plummet, at the same time noting how far you have to raise the rod tip before the float can be seen. Now wind in the tackle and raise the float by the estimated amount you lifted the rod. This should not put the tackle at about the water's full depth.

Repeat the same process. If the float now sits flat on the surface (B) you have overdone the depth estimate. Raise the rod again and try to gauge how much the float can be lifted before weight is felt. Shallow off accordingly and repeat the whole operation again until such time as the float can be seen just above the surface as it would appear under normal fishing conditions. This will now be the depth of the water, and extra inches can be added or taken off according to the requirements of the day.

Use the plummet also to test the entire swim. Swing it in at the top of the swim and at several places along it. You may find a hole or a rising shallow, and all the time you should be building up a mental picture of the contours of the bottom. Try a few swings both closer than, and beyond your expected fishing line. It is just possible you will find a ledge or some other feature that may be worth exploiting before the day is over. Above all, don't rush things. Take your time – it will be an investment – and try to do everything without making too much disturbance.

Size of plummet will be determined by the sort of swim and water you are fishing. A fast and deep swim may need a fairly heavy plummet in order to obtain an accurate 'feel' – the rule is, use one just big enough to cope and heavy enough for you to feel, without pulling it along the bottom. In very fast, deep and powerful swims there will always be some slight difference between actual depth and the depth you arrive at by lifting for the 'feel'. This is because the flow will cause a bow or angle to form in the line between float and plummet within seconds of the weight reaching bottom. In such conditions try to get a reading as quickly as possible and don't be afraid to double check. And in

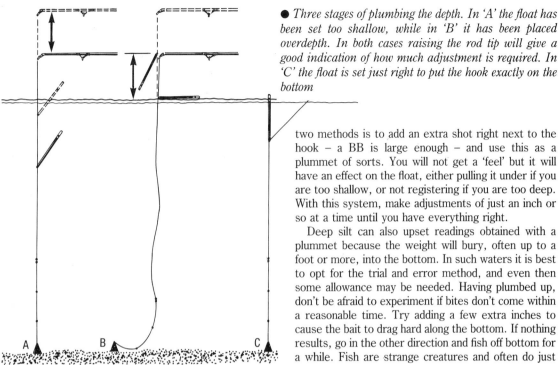

● *Three stages of plumbing the depth. In 'A' the float has been set too shallow, while in 'B' it has been placed overdepth. In both cases raising the rod tip will give a good indication of how much adjustment is required. In 'C' the float is set just right to put the hook exactly on the bottom*

two methods is to add an extra shot right next to the hook – a BB is large enough – and use this as a plummet of sorts. You will not get a 'feel' but it will have an effect on the float, either pulling it under if you are too shallow, or not registering if you are too deep. With this system, make adjustments of just an inch or so at a time until you have everything right.

Deep silt can also upset readings obtained with a plummet because the weight will bury, often up to a foot or more, into the bottom. In such waters it is best to opt for the trial and error method, and even then some allowance may be needed. Having plumbed up, don't be afraid to experiment if bites don't come within a reasonable time. Try adding a few extra inches to cause the bait to drag hard along the bottom. If nothing results, go in the other direction and fish off bottom for a while. Fish are strange creatures and often do just the opposite to what we expect.

Having spent so much time plumbing, it would be foolish to start shifting the tackle around without first making some sort of check on the original reading obtained. To do this, the first job after plumbing is always to wind the float along the rod to a position you can remember later. On deep waters this may mean winding it right to the tip ring. A ferrule or rod ring will do, so long as you remember which one. With the float in this noted position, hold the hook and check where it comes down the rod. Mark this spot either mentally or by means of a piece of sticky tape, a blob of Tipp-Ex or any method you like. You will now be able to re-set the rig even after breaking down and completely changing it several times.

A check on the depth in this manner is also something that should be done every so often, especially if bites stop coming suddenly. It is possible that locking shots have shifted and allowed the float to move during casting. Minor adjustments to depth should be made in small stages – an inch or two at a time is the way to go about searching a swim. Alterations made by the foot will rarely be as effective when it comes to finding a few fish on hard days.

A word of warning, too. Plummets are heavy and even the smallest is too much for a match rod to throw safely overhead unless you are a very good and confident caster.

flowing water a waggler with plummet attached will quickly be pulled under by the current, so concentrate and think about what you are doing right from the off.

An alternative to all this swinging about with a plummet is to adopt the expert's trial and error system mentioned earlier. To do this, just start fishing at the estimated depth and allow the tackle to move through the swim unchecked. If it runs through and shows no sign of catching on the bottom, add a few inches at a time until contact with the bottom registers by the float being pulled under or checking slightly as it moves downstream.

Should the float not run through evenly from the start, it is obvious you are too deep, so reverse the process and try again. It can help here to move a shot down close to the hook in order to get a more accurate reading, but don't forget to move it back to the correct position before fishing begins.

This method does take a bit more time and perhaps experience, but it also has the advantage that you may find fish feeding higher in the water than you had expected, and in any case the swim will be disturbed less – an important point if you happen to be fishing for shy species such as chub or carp in shallow water. A shoal of bream may also not take kindly to being bombed by a big plummet. A compromise between the

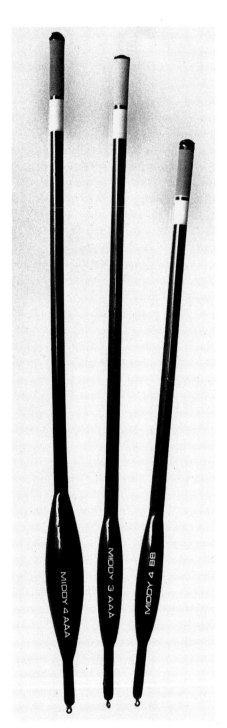

● *Commercial floats are usually marked with shot loadings, but use them only as a rough guide to the total load required*

A bottom shot moved a little nearer to the hook may be all that was needed to steady a bait slightly. Or giving a bit more room from the hook could tempt shy fish to take a bait which had been ignored before. Maybe bites have been hard to detect and maggots have come back chewed without a bite showing on the float. This is the time to move a shot closer to the hook, or maybe in severe cases, even bring down a second one to add to the lowest, thus exaggerating the effect a bite has on the float because more weight is being moved in one go.

These principles are very basic but will see you through many situations; you may want to make slight adjustments to suit your own waters. At this stage it is worth noting that many commercial floats have some form of shot-loading guide printed on them. A float that shows, for example, three AAA as its load will still need to have that total broken into

Sure Shots

A few little tricks are also worth using to ensure you get the best out of your shotting. As well as being perfectly round and evenly cut, it also pays to get split shot on the line in a certain manner. Where two or more are used together in a bulk, try to get the splits all facing the same way – this will help stop any spiralling effect. Take time to get each shot centrally located on the line, too. With long bulk shot groups there is sometimes a tendency for them to twist over each other, though much of this can be avoided by pushing them right up tight – there is no point in having any gaps.

If a shot group persists in tangling, slip a length of silicone rubber over them like a sleeve; alternatively, replace the whole lot with a piece of tungsten tubing, stopped with a small shot at either end or a piece of cocktail stick pushed down the bore. With locking shot there is often a problem with them sliding about. The cure is usually to replace the large size with two smaller ones, or at least add a no 8 or 10 above and below, reducing the other shot by the same amount.

Some anglers (although I can't ever remember having to do it myself) use a 5mm length of silicone tubing slipped on the line below the float which is intended to act as a shock absorber against the float on the strike. This idea may be a good one to try when fishing with very heavy wagglers on deep water, the sort of conditions that demand a hard strike to set the hook.

more manageable sizes, so it is vital to have a working knowledge of the equivalent shot sizes.

The following table is a good guide and maybe one you will want to copy and keep handy inside your float box lid. But never use commercial markings as anything more than a rough guide. With home-made floats it is an easy task to load and mark each float individually, but on a commercial basis an overall average is about all that is practical because variations between materials cannot be taken into account.

Shot equivalent guide:

1 swan	=	two AAA or four BB
1 AAA	=	two BB or three no 1
1 BB	=	two no 4 or four no 6 or seven no 8

Deciding how much shot to use is probably something that only comes with experience, and is matched to the ability of the angler. But always decide how much shot you need for the conditions facing you, and then find a float to suit. Never select a float because you like the colour and then shot to balance it; and if a swim demands four AAA, it is no good trying to struggle through with half that amount just because it happens to be the loading of your favourite waggler.

Styl weights

Another form of weight that is very handy is the 'styl', cylindrical in shape but with a split just like a conventional shot. These are ideal for use with hemp or tares, baits that can lead to shot bites if ordinary shots are used individually. Styl weights are used a lot by pole anglers, but they are a handy means of creating a slow-falling bait if used instead of normal shots.

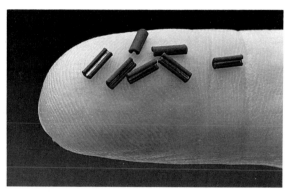

● *Styl leads are ideal for use when hempseed fishing and are also a favourite with pole anglers*

● *Special pincers are required to fasten styl leads to the line*

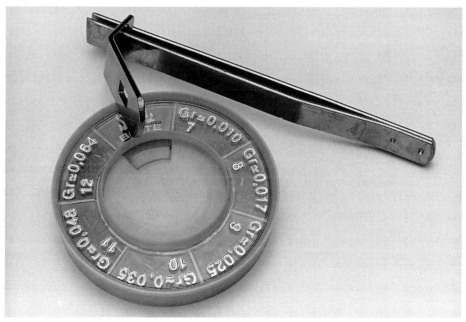

Tackle Layout, Shotting Principles and Casting

To attach styl weights you will need a special pair of pincers, available from tackle dealers. Picking up the smaller sizes can be difficult, but a good trick is to tip a few out onto the dispenser top and give it a gentle shake or a couple of taps with your finger. This will cause the weights to flip over and land split downwards, a position which then permits you to pick them up easily. Pinch them gently on the line, keeping them as central as possible. Styl weights also have the advantage of spreading the load along a lower length of line, thus reducing the chance of damage to low breaking strains.

● *The most vital of all shotting principles is the 'mid-water' rule if tangles are to be avoided. By ensuring the bulk shotting is below half depth the hook cannot catch on the float during casting*

The mid-water rule

No matter which type of weight you use it will cause problems if not located correctly within a shot pattern, and we have already looked at the principles of how much weight can be used down the line and the need to balance this against a larger quantity at the float.

In waggler fishing, the usual style is to lock the float in position with a fair proportion of the total load – two-thirds is the suggested minimum to ensure smooth casting. Equally vital is that the remaining shot down the line is positioned with the 'mid-water rule' in mind. It *is* possible to fish with a whole line of small shot spaced equally from float to hook, but sooner or later the hook will fold back during casting and catch on the line near the float. In order to

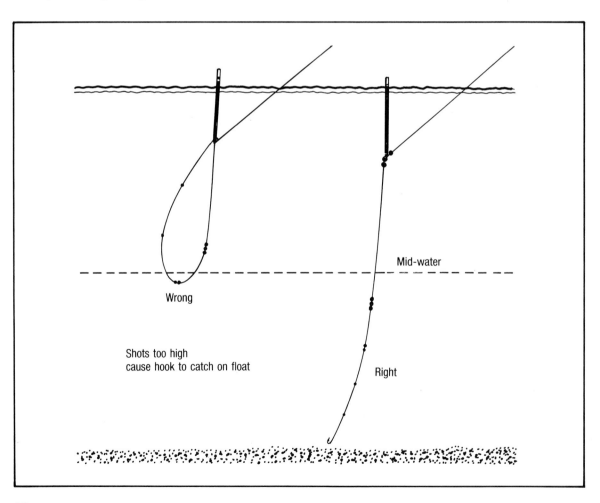

Wrong

Shots too high
cause hook to catch on float

Mid-water

Right

Self-cocking Floats

Self-cocking floats have a lot in their favour and at times a good one can be hard to beat. They do, however, have a few bad qualities.

Self-cockers are usually made with a short base stem of brass or with a weight of some description built into the lower part of the body – a length of quill with some wire wrapped around the bottom will cast as far as any float I know. But once it lands on the water it will dive beneath the surface for a second or two – not a good thing if you happen to be fishing a shallow, clear-water ledge for shy chub. Reason for this is the very streamlining built into a self-cocker. A similar float without load but locked in position with shots will tend to stay on the surface when it lands.

Shot has further advantages: a reasonable self-cocker is one that has, say, half its total load built in. The rest can then be added in the form of shot, which can be moved around should conditions or the feeding habits of a shoal change suddenly. Also, if locking shots are used to add some weight to a stem they can be kept down to a much smaller and more manageable number, thus reducing the possibility of tangles caused by twisting.

The best self-cocking floats are those which have the weight loaded as near to the base as possible – built this way they fly like a dart and cast truly. But with any self-cocking float you must learn to use it only when conditions are right, bearing in mind the shortcomings just outlined.

prevent this, apply the 'mid-water' rule: position the first shot below the float no higher than midway between float and hook and ideally slightly nearer to the hook. Such a simple thing to remember and certainly something that will make all your waggler fishing so much easier. Once that main bulk is in position the rest can go in a string below until the final 'tell-tale' shot is reached nearest the hook.

The whole idea of this pattern of shotting is to use plenty of bulk at the float to provide weight for casting, and to give the tackle stability in the water. The shots beneath the surface are there to present the bait in a way a fish might expect to find it, that is to say in the most natural manner possible.

Before any shot is placed it should be known what its effect will be on the tackle in general and if in fact it is needed at all. The best shotting is often the most simple, and should you ever feel your rigs are getting out of hand, try going back to the very basic principles and start again.

Know your float loadings

Experience will eventually enable you to have a fairly accurate guess at how much shot a particular float will take, but ideally every one in your box will be accurately marked with its load. Shop-marked loads are fine, but are often way out due to variation in material density and the thickness of paint used on that particular batch.

Most of my floats have been marked using paint and a very fine brush. I mark each one with the total load, using my own code: 1A, 3x8 will mean a load of 1AAA and three no 8s. A equals AAA, B a BB and the other marks are shot sizes preceded by the number required. You can make up any code you like. Some anglers develop a colour code of dots – say, two red dots indicate two AAA, blue will be for BB, and so on. How you arrive at a load does not matter, so long as you can understand it.

Self-cockers can be a problem unless you give them the same treatment. I mark mine with an 'L' to stand for 'loaded', and then indicate how much extra weight is needed to fully cock them. Loadings on some continental floats and in particular on pole floats is usually shown in grammes rather than in our shot sizes. This is fine so long as you are going to use olivette weights that are also coded in grammes, otherwise give them the personal code treatment and save yourself a lot of time later on.

CASTING

Casting a waggler

The most common fault with the less experienced caster's technique is that it has a shallow trajectory and as a result lands with too much force. What we are looking for is a higher arc, giving the tackle sufficient height to carry it the required distance but with just enough power so that nearly all the energy transmitted through the rod has been used by the time that distance is reached. Several different types of cast will be needed in order to cope with all types of swim, conditions and even float patterns. So let us begin with the basic principle of casting a waggler to give distance over a swim that is snag-free and has no unmanageable wind problem.

Assuming you have selected a suitable float for the job and that everything is in order – such as the shotting and the reel spool being fully loaded – it is a case of getting the cast itself running to form. For really long-distance fishing it may pay you to fish standing up, but that choice will be yours depending on bank conditions at the time and how well you can perform sitting down. Incidentally you will usually see bites better from a standing position when fishing at long distance. Casting is not a strong-man's sport. Try to get distance through sheer

effort and you will probably end up with a shorter rod than you began with, and that's expensive.

Assuming you are right-handed, that is to say you wind the reel with your left hand, begin by winding the float well up the rod – about a couple of feet from the tip is about right, but this distance will need to be shorter if the swim is very deep. Position the right hand on the handle directly above the reel, and the left right at the bottom of the butt.

Now, trap the line with the index finger of the right hand and open the bale arm (we are assuming at this stage that the reel is not an automatic). Bring the rod up almost to the vertical and with the arms reaching high, move it backwards to about 2 o'clock. The forward movement begins to bring it over the water again, the right hand pushing the handle forward and slightly downwards as the left pulls backwards and slightly upwards. It's a sort of 'push-and-pull' motion between the two arms.

The rod and tackle are both now moving forwards, and once the rod tip reaches a point between 10 and 11 o'clock, line is released. Continue to follow through with the rod until its tip almost touches the water, and your left hand (which is still holding the extreme butt) has ended up under the right armpit. It sounds complicated, but it is all really very simple.

Now cast again, and as the tackle is about to hit the water try 'feathering' the line, the right hand

index finger acting as a brake, checking the line slightly as it runs off the reel spool lip. Done correctly this will slow the tackle down in its final stages of flight, causing it to land in a nice straight line.

Throughout the casting operation always keep your eyes on the float, following it through every stage of its flight. And with the overhead cast just described, the rod should stay as near as possible in a straight line from the vertical to the end of the cast – allow it to wander around, and accuracy will be lost. Timing is the key to any good casting operation and as you improve it will all become second nature.

● *Casting a waggler is done with an overhead action. Begin with the float wound to within a metre or so of the rod tip, and with one hand on the extreme butt and the other controlling line on the reel spool.*

The arms are raised as the rod is moved backwards to between 10 and 11 o'clock.

As the rod is brought forward the hand on the reel pushes forwards while the butt-end hand pulls backwards.

Line is released as the rod builds up power (right) at around 1 o'clock and is then checked as the float reaches its destination.

The final position as the float lands is with the rod pointing slightly tip down from horizontal and the butt stopping just beneath the armpit.

So far, the cast has only put the float and tackle in the required position. Keeping it there for as long as possible before wind takes control of the line and begins to pull it away from a true path will call for one more little trick. Cast again but this time, just as the float lands, push the rod tip a foot or so beneath the water surface and give the reel handle a few quick turns. This will cause the line to sink beneath the surface and out of the wind's skimming effect. So as not to lose accuracy, you may need to cast the tackle a few feet beyond the required fishing position and then wind back briskly as the line sinks.

On open water this method of tackle control is fine, but the luxury of over-casting will not be possible for example when fishing close to the far bank, as may be required when chub fishing. To overcome this problem, cast, and when the rod tip is almost touching the water, give it a couple of sharp twitches by moving the right hand quickly sideways. The tip will react violently and pull just enough line

● *When there is a strong downstream wind line will quickly form a bow if the float is cast to 'A'. By casting slightly downstream ('B') the bow will take longer to form, giving slightly more effective fishing time*

under the surface without pulling the float away from the bank.

A howling downstream wind is always difficult to combat, and you must be prepared to have less fishing time before it takes control and ruins presentation. This will mean more casting and a lot more work, but it will be rewarded with more bites, too. However, casting and then allowing the tackle to be pulled around by the wind at an unnatural pace or across the flow will fool very few fish.

Coping with such a wind is never going to be easy, and you may have to decide to fish a much closer line in order to make the best of a bad job. In the case of waters where long distance fishing is a must, cast slightly downwind so that you are behind the tackle as it begins its journey downstream. You will lose out by not fishing the top end of the swim, but overall presentation will remain good for the maximum length of time.

Narrow rivers and canals that demand a small waggler can often be tackled best with a different cast to the one we have already considered. A cast of three or four rod lengths out can be achieved by a sideways style, similar to the one we will be using

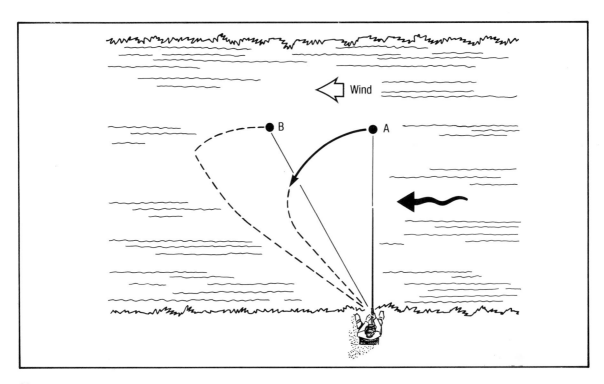

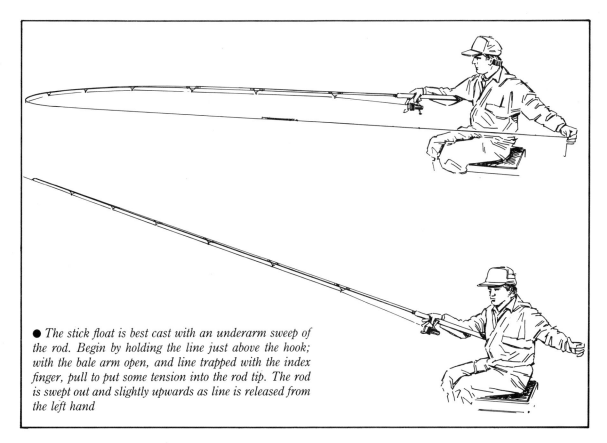

● *The stick float is best cast with an underarm sweep of the rod. Begin by holding the line just above the hook; with the bale arm open, and line trapped with the index finger, pull to put some tension into the rod tip. The rod is swept out and slightly upwards as line is released from the left hand*

when we begin stick float fishing.

Instead of opening the bale arm of the reel and launching the float from a high position, start by opening the bale arm, with line trapped by the index finger. With the thumb and finger of the left hand, grasp the line a couple of inches from the hook and pull slightly to put a curve in the top section of rod.

With the rod to the left, almost parallel with the bank and in a horizontal plane, the cast can begin as a sort of underarm sweep. The tension in the rod tip caused by the left hand will start the cast, then all that is needed is a follow-through until the rod is almost 90 degrees to the bank. Accuracy will again depend on timing, and in particular on releasing the hook and line controlled at the reel just at the right time.

This is not a cast for long distances, but it does have the bonus of causing very little disturbance, an essential requirement on hard-fished canals and shallow rivers.

Casting a stick float

Stick floats and other 'top and bottom' patterns will need a different casting technique to the one used for wagglers. The stick float takes a lot of mastering in order to be cast overhead without tangling. It *is* possible and a lot of good anglers do it well, but only because they have perfected their timing down to a split second and can control feathering of the line accurately.

To begin stick float fishing, it is best to master the underarm and sideways technique. It will lay line out well, and because a stick float is not the tool for distance work anyway, there is no problem in getting enough range. The principle is similar to that for casting a small waggler on a canal (see p. 116). The rod is used as a spring and the tackle casts from a rod held nearly horizontal.

Begin by holding line with the right index finger against the spool lip while the bale arm is released.

Or in the case of closed-face reels, press the release button but keep line pressed to the housing so that it cannot run off. The hook should be about level with, or just below the reel position so that it can be reached easily with the left finger and thumb.

Grasp line just above the hook, pull to build up a little tension in the rod tip, and begin the cast with the rod facing to your left, along the bank. The cast begins by a sweeping movement of the rod that brings it out over the river in front of you. The hook is released from the left hand and allowed to fly out over the water as the right index finger releases line at the spool.

Throughout this operation the rod has been moving outwards in an arc until it reaches 90 degrees from your bank position. For a little extra distance the tip is also allowed to move upwards, so that the rod ends up about 30 degrees from the horizontal.

As soon as the float lands, raise the rod tip and 'mend' line to bring it all straight and behind the float. You will need to repeat this flick of the tip every few yards or so as the float travels downstream and a bow begins to form. Never allow the bow to be in advance of the float because this will act as a sail and pull the tackle through at an unnaturally fast pace; it will also drag it round in an arc across the flow. At all times you should be working hard to get the bait to follow a natural direction, as it might be carried without any external interference.

Mending line correctly is one of the great skills that must be practised in order to become a skilled stick float angler. Done correctly, it should be possible to keep line behind the float at all times without upsetting the float's travel – overdo it, and every time line is mended the float will be moved, too.

Overhead casting of a stick float is not often called for, but if you feel it is essential, the principle is the same as for wagglers. Keep the cast fairly high, but follow through well and check the fall to allow the shotting to straighten out fully – otherwise the whole lot lands in a heap, and since it is usual to have a string of small shots with this float, a lot of time can be lost sorting out the mess.

● *Mending line involves a sweeping flick of the rod with the arm outstretched to lift line over the float and keep it all upstream and free from a bow*

Larger floats such as the Avon do not demand such delicate shotting rigs, and can be cast either under- or overarm without too many problems. Blustery conditions can also be beaten with a modified sideways cast that is a mixture of both the under- and overarm styles.

This cast begins exactly as a conventional stick float side cast but the rod is moved in a sort of loop, moving the butt towards your body and then flicking the wrist to make the tip describe a circle. The tackle is released as the rod reaches the lowest and most forward position in its circle. Result is, the float passes over the top of the rod instead of beneath it as it would normally and lands on the water before the rest of the tackle. By falling in this order there is less time for wind to pick up on the line. It works well enough, but this cast is not to be recommended except for close-in fishing. Don't use it, either, if shot is heavy down the line because the flight will be upset and everything will land at the same time and in a great heap.

4

Feed and Baiting

Although good float fishing skills – presentation, shotting and casting ability – all add up to a fairly effective fish-catching package, there is another area that needs to be looked at in some depth in order to capitalise on them fully: groundbaiting and feeding of a swim in a manner that will attract and hold fish for long periods, feed but not overfeed them, and stimulate them to search out your hookbait.

FEEDING A SWIM

'Little and often' is the way I was taught to feed a swim during my early angling years. In those days, however, that might have meant an egg-sized ball of groundbait every couple of minutes. Things have changed a lot since then and the advent of catapults and throwing sticks has changed the overall feeding pattern a great deal.

One of the best ways to learn good feeding habits is to go along to an important match and watch a top angler at work. What you will see is a machine operating smoothly and regularly, changing gear to suit the pace of the action, speeding up when fish are coming quickly and slowing down if things get hard.

So what is the objective when we feed a swim, either with loose feed or a groundbait mixture? The answer, of course, is to attract fish to the fishing area or to stimulate those that are already there into feeding. It is not a free handout that becomes an alternative to your hookbait.

Imagine for a moment what goes on beneath the surface in a swim containing a shoal of roach about a hundred strong and averaging a couple of ounces each: You *could* fire a catapult pouchful of maggots into the water – that's maybe 150 maggots that sink to the bottom, attracting the attention of the shoal. The quickest fish grab two maggots each, while maybe half the others get an odd one each. Those that got two have done alright, while the slower ones start searching for more and maybe you catch a few as a result during the next five minutes, after which you feed again with another 150 maggots. The fastest fish zoom in and grab another one or two apiece while the others also get a second helping, having digested the first.

Now at this rate, it doesn't take a 2oz roach very long to eat its fill, and as more and more maggots pour in as a result of regular feeding from above, the shoal slows down its feeding frenzy and becomes more selective. Result is, bites become few and far between and eventually stop altogether. What has happened is the shoal has been overfed and has 'gone off'.

Now, let's take the same swim and do it properly: the first pouch of bait is limited to ten maggots, which means that only ten or so fish get a small free feed. The others dash around searching for their

share and one takes the hookbait in its haste. You catch a couple more, and then feed again with another ten maggots after catching, say, four fish. The process starts over again and still a lot of the shoal is left searching for a maggot.

Continue in this manner and other fish may see the activity and become curious, moving closer to see what's happening. These may be larger fish, that until now have kept out of the swim and are only coming into range because of the extra confidence the other feeding fish are providing. The swim is now building, instead of dying on you, yet the total that has gone into the swim is probably less than the three pouchfuls introduced in the first example.

What we achieved the second time round was to construct a pattern that kept only a few of the total fish population with food to eat. The others therefore continued searching longer, and were encouraged to keep hunting every time a few more free offerings arrived. In some ways, feeding a swim is like setting odds against a fish taking your bait. Feed two hundred maggots in one go and the chances are high against one of the shoal taking your bait. Reduce that feed to a hundred and the odds drop by half – and so on.

The key to all this is to be able to read what is happening and feed accordingly. A swim that is producing regular bites only needs ordinary treatment until bites begin to slow. Once this stage occurs, the usual trick is to cut down the feed rate to half the amount or less until bites pick up frequency again. What you do not want, in most cases, is a great mass of bait just sitting there on the bottom waiting to be eaten.

However, as with most things in angling, there are exceptions to this rule. Chub are a classic example of this, in that a swim full of them will often not respond until a lot of bait is piled in. However, the gently, gently approach is still the one to begin with unless you know the water and its habits well. Remember, it is very easy to put feed into a swim . . . it's very difficult to take it out again if you get things wrong!

Many anglers get off to a bad start with their very first feed of the day. Too often a pouchful of bait goes in before they have first had a few runs through

● *A fine carp, the class of fish that often falls to the attraction of a golden grain of sweetcorn (Chapter 5)*

with a float to search out any hidden problems. Result is, that bait has been fired in totally the wrong place and has actually taken fish away from where they might have been caught.

Not only can fish be stimulated into feeding by what you give them as free offerings, they can also be moved around to feed in the place that suits you best. In the case of match fishing that spot will be as close to you as is practical in order to reduce the time taken to land them, and also to keep them well out of range of the anglers at the pegs either side of yours.

Catching fish right under the rod tip is fine until you drop off one or two straight on top of the feeding

---

● *Norfolk tackle dealer Tom Boulton tries a bread punch at the start of a day's sport. The groundbait and casters will be used as a second line of attack if the bread fails to bring a quick response (Chapter 5)*

● *In goes the first ball of groundbait, but unless it is in the right place it will do more harm than good*

shoal. In my opinion it is far safer to get them feeding a few yards below you so that a hooked fish can be drawn away upstream and well out of the way before it hits the surface.

So, not only do you have to get the amount and frequency right; you also have to judge where to feed. Obviously, a loose maggot fired into a 10ft-deep swim that is pushing through hard, will end up a very long way downstream before it reaches bottom And just to complicate things even more, different baits will fall at varying rates. Hempseed, for example, is very heavy and falls through the water much faster than maggots or casters. Old maggots also fall quicker than fresh ones – something to use to your advantage when fishing a winter flood or a fast swim.

On a swim where you begin by catching well downstream, the trick is to gradually move fish towards you by feeding higher up your pitch. Don't try to do it all in one go, because that only creates a patch of feed too far away for the shoal to find. Far better to do the job a foot or so at a time by moving up just that much with every feeding.

Loose feed can also cause fish to rise up in the water, especially at times when water temperatures are reasonably high and fish are constantly changing their swimming depth. So if bites suddenly stop, don't automatically change feeding patterns until you have shortened down a foot or so, or maybe moved the bottom few shots higher up the rig to give a slower drop to the bait. The change this can bring about is often dramatic, but remember the fish might drop down again without warning and especially if you forget to feed for a while.

So far we have looked at how often and where to feed. The next consideration is when. The little-and-often principle is not likely to let you down that often and it is certainly going to be far better than a great big pile every hour and then nothing.

You can add to the effectiveness of the regular feeding pattern by linking it to your casting. In the days of caster fishing for roach on the Trent, before chub and other big fish took over the river, the usual tactic was to fish a single caster on a delicate, lightly shotted stick float that was eased gently through the swim and checked regularly to cause the bait to flick upwards in an attractive arc. Bites usually came as the check was made or directly the float was allowed to run through again. But in order to make this method work well, feeding had to be timed just right. That meant feeding half-a-dozen casters and then casting into them. What happened was, the hookbait was falling with the loose feed and becoming part of the overall feeding pattern. Done in reverse – that is, casting and then feeding – would result in fish moving up in the water to intercept the loose feed when the bait was just about on the bottom, leaving it totally ignored except perhaps for a gudgeon that thought its luck was in.

So apply that feeding principle whenever possible – feed and then cast; it's surprising what a difference it can make.

Feeding loose hook maggots, casters or hemp is straightforward enough, but when you start adding them to groundbait it becomes a different ball-game.

Big hook maggots need to be used in this way with great care, because too many in a ball will cause it to break up in mid-air. Pinkies are smaller than hook maggots but are still strong enough to have the same effect on a lightly mixed groundbait ball. Squatts, however, are small and tend to move about a lot less than their larger relations; for this reason alone they are the easiest to use with cereal feed.

Which type of maggot you use for feeding is also going to be controlled by the pace of the river and its depth. It goes without saying that a tiny squatt will stand very little chance in a big powerful river, and a hook maggot is the last thing a fish-starved canal needs as feed.

Pinkie maggots and squatts react differently on the bottom, too. Pinkies quickly bury themselves in bottom silt but the squatt stays above it, and I believe it is for this reason that squatts make a superior feed for bream which like to browse along the bottom and suck up anything in their path. The smaller maggot is also more likely to be disturbed by passing fish movements – the lightness of a squatt will allow even a swirl from a passing tail to lift it up, which is attractive and pulls other fish into a swim.

So far we have looked mainly at loose feeding, and for much of your float fishing this is likely to be the main line of attack; however, there are always exceptions, and you will certainly use groundbait. Groundbait, or any form of cereal feed, will eventually take the edge off a fish's appetite, and so must always be used in only enough quantity to do its job – in many cases it is often nothing more than a means of transporting other feed such as maggots into the desired position. It may be that groundbait is needed in order to take maggots down through deep and fast water and deposit them in just the right place. Or perhaps the catching area is beyond loose feed range and the ball of cereal is used to reach the target.

Of course, groundbait in itself is attractive and some fish – bream in particular – will respond well to its presence. How it is fed can play a big part in how long a swim will continue to produce fish. Its use will also be governed by the amount of fishing pressure a water is subjected to – a hard-fished water will require only a small amount, and any hint of overdoing it and your sport will be finished. It is possible to throw in a large amount of cereal without realising it, but as a general rule nothing much larger than an egg is required. Even the big bream shoals that thrive on cereal will not always tolerate cannon balls being dropped on their heads!

If you arrive at a swim that is obviously full of fish, extra care is going to be needed. A shoal of bream in front of you can only be scared away by a bombardment from above. So in such a case, take things very steadily indeed and only step up the size and rate of feed when you know for sure the fish are really keen to feed, when a fish is coming every cast and very soon after the bait has settled.

It is possible to 'read' the reaction to cereal – or for that matter any form of feeding – by the bite response. For example, if a ball of feed is introduced and then quickly afterwards there is a succession of bites that taper off after a while, it shows fish are responding to your feed. If, on the other hand, feeding actually slows down the catch rate, there could be one or more reasons; the obvious one is that cereal groundbait is not to their liking – if that is the case, then loose feed is the only alternative. But before making any change to a feeding pattern you must firstly be sure of the real reason that has slowed the fish down.

Think about the feed you have introduced. Is it getting to the fish in the area you are fishing? Could it be breaking up too high in the water and then either being carried downstream, causing the shoal also to drop down? Has it broken high in the water and brought fish up, away from the bottom? Have you mixed it too stiffly, and is it laying on the bottom in a solid ball at the head of the swim?

Consider all these possibilities and act accordingly It is a bit of a gamble what you choose to do, but some thought before the decision is made increases the odds that you are going to get it right. Try the easiest option first, that is to fish the swim lower downstream. If bites come again you will know that fish have dropped back, and that you have to feed a firmer mix right at the head of the swim to gradually work them back towards you.

The possibility of fish rising in the water is easy to check out, and you can test this by altering shotting to give a slow drop and maybe shallowing off a couple of feet. If they *are* found high in the water, cut down the feed rate by half and introduce a firmer mix to pull fish back to the bottom (see colour photograph on p. 34). Cut out loose feed, too, as this slower-falling food will bring them up again.

If you test both these options without positive

'Panic Feeding' Trick

A tip worth storing away for match-fishing use is the 'panic feeding' trick. This is one to use when the next peg has bream in it and the angler there is catching, but you are not – and don't look like making an impression on the result. What happens is, you mix up some cereal and lace it with casters, maggots or whatever your hookbait is. In go four, five or six good balls in a matter of seconds. The angler who is catching panics, thinking you are about to pull his fish away. He responds by feeding cereal into his own swim – right on top of the shoal, which is probably already getting a little fickle having had a few of its members extracted.

If all goes to plan, the cereal your neighbour has thrown in will be the last straw and the shoal moves off. The gamble, of course, is that the shoal can go either way, towards you or away in the opposite direction. However, I've used the trick many times and it has worked often enough to have made it worth taking the risk. Should it work, you must now treat the shoal with extreme care. Don't feed more cereal otherwise you will be making the same mistake as the angler from whom you have just drawn it. Loose feed and plenty of it, is what needs to be given instead. And whatever you do, don't lose a fish because that really will be fatal.

results, it is worth checking that your groundbait mix is correct for the job it is supposed to be doing. Be certain it is not cloggy and heavy when a fluffy texture is needed. If things appear fine, then the solution is to stop feeding it altogether and put faith in loose feed, starting off very gently until you have some response. The whole secret of good feeding is not to put in anything which isn't going to be cleaned up quickly; it must leave the shoal still searching. Putting bait into a near-barren swim is not going to do anything other than reduce the chances of catching fish even further.

On a more positive note let us consider a few situations where there is a good chance of catching a lot of fish. Feeding should be accurate, but that does not always mean every ball of cereal has to go in at exactly the same spot. In the case of a swim that holds a lot of fish, it may pay to feed to a pattern that gives, say, four possible areas of fish concentration. This system works particularly well with big bream shoals and allows the angler to 'rest' the swim without reducing the catching rate.

By feeding a diamond shape of four corners, fish will be held in four different places and by working around them by casting to each in turn, it is possible to keep fish coming for long periods. With this system it is always best to start at the nearest of the four corners, catching a few fish and then moving to the next nearest, and so on. The final place is the most distant one, and this is used only when the others fail to respond. If fish are taken from it earlier they are going to be drawn through the rest of the feeding shoal with the possibility of scaring them off for good.

Use this method of feeding but be careful not to get fish spread all over the place, and in the case of a match, don't put them within reach of the anglers pegged on either side!

Hopefully by now the value of a sensible feeding pattern is easy to see. How much feed to use is something that comes with experience, but thinking carefully about what has happened during a day's fishing will help to develop a greater understanding of what really is one of the great arts of angling.

Feeding Rules

Basic rules to follow are:

1 The colder and clearer a water, the less feed will be needed.

2 Clear water is best loose fed rather than ground-baited.

3 Coloured water will take cereal, but be sure the colour is not being caused by a feeding shoal that might be scared by heavy cereal.

4 Cold weather slows fish down, they use less energy and therefore can be overfed more easily than when temperatures are higher.

5 Very hot weather may also reduce activity so feed accordingly.

6 Don't feed unless you are sure what is happening.

7 The faster bites are coming the more feed can be given.

8 If bites slow, reduce the amount of feeding accordingly.

● *In a swim holding a lot of fish it will pay to feed a slightly larger than normal area, concentrating on four areas and then working round them in the order shown*

Flow

GROUNDBAITS

Feeding patterns have rules that can generally be applied to good effect – as already mentioned, the one you have probably heard of is 'little and often'. But even before getting the pattern right, it is vital that the groundbait mix itself is correct and fully understood.

The simplest of all groundbait is a breadcrumb base, whereby slices of bread are dried to remove all moisture and then ground to a fine crumb. Not so many years ago only the very whitest crumb was considered to be suitable. We know now that this was far from the right thinking, and probably did as much to reduce our fish-catching chances as improve them. White crumb contains a lot of fat, and no matter how well it is mixed, will clog into very firm balls that will not break up effectively. Brown crumb made by drying off white bread until it begins to roast, as opposed to brown bread, will produce a more versatile groundbait and certainly one that will break up quickly in the water.

Most groundbait of this type purchased from a tackle dealer or bakery will feel reasonably fine, but it can be improved further by putting the whole lot through a fine-meshed riddle. Do this, and you may well find that the good-looking stuff you paid money for has got bits of wrapper in it, coarse crumb and large pieces of crusty material. Pure breadcrumb is what is needed. You will probably find blends containing all sorts of rusk, biscuit, cake and other edible products but if they contain fat it will make good mixing difficult.

Mesh size of your riddle will, of course, depend on the waters you fish. A small canal full of tiny fish will need a much finer groundbait than, say, a deep and powerful river where fish are large. So a canal-bait riddle can be a kitchen type as used for flour, but for a river or lake go for a mesh about 2mm square and if possible in stainless steel or other rustproof material such as zinc. Riddle the bait off and either discard the rough crumbs or put them through a coffee grinder, blender or old-fashioned mincer, and riddle again.

The finished crumbs will need to be stored in a dry place, and one that is mice-proof is also a good idea – I keep most of mine in large plastic bins that have airtight lids. Keep a stock of brown crumb and a smaller amount of pure white; you will need both in order to be able to blend mixtures of different textures and characteristics. The more white there is in a blend, the firmer it will mix.

For much of your fishing on slow or still waters a pure brown crumb will be fine. Don't worry about the mix being dark – in fact, I believe this is a bonus because fish that have to swim over a light patch of bait on the bottom will be nervous and shy, knowing they are easily seen by their enemies such as predatory fish or birds. So use brown whenever possible, adding just enough white to achieve extra stiffness if needed. Usually one part white to four of brown is sufficient, and even that will make up to a very stiff groundbait if too much water is added. Mix the two groundbaits dry first of all, and be sure to get them evenly distributed otherwise the mix will be lumpy when wet.

Having decided on the mix you require, the next stage is to add water. This can be done either by adding groundbait to water or water to groundbait – the choice is really yours, although the bait-to-water method is probably slightly better for getting an even mix. However, adding bait to water means you must have a fair idea of how much water is needed

● *All groundbait, even the pre-packed varieties, will benefit from a riddling*

● *A large, shallow bowl is a must for good groundbait mixing. Buckets and narrow containers will result in a lumpy mix*

for a given amount of bait. Too much water, and you're forced into making up far more bait than is needed.

Mixing is an important part of the preparation. It should not be rushed, and it must be done in the right type of container. There is no place for deep, narrow buckets when it comes to either mixing or using groundbait. A shallow, wide tray or bowl is what is required, in order to get an even distribution

of water and also to stop any maggots that may be added later from working to the bottom and all ending up in the last few balls. Add water slowly, a little at a time, and work it through the crumb with your fingers, working it around like a chef makes up a pastry mix. Use your fingers and keep everything moving around, paying special attention to the corners if the bowl is a square one.

The final mix will depend very much on the water to be fished, but a good groundbait that is required to break up almost on impact with the water will feel almost alive in your hands. A ball made up lightly will begin to burst open if held in an open palm. A little more water, and it will hold together just long enough to reach its target, and only begin to break up as it sinks. Result of such a mix will be a dense cloud that hangs in the water for long periods, attracting fish to your swim.

Even a fairly dry mixture like this can be thrown a long way by forming a ball and then moulding it again with wet hands – the extra water will form a 'skin' on the ball which will hold it together long enough for it to be thrown or catapulted. If you use this little trick it will pay to keep a bait box full of water next to your bowl. If you intend to mix up groundbait at the waterside it should be the first thing you do before setting up any other tackle. The extra time the bait is allowed to 'soak' will allow a better distribution before use, and will give you the chance to see if more water is needed by the time you are ready to begin fishing.

The very best groundbait mix will be the one that is made up at home, but in order to do this you must be sure of the swim and conditions which will face you later. Mixing at home is no different to doing it at the waterside, but the extra time it has to soak will be a bonus. In fact, many continental anglers insist that groundbait should never be mixed on the bankside, maintaining that the sharp crumbs will not have had time to soften and that the fish will not eat it so readily. I'm not convinced, but it's something to think about. Should too much groundbait be mixed up by mistake it can always be frozen, but only if no maggots or casters have been added.

After mixing, force the whole lot through a riddle – the one you use for riddling maggots will do fine. This extra operation will help spread moisture evenly and also ensure no lumps have formed. Try mixing up a batch and then inspect it closely both

● *Groundbaits and additives come in hundreds of flavours and textures. Most anglers have faith in just one or two favourites*

Certainly a few different flavours are worth trying, if only to give yourself a bit of confidence and something different from other anglers around you. Over the years I have tried just about every continental bait that's ever been made, and I've caught a lot of fish with them, too. However, how many I would have caught in the same swims at the same time without anything more than crumb I will never know.

Many of the additives are supposed to act like a rapid laxative on the digestive system of the fish; this purging then stimulates them into a feeding frenzy. Other ingredients take in water at different rates which results in a constant stream of tiny particles rising and falling through the water. The best blends seem almost alive in the water, and it is possible to see the various oils and extracts forming blobs on the surface.

A worthwhile tip is to add a little of one of the special baits to a plain breadcrumb mix. This is a cheaper way of using the rather expensive pre-packaged products, and a dilution of three or four to one with crumb does not seem to detract from the effectiveness. Hemp oil, aniseed, vanilla, caramel, amino acids and all sorts of magical chemicals go into some baits. Most have some use, but none will compensate for a lack of basic angling skill.

Colour is another thing. I believe fish get used to a particular colour and after being caught a few times get very wary, so a change to something new will often work wonders for a season or two. Then as others begin copying your ideas the effectiveness will be lost, and you may need to start again with a new trick.

I am a great believer in red as a base colour for my bait. It is a colour that occurs naturally in water – bloodworms, for example, one of the most natural of all fish foods, are brilliant red, and berries, worms, even the tails and eyes of some fishes are red. Yellow has some uses, too. In really coloured water it is the most penetrating of all colours, while the good old standby, bronze, seems to be a favourite of roach and chub in particular.

I have one rule with all these: the hookbait, and if possible anything that goes into the groundbait is of the same colour. Red, for example, will be fished with red squatts, red pinkies or casters; bronze goes well with bronze samples of the same maggots and bronze hookbaits – and so on. My thinking is based

before and after riddling. The difference in texture will convince you the job is worth doing. With all groundbait mixing you should be aiming to produce a mix that is completely lump-free, evenly soaked and of a consistency that will 'work' in the water and not lie for hours as a collection of dead lumps on the bottom.

Additives are a matter of choice – some anglers swear by them while others are not convinced.

on the assumption that fish get 'locked' onto one colour and can easily get confused by too much contrast. This rule, however, like so many in angling, is not infallible, so don't hesitate to switch to a bronze hook maggot if the red one is not working. Theories are only any good if they work on the day.

Getting a particular colour is not difficult, thanks to the modern pre-packed groundbaits that often come with a very powerful colouring of their own. 'Masterclass' is one that springs readily to mind, and even when blended at two to one with crumb will give a dense shade.

Liquid colourings can be cheaper and there are several of these on the market. Many are nothing more than colourings and will not add the other flavours found in pre-packed groundbaits; but that is a matter you will have to decide for yourself. Good shades of dye can also be found in the food colourings that line the shelves of our supermarkets.

● *Extra-fine groundbaits such as those for canal use need a fine spray to ensure the mixture is damped evenly.*

One other mix that you may find useful is the shallow canal special. A real problem to mix, but get it right and it will catch fish on the hardest water. Originally developed for fishing very close-in with a pole, it will work best in coloured water of no more than 18in or so deep. And believe it or not, white – pure white – has been the best cereal I've used for this mix.

Begin by riddling a pound or two of the best white crumb through a kitchen sieve. The mesh must be fine, and it will take some time and produce a fair amount of waste, but the cereal obtained will be excellent for the job. Mix it with care, adding just enough water to make it damp – it will certainly be much drier than anything you would expect to use on a river. The best method to get the right amount of dampness is to use a plant sprayer which gives off a mist of water. Keep spraying as you work the batch of cereal with your fingers, adding spray until the crumb will just hold together in very tiny pieces. When fishing you will need to use no more than a pinch the size of a thumb nail at a time.

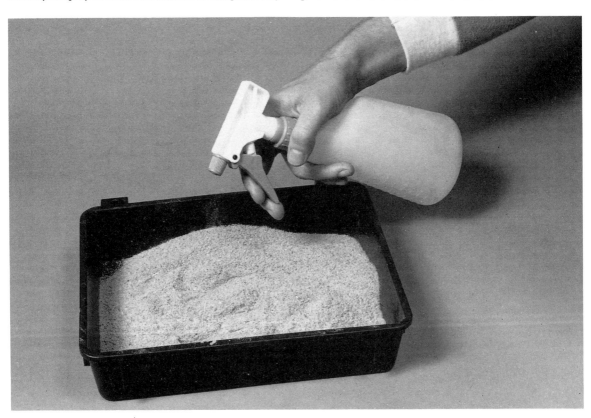

Catapult Accuracy

Accuracy with a catapult is something that you must develop. Aim well above the proposed fishing area and try to find a marker at which to aim. A thistle, tree or bush on the far bank, a weed bed or anything similar will do. Check how far back you need to pull the elastic and then stick to it every time.

In a head wind or at extreme range even a catapult will not do the job. Remember, you are looking to concentrate feed in a tight area, not spread it all over the river. A dodge under these conditions is to riddle off some hook maggots and place them in a clean bait box, dampening them just very slightly with a spot or two – no more – of water. Next, add some dry Horlicks, malted milk or if you can find any, a product called 'Stickymag'. A few minutes in any of these and maggots – or casters – will acquire a sticky coat and will then hold together in balls which can be fired with a catapult a long way.

Go easy on the size of ball you use, as otherwise a lot of bait will land in a small area and may be cleaned up in a single mouthful by a feeding fish, filling it for the rest of the day. Take care also not to overdo the malted milk etc, or you will have a job scraping the bait off the bottom of the bait box.

● *A couple of good catapults are an essential part of the float angler's kit. These examples have small cups which prevent bait from scattering in too wide an area*

This is a mix for close work, and any more than a metre from the bank will be too far for it to carry in this state. You could add a little more water for deeper or more distant fishing, but always use the minimum possible.

It sounds very specialised, and that's just what it is. I have used it to good effect when match fishing for gudgeon with a single squatt as hookbait. A mix of a pound of dry crumb will be enough for a five-hour session, and like all groundbait it will need running through the riddle again once it has been dampened – you can use the same fine kitchen sieve. Because the mixture is so dry it will pay to keep the spray handy while fishing and give the crumb a little freshener from time to time.

Effect of this ultra-dry mixture is a very fine cloud which hangs in the water and then settles very lightly on the bottom silt. A heavier blend would not only overfeed tiny fish very quickly, it would also be lost in the silt. But should a boat pass through you will have lost the whole lot and feeding will need to be started over again. Remember, it is a pinch at a time and no more.

Let us now move to the opposite end of the feeding scale, one that calls for mixes of great stiffness, able to get through deep and very fast water before breaking up. White crumb can be made into very firm balls, and can be made like concrete by adding some flour before wetting. Ground rice has the same effect.

Often firmness needs to be only part of the plan. Conditions may call for a groundbait that is heavy enough to get down to the bottom as a solid ball before being swept away, and in this case don't be afraid to add a heavy soil as a binding agent. The French use a clay called 'leam', but any soil will do the job – mole-hills are good because the soil is usually fine and lacking in stones. Even so, a riddling is essential before adding to the crumb.

My Peterborough team once used another trick to fish a National Championship on Norfolk's tidal Broads rivers: we added cooked, mashed potato to our mixture. This made up into very heavy balls that sank with unbelievable speed and got through the tide race to reach the bream that lived in the deep water. It proved a good idea, too, and we finished second, beaten (in those days before a points system) by just 2½oz by Leighton Buzzard. As a result of that match, Robin Harris – a member of our spud-throwing team – went on to earn an England team place and ultimately a world individual crown.

I am telling you of these rather strange mixtures only because they may one day solve a problem on a hard water. Try other binders such as scalded bran, maize meal or even pig meal, but in every case use them as a last resort and only after more conventionl groundbaits have failed to cope. On some waters no groundbait at all is the best approach. Loose feeding may be all that is required, and provided the fishing area is within catapult range there should be no problem in getting offerings such as casters or maggots into the water.

A final word of warning on adding maggots, casters or other hook samples to groundbait: never put in a whole load of maggots or casters at a time. Maggots will work to the bottom of the bowl, and in any case will absorb water from the mixture and then float when cast or at best sink very slowly; casters left lying on top of the groundbait will tend to dry out and float, too.

Keep your groundbait neat, and add only a few maggots, squatts, pinkies or casters to the corner of the bowl from which you are about to make up a ball for feeding. And even doing it this way you will still need to stir things up from time to time to prevent the surplus finding its way to the bottom of the bowl.

And on the subject of surplus, never throw left-over cereal into the water when you pack up for the day. Bait dumped in the margin is unlikely to be eaten and may even turn sour and spoil the water. Far better to tip it on the bank where it will become a welcome meal for birds and wildlife. But please: *no* other litter!

BAITING THE HOOK

All the time, preparation and cash that is put into obtaining good bait can be wasted if it is badly hooked. Bites will be missed, fish will come off for no obvious reason and the bait will lose much of its attractiveness. Good tackle and superb presentation will not cover up the faults if this important part of float fishing is overlooked – yet I have seen even the most experienced anglers hooking a maggot wrongly and in a manner that is going to cause all sorts of problems that could so easily have been avoided.

Correct choice of hook pattern can also play a part, and in some cases is essential if the bait is to remain in ideal condition. Relating hook size to bait is obvious enough. You would not fish a lobworm with a size 20 hook or a single maggot on a 10, but the subject goes deeper and is one that will earn a lot of bonus if considered sensibly from the start.

Maggots will make a good start, in particular the large, commercial hook maggot. Most anglers already know that the hook is passed through the ragged piece of flesh that protrudes slightly from the blunt end of the maggot, and that it is the best way to keep a maggot lively. But even attached in this manner there is a right and wrong way.

Take a maggot and hold it between finger and thumb ready to hook it. Apply a little pressure and the ragged, fleshy protrusion will extend a little, making hooking easier. Now think about the direction from which the point should be inserted. Hooked from the outside, so that the point crosses the maggot's body, the point will be just beyond centre. Left like that the maggot can turn up and hook itself again at the opposite end, completely covering the point in the process.

What has to be done is to pass the hook through the protrusion from the bait's centre so that it passes out away from the maggot. In this position the bait cannot work itself over the point again and the hook will be better placed to ensure good contact when a strike is made.

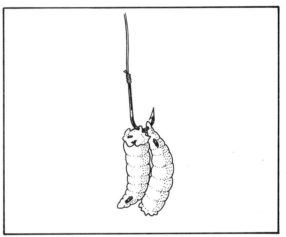

● *Twisting of the line can occur when using two maggots. Prevent spinning by hooking the one nearest the hook point through the pointed end*

When fishing two maggots at a time, hook one in the manner described and the other just through the extreme tip of the pointed end. This will not enhance the 'tip'-hooked maggot's performance but it will ensure the two are evenly balanced, which in turn helps prevent line twist on the retrieve. Try always to hook a maggot so that it is damaged as little as possible and the internal juices do not spill out. A dead maggot is rather unattractive bait when compared with one that wiggles enticingly.

On rare occasions fish will not take in the whole maggot, and instead just nip on the end. If this results in missed bites try hooking through the skin

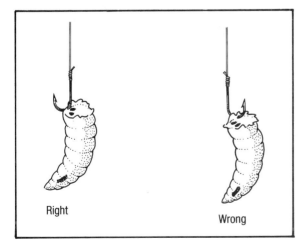

Right

Wrong

● *Fewer bites will be missed if maggots are hooked correctly. Pass the hook through the skin on the blunt end so that the point faces outwards*

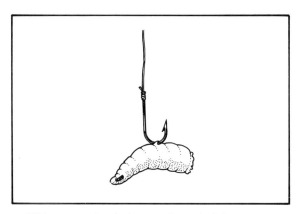

● *If bites are only nipping out the end of the maggot try hooking one through the middle of the skin*

midway along the body. Again it is not the best way to attach a maggot but it can often solve the problem.

Choice of shape for a hook best suited for maggots is rather a personal one. Some anglers like a round bend pattern so that the bait sits neatly in the bend and leaves a lot of point clear; others go for a crystal hook which places the maggot much closer to the point. I am not bothered which I use, but I do believe the hook weight is of much greater importance. I try always to use the finest hook possible in relation to the fish I expect to catch. A fine wire hook will be fine if average-sized roach are the target, but for chub or large bream then I step up to a forged pattern.

Shank length for maggots is a medium one, although for years I seemed to fish a short one without too many failures. The good thing about a longer shank is that it makes baiting easier and quicker, and for some mechanical reason a fish is less able to pull off a longer shank, something to do with leverage.

Pinkies are hooked in exactly the same manner as the larger maggots, but results will be improved if the hook size is kept in proportion. A double pinkie bait will often be worth a try as the next line of attack when a big hook maggot fails. Continue down the range, reducing hook size as you go, to a single pinkie – a 22 is about the largest hook I would want for this bait, and a 24 makes me feel a lot more confident.

Nor should squatt be overlooked as a possible hookbait. Like the pinkie, it needs a tiny hook and will be best when fished on very fine tackle. The blunt end of a squatt is more rounded than that on a larger maggot and it is also lacking in any visible ragged flesh through which to pass the hook. Squatts are tough, however, and it is no problem just to hook them as close to the end as possible.

Casters, although lacking in movement, still need some care when being hooked and if this is done incorrectly the whole thing will just collapse and you will be left with a broken shell which has lost all its contents. For caster fishing a fine wire, round bend, long-shanked hook is best – the fine wire helps keep the bait light and looking natural in the water, the round bend sits best inside the shell, while a long shank helps to hold the caster in the correct attitude and prevents the hook sliding to one end.

To hook a caster, first insert the point in one end, then turn the hook inside the shell and push it down so that the spade end sits just inside the top of the shell. Done correctly, the caster will look perfect, and the only indication that there is a hook inside will be the line protruding at one end. The whole idea is to do as little damage to the shell as possible and as a result keep all the juices inside. A caster that has been attacked by a fish will come up crushed or with the end nipped out, leaving only a ring of shell on the hook.

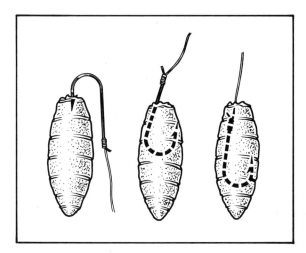

● *The hook can be buried completely inside a caster if threaded down gently from one end*

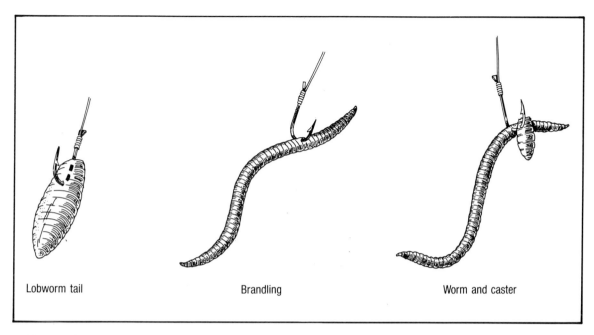

| Lobworm tail | Brandling | Worm and caster |

Keep a few of the darkest casters to one side. These are usually 'floaters' and because they either float, or only just sink, will be perfect for hookers, the extra weight of the hook making them fall at the same rate as loose-fed casters.

Worms are not the easiest of baits to deal with, though lob-tails are no problem and are hooked by burying a long-shanked pattern down from the cut end and then turning to break the point out through the side.

Redworms and brandlings need to be hooked in a manner that lets them work for you – threading them on, or attaching them in a loop by hooking at both ends, is certainly not the way to do it. I like to hook mine just once, about a quarter of the way along from the head. Tipping the hook with a caster or a small maggot is one way to ensure that a worm stays on if casting a long way. Use a hook matched to the bait's size; it must also be a barbed version to prevent it working itself off.

Hooking just once will leave a large portion of the worm free of the hook, and although this may look like a way of missing bites it does work well, maybe because the fish takes in the worm boldly once it gets hold of it. I believe some of this confidence is forced upon the fish which fears it may lose this meal

● The correct ways in which to hook worms. By hooking them in just one place they remain lively. A caster is a good means of 'tipping' a worm to ensure it stays on the hook during long casts

that has enough strength to try and wriggle free of its jaws.

There is also the 'octopus' bait – two or more small worms used at once. These, too, should be single-hooked and allowed to thrash around as much as possible to create the maximum amount of attraction.

Wasp grubs need less effort since they are not going to move at all. But they are very soft, and it is best to use a large hook baited with three or four at a time in the hope that at least one stays on throughout the cast. The hook needs to be sharp to prevent too much damage to the delicate skin of the grub; hook them through the head end if possible.

Hempseed is a tiny bait and is best fished on a 20 or at most an 18. I find a fairly fine, but flat-forged pattern is good because the flats caused by the forging help to keep the seed in place. To hook a grain of hemp, hold the seed at either end of the split between finger and thumb. Squeeze gently to open

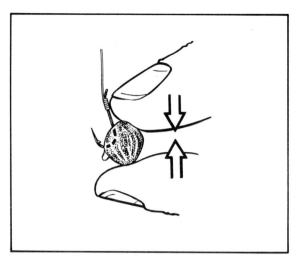

● *Gentle finger pressure will open up the split in a grain of cooked hemp so that the hook can be pushed inside*

up the split and then insert the bend of the hook, leaving the point clear. When finger pressure is released, the grain will jam itself on the hook. Slightly undercooked grains are the easiest to hook in this manner.

Tares are tough things and the hook is passed through the skin only. Use a black or dark-coloured hook if possible, to match the grain, and don't be afraid to go a little on the large side. A 16 is the smallest to use with a tare and a 14 is not really out of place. The pattern I prefer is a round bend because these usually have a wider-looking gape and seem to hold the tare in the best position.

Sweetcorn is one of the easiest of all baits to handle. It is soft but with a reasonably tough skin. Use size 16 to 12 hooks and ideally forged, gold patterns, passing the hook through the skin and out in a manner that ensures the point is well clear.

Bread calls for several approaches since it comes in so many different bait forms. Paste, should you decide to give it a try, needs nothing more than a hook to match bait size. A long shank gives more support to the bread and helps reduce the chances of it coming off in flight. The point is best left protruding slightly to give a clean strike and maximum hooking possibility.

Flake demands the same rules and certainly long-shanked patterns are best. Pinch just enough of the bread around the shank to get it to hold, while leaving a good proportion as fluffy as possible so that it can 'flake' away. Try to protect the bread from drying out by covering with a slightly damp cloth, and each time only pull off enough for a single bait.

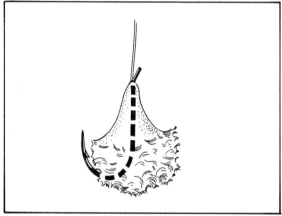

● *A piece of flake pinched on a hook so that it is firmly held by the shank but still able to remain fluffy around the bend*

Punched bread needs a flat surface on which to be cut out with the punch. I must admit I have ruined a few float-box tops in this manner, and would suggest a piece of flat wood is a much better idea. Push the selected size of punch into the bread so that a disc is cut free, and then with the bread still inside, pass the hook – a long shank – through the silt in the punch's side and ease it into the bread with a finger-tip. It can now be pulled free of the punch and carefully eased round to the bend of the hook. Try to handle the bread as little as possible throughout and again, watch the slices are not allowed to dry out.

Bloodworms can be really frustrating. They are soft, small and very easily damaged and hooking calls for care, a certain amount of technique and above all a very sharp, fine wire hook. Special red bloodworm hooks are now available, but I feel the quality and pattern are both far more important than the colour. Pick out the bloodworm to be hooked, and gently hold it between finger and thumb so that the hook can be inserted through the correct end – this end

84

● *The author lands a chub from a fast river. On this occasion the float had been discarded in favour of a swimfeeder rig. Float fishing for big fish such as chub, carp, barbel and bream may demand large quantities of bait in order to keep them shoaled tightly in one swim. The trick is being able to work out what is going on beneath the surface and feed accordingly. If few fish are present the feed rate is reduced. A lot of big fish and more will be needed to keep them occupied*

Feed and Baiting

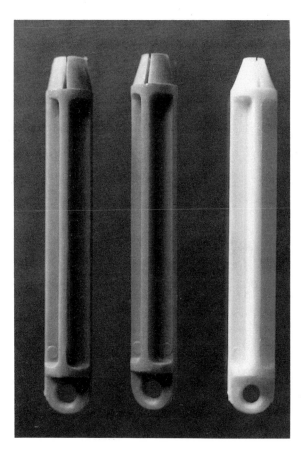

● *Plastic bread punches like these are cheap, effective and come in a variety of sizes*

● *Bread punch correctly positioned on the hook so that the point is clear*

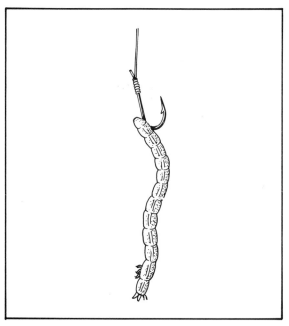

● *A bloodworm hook must be very sharp and preferably have only a small barb. Hook the worm through the slightly darker head end*

should be the slightly darker, greenish head-end of the worm. On close inspection you will see the whole body is made up of small segments – the hook goes through the second segment at the head-end. At least with bloodworms you know if they have been hooked badly. Get it wrong, and the whole worm is reduced to a blob of liquid and a small piece of skin.

Wheat is not a difficult bait to use if prepared as described on p. 100. A gold-coloured hook is best, and because wheat usually attracts fish of good quality, it should be of a fairly sturdy pattern. I like a round bend, but a crystal will work just as effectively.

Pass the hook point into the grain from the side opposite the split, passing it out again so that it sits actually in the soft white inside of the wheat where it has burst through the split. It's a good idea to use at least a 16 for this bait.

● *A swim with a strong but even flow like this one is home to the stick float. The angler pictured using a long pole will be limited to a much shorter run though (Chapter 6)*

5

Baits

Float fishing is all about presenting a bait in a natural manner but if that bait is of poor quality or wrongly hooked it will be unattractive and therefore unlikely to bring success.

Preparing bait carefully, and taking it to the water in the best possible condition, is one more way of stacking the odds in your favour.

This chapter deals with ways to get a wide variety of baits into prime condition and how to obtain and prepare some of the often overlooked ones that can bring success in return for a little extra work.

● *A catch of small fish for Wisbech angler Dick Pinning. On the windswept waters of his fenland home a bodied waggler is a favourite choice (Chapter 6)*

HOOK MAGGOTS

Without a doubt the humble maggot is the most popular and effective of all baits. Every weekend thousands of gallons are sold by Britain's tackle shops and I suspect that they have become a major part of our fish stock's staple diet. But there is a lot of difference between a fresh maggot and one that has been allowed to deteriorate to a stage where it is about to pass into the next stage of its life cycle – the chrysalis, or caster.

A commercial hook maggot is the larval stage of the large housefly or bluebottle. They develop from tiny whitish eggs that are laid on dead flesh by the adult fly. The eggs take about a week to hatch, after which the tiny maggot spends another week or so feeding on the meat until it reaches full size. A few days later it will leave the meat and after absorbing the food it has ingested, will develop into a chrysalis and a week later to the adult fly. It is at various stages during this life cycle that the maggot is used as bait.

Maggots purchased in a tackle shop will probably be a few days old, having been bred on a commercial maggot farm, cleaned of grease and fat from their 'host' meat and transported in sawdust to the dealer, often passing through the hands of a 'middle-man' en route. As anglers, we must check before buying that the bait is of an acceptable standard and not unduly old. A fresh maggot is lively, large and shows a black spot at its pointed end. The larger this spot the fresher the maggot – that's the one to buy. If the spot is missing the maggot is old, soon to turn to a caster and will probably be less lively and have a tough skin.

A tough-skinned maggot is not a good bait and has only one or two special uses. If the skin is tough a fish will take in the bait and reject it much quicker than if it were soft – a soft maggot will burst as the fish sucks it into its mouth, juices will be emitted and the fish will hold on, enjoying the rich protein source it has found. The only exception to this need for a soft skin is when a bait is to be used for speed fishing, such as when bleak or dace are the target. In this situation a tough maggot will withstand the catching of several fish and the angler can take several before changing baits – a great time-saver in matches.

Coloured Maggots

Coloured maggots are popular and my own obsession is with red and bronze ones. Most shops sell these colours ready dyed, but if you purchase them be sure to find out what the colouring agent was. If it is one of the aniline dyes such as chrysoidine (for bronze) and rhodamine (for pink), don't buy them. Although many anglers have been using these dyes for years, they have now been shown to be carcinogenic and too dangerous to use. They are particularly dangerous if they have been applied to the skin of the maggot rather than fed into it at the stage when it was living off meat during the growth period – this is usually the case with chrysoidine.

Alternative dyes are constantly appearing; some work better than others, but I have been using several without any reduction in my success rate. The good things about them, too, is that they wash off both clothing and your hands much easier than the old anilines. Successful colouring takes a little time and the instructions must be followed closely. Usually the colour obtained when first dyed will fade after a few hours, so try initially to get a darker-than-required colour.

With coloured baits I always change the bran several times so it can carry away any left-over colouring that may be on the bait. And even with farm-coloured or white maggots I still change the bran at least once just before setting off for the river; that way I know my bait is clean and free from any tainting left by dirty bran.

Having purchased a good, fresh maggot we can do quite a lot to keep it in good order for the next few days. A fridge is a good investment and it is usually easy to find one, either free or for a few pounds, that is still serviceable·but beyond kitchen use. Mine lives in the back garden, protected from the weather by a box-like construction built around it.

But before committing your maggots to a cool place they must first be riddled free of all foreign material. Riddle off the sawdust and discard it. Next, put the maggots back on a riddle through which they can just crawl into a container below; those that

● *These maggots are large, but are lacking in the dark feed spot that would indicate their freshness. They would also be improved by a thorough cleaning*

remain on the riddle are either dead or past their best, and can be fed to the birds. The neat maggots now need some new material to keep them fresh and sweat-free. Clean sawdust is fine, but because it is sharp it will toughen their skins slightly. I prefer fine bran, which can be bought from most pet shops or corn merchants.

A pint of hook maggots needs a container at least twice that capacity, and the larger the better. Sprinkle on a handful of bran to the pint. The bran can be dampened – but only very slightly – in order to prevent too much moisture being drawn from the bait and causing shrinkage. However, get them too wet and they will either climb out of the container or float when used – either way they won't be much use.

A fridge enables hook maggots to be stored for several days in good condition, but don't get the temperature too low. Start with one of the highest settings on your fridge and work downwards – the idea is to keep them just cool enough to prevent them progressing through their life cycle. Store them with the lids off, too, so that plenty of air can circulate. In fact all my bait gets transported to the river in open containers whenever possible, though watch out with pinkies (see p. 82)!

The final riddling will leave you with good, clean bait, free from dead skins, turning maggots or debris. To take them to the waterside add only a little bran so that you can see what you are selecting every time during fishing – you should not have to fumble about through a layer of bran in order to find a bait.

After fishing, don't throw away leftover maggots. They can be brought back home and fridged for use as feeders next time – remember, older maggots sink faster than fresh ones. You can also produce your own casters by taking just a little trouble in the week that follows.

Gozzers

Another form of hook maggot, but one that will not be found in the average tackle shop. It is bred at home from a certain fly that only lays eggs – or 'blows' as they are called – in the dark. The gozzer is a very soft, rather dumpy maggot that has proved a great advantage with bream. Breed a few for the hook by setting up a little area in the garden shed or garage. Done correctly there will be little smell or mess, and the result will be a few hundred hook maggots of the very best quality.

Start by buying a sheep or pig's heart. Chicken portions are also good, or you may know a source of cheap pigeons. Place your chosen meat in a large bait box that has a couple of inches of bran sprinkled over the bottom. The box is then covered by placing it under a bucket or larger container – anything that makes it dark inside will do – and the top covered with a piece of wood. Hold the wood down with a brick or two to keep the cats out, but ensure there is one tiny opening, just room for a fly to get in.

I have found that warming the meat in the oven for a minute or so usually results in a more rapid 'blow', maybe because warming causes more scent to be given off which in turn attracts the gozzer fly. Check every couple of hours to see if there are any signs of 'blows'. Only a few are needed; too many, and the young maggots will run out of food long before they reach full size. Allow just enough blows to cover a fingernail and you will obtain all the hookbait you need for a couple of days' fishing.

Once blown, wrap the meat in several layers of newspaper and place it inside a tin with the bottom covered with plenty of bran. Seal on the lid, but be sure there are plenty of air holes; then leave well alone until some five days later, at which time it is worth checking to see all is well. If after five days the maggots are visible and there is meat left but the young have not reached full size, give them another day or so. Properly judged you should end up with large maggots and only a few threads of meaty fibre left to discard.

Timing will vary according to temperature, as both the speed in which the first 'blows' are obtained and the growing time of the young maggots will be more rapid in warmer weather. Once happy that the maggots are ready for use, it is a case of tipping the meat on a riddle and leaving the maggots to work through into some clean bran. Be sure to shake the remaining meat well to extract all the maggots that may be inside. A few changes of damp bran and you will have the softest, whitest maggots possible.

Pinkies

The smaller relation of the hook maggot, the pinkie comes from the greenbottle fly, a smaller creature than the bluebottle and therefore producing a smaller maggot that looks a bit like a half-grown hook maggot but is flesh-pink in colour. The depth of this colour is a good guide to age. A pinkie fresh from the 'host' meat will be almost white to cream (not unlike the hook maggot), but as it ages so the pink darkens.

Because the pinkie is used mainly as a feed maggot it is beneficial to have it slightly older in order to ensure a rapid sinking rate and reduce somewhat its tendency to bury into the bottom. It is the toughest of all maggots in terms of life span, and can be fridged for weeks at a time – it will still emerge in good order, having only lost maybe a slight amount of size. In a fresh state a good pinkie is a fine hookbait, and will get a response where a larger hook maggot has failed. They colour easily, too.

If it has one fault it is its ability to escape from bait boxes. Leave pinkies to sweat up in a sealed box and they will find a way out. They climb anything, even a window is not too smooth for a damp pinkie to tackle . . . so don't say you haven't been warned. Pinkies taken into the house must have been responsible for the end of many a happy marriage. Treat pinkies much like hook maggots, except keep them very dry to prevent their wanderings. Again, it is best to keep the lids off to help reduce sweating or condensation forming inside the fridge.

A good method of transporting pinkies – or for that matter, any type of maggot – for long periods is in a cotton pillow-case that has been double stitched at the seams. The nearly neat maggots are placed in the pillow-case and the top tied securely with string or a few elastic bands. Kept like this on the cold floor of a coach or in the boot of a car they will be fine. If you have travelled overnight to a distant venue it is no problem to find a cold garage floor on which to lay your pillow-case. But keep 'em dry, or you are in real trouble.

Squatts

The smallest of the three common maggots used by anglers, and in many ways completely different from the other species. For a start, they do not breed from meat 'blow' but from eggs laid by a very small, dark fly which prefers rotting material. In fact you may find a few in ancient manure heaps and sometimes under dried cowpats.

Breeding them at home is not practical, for obvious reasons, but they are now widely available through tackle shops – although many suppliers still require orders a week in advance. Keeping squatts in good order is also more difficult than with other maggots. They do not tolerate fridging well, though they will cope with a day or two providing they are placed right at the bottom and given plenty of space and air. The fridge also needs to be a little warmer than is ideal for other maggots.

Supplied in a dark brown sand, squatts should not be allowed to dry out. Keep the sand just moist, but never wet. Overdo the fridging and you end up with 'stretchers' – a state where the squatts stretch out straight as if dead. Left like that for long and they *will* be dead, but if you rescue them by leaving them in a shallow container outside the fridge they will come back to life after a couple of hours. If after that time they remain 'dead', they are useless.

Primarily a maggot for feeding, the squatt can be a hooker too, especially on those really bad days when the water is cold, clear and unproductive. Because they are so tiny it goes without saying the hook will need to be small – a 22 is the maximum and a 24 or 26 is more in keeping. Go for a fine wire pattern, too, to prevent damaging the tiny creature.

Squatts come into their own when fished in conjunction with groundbait. Loved by bream and yet just as deadly on a tiny fish water it is, without doubt, the supreme feeder maggot. The dark sand in which they are sold can be used in with groundbait, but don't include large amounts as it can taint the flavour – it will contain a lot of ammonia that has been given off by the maggots.

If the sand is suspected of being too tainted to use, riddle it off and replace with slightly damp, fine groundbait, but don't do this until just before leaving for the water. And any unused squatts will need to be transferred back into sand before the groundbait goes sour. My own favourite is a deep red squatt, though in their natural state they are yellowish in colour and do not possess the dark feed spot found on other types. The deeper the yellow the older they are likely to be.

Casters

The bait for quality fish, loved by big roach, chub and bream, casters can be an amazing bait one day and almost useless the next. It's strange, too, how they seem to fall from favour every so often on waters where they have ruled for several seasons. There are plenty of theories as to why this happens; the most popular is that a lot of sour casters are introduced by anglers who have not taken enough care of them – casters are a demanding bait. I'm not sure this idea is correct, although I do agree that casters should be as fresh as possible. I think a water where a lot of maggots go in every week will be slow to respond to the caster because it is a bait lacking in movement, and thus less attractive when compared with a maggot that wriggles.

What is important is that casters are living things just like maggots, and unless they receive attention they will either die or continue their life cycle into the fly stage. For convenience sake casters are usually sold commercially in plastic bags which have been sealed after most of the air has been excluded. Such a home is fine for a few hours but like all living creatures casters demand air and left without this vital supply they will cling to the bag and dark 'burns' will appear on them. Never buy casters in this state – it's a sure sign they are past their best.

The ideal caster should be a light orange to red; the darker they are the closer they are to becoming 'floaters'. And even fresh ones will go soft in a bag if left for too long. They are alright to use in this soft state but the best casters will have a crisp shell that bursts open the moment it is taken by a fish.

So, having purchased a pint of casters the evening before fishing, take them home and empty the bag onto a sheet of newspaper. Spread the casters thinly and pick out all the skins, dead maggots and bits of debris. The clean casters that are left should be washed off in clean, cold water and then packed into a bait box right to the brim. This complete filling is very important because too much space at the top and they will continue turning. Place a piece of wet newspaper on the top and cover this with a piece of plastic bag before fitting the lid. Left like this in the fridge they will have just enough air, and by the following day will have turned to a uniform colour and become crisp.

Once at the waterside it is important to keep casters wet, and if they are already getting a little too dark, cover them completely with water. Casters that are too light can be darkened off by taking them to the water in a wet towel. But an hour

or so is all they will need in this state, so go prepared with a spare bait box.

Producing your own casters takes a lot of time, effort and patience but the end result will be a far superior bait to the commercially produced item. A fridge is essential, as is a riddle large enough for hook maggots to pass through; also, a large container to catch the maggots as they work through the riddle and a supply of clean sawdust will get you going. Some plastic bags will also help save on waste when the casters begin to appear.

Casters are best produced by buying maggots two weeks prior to the day they will be needed as casters, and keeping them fridged for a week at least. Actual production time will vary according to air temperature and humidity, but as a rule the bulk of the casters will need to appear in the couple of days before fishing is due. Buy big, white maggots for caster production and riddle them clean of sawdust, dead skins and rubbish before placing them in a large open container – a gallon of maggots will produce only about six pints of good casters, so order accordingly.

To the clean maggots, add an equal amount of fresh sawdust and dampen it slightly. This dampness will help stop shrinkage and produce a big caster. And after using the sawdust don't throw it away – it will have taken in a lot of moisture during its time in the fridge and will be even better for caster production the following week. I have used the same batch of sawdust over and over again for weeks on end – only when it gets very dark-looking and smells does it need throwing away and replacing.

Take the caster maggots from the fridge on the Tuesday before fishing on the Saturday or Sunday, and leave them in a cool place. Now the work really starts, and the more often they can be attended to, the better will be the casters produced. After they have warmed to air temperature, run them through the riddle and remove any skins and casters that may have formed. These are thrown away. Check again a few hours later, and if casters are showing run them off but this time save them in a plastic bag and store them in the fridge. They will be fine, because the bag will be opened again in a matter of hours to add more. Repeat the process until the very last minute, and you will have plenty of casters of the highest quality. However, don't forget to box them as already described for the last few hours.

If you finish up with more casters than you expected it is worth using some as feed, though not in the usual manner. After mixing up cereal in the normal way, add a generous number of casters – several pints can go into a full bowl of groundbait – but as they are introduced, crunch them up until they are nothing more than pulpy liquid. What you have now made is a strongly scented and powerfully attractive feed that is almost pure protein. In the water it will produce a cloud of caster juice that will be carried through the swim and draw fish from a wide area.

WORMS

Three types of earthworm are commonly used by anglers, the biggest being the lobworm and its two smaller cousins the redworm and brandling.

Lobworms

These account for a lot of very big fish in the course of a season and I doubt there is a sizeable species that will not fall to it at some time during its life-span. Used whole, it is a bit of a handful for the average float fishing rig, but those intended for fish such as carp or tench will cope. Otherwise it is a killer with big chub if used whole or just the tail-end on a size-able hook.

The tail of the lob is traditionally considered the favourite end of this worm, which can grow to well over a foot long. The tail is the lighter coloured, flat end but why fish should show a marked preference for it has never been established. Maybe it is something to do with the bitterness of the head or simply because the flesh at the tail is softer. From the angler's point of view it doesn't matter much why it works, suffice to say it does. Lob-tails come into their own on flooded waters. The Trent, for example, responds very well to a lob-tail trundled along the marginal rocks. Reason is possibly because other worms are constantly washed into the river by the rising water.

Best way to collect a reasonable number of lobworms is to stalk them on a short-cut lawn after dark. A damp night is best, but a good watering of the lawn during late afternoon will usually bring them up later. Go armed with a bait box, a torch and a pair of slippers. Worms are sensitive to vibration and a heavy footfall will send the whole lot underground within seconds, so walk carefully and go easy with the torch. When a worm is spotted, grasp it quickly and firmly nearest to the end still in the ground and apply a constant and even pressure. Eventually the worm will loosen its grip and can be pulled free; some anglers wear a thin glove in order to get a better grip. Although I have not found any great problem collecting worms in this manner, I know anglers who prefer to trap the tail end of the worm and then, as it contracts, gently hold the head and lift it away from the ground.

After collection, lobworms will survive for a reasonable time in nothing more than a layer of earth. But to really bring them into condition and scour their skins to a bright finish, cover them in a few layers of damp moss. This will encourage them to eject any soil that is passing through their bodies and will leave you with a superb bait.

Should the lawn method of collection not be practical, you can still find lobworms by digging in any wet and heavy-soiled part of the garden. A clay-like soil is a favourite but it must be permanently wet.

Brandlings

The most common worm used by anglers but not, in my opinion, the best. Much smaller than the lob, this worm is found in rotting heaps of manure and garden refuse and you will recognise it by the bright yellowish bands that run around its body. These emit a rather foul-smelling yellow fluid when the worm is handled and it is this that probably reduces the effectiveness of the worm as bait. Brandlings also tend to die rather quickly once hooked. Worms purchased from tackle shops are often brandlings and they will work well enough but are a second-class alternative to the redworm.

Redworms

The most versatile of the earthworms, this one is a deep red in colour and very similar in size to the brandling but lacking the yellow bands. Like the brandling, it is found in manure and garden rubbish heaps but is a much tougher customer and will perform better as a hookbait for that reason.

95

Once a supply of good redworms has been obtained it is worth creating your own source in a well-cared-for heap. Worms will also do well in an old fertiliser sack that has been filled with good quality compost and is kept fed with kitchen scraps such as potato peelings, green vegetable leaves and fruit skins. It must be kept damp – but not soaking wet – at all times, and in a fairly shaded spot. In winter it will also need some protection from frosts.

When collecting worms from a heap always work from one corner and cause as little disturbance as possible. Replace the disturbed area when you have finished and press it down firmly with your boot – this will help retain the moisture and heat which is so vital to a thriving wormery. I treasure my worms so much that I also return any unused ones back to the heap to help keep up stocks.

Storing worms in bait boxes is not difficult during the colder months and they will survive for a few days with no trouble. If the weather is very warm then the bait must be kept as cool as possible and never allowed to dry out. Fridging is not really a success and is more likely to land you with a few shrivelled specimens.

A word of warning, too: there is nothing that smells worse than a box of worms that has been forgotten and left to die in the bottom of your kit. They quickly turn into an evil liquid that will leave its odour behind for weeks. So keep a regular check on any worms you have collected and remove any that have died as quickly as possible. One dead worm in a bait box will very quickly kill off the rest, too.

The largest brandling or redworm is not always the best. Take along a few very tiny ones and fish them on a small hook just like a maggot. Two, or even three on the hook are a real bream-killer and will often get bites where a single, larger worm has failed.

WASP GRUBS

I have used this bait a few times but my hatred of wasps tends to prevent me collecting the grubs unless I'm desperate, which isn't often. The big white grubs are supposed to be deadly for chub, but I reckon a good caster or well-presented maggot is just as effective and certainly far less of a risk if

things go wrong. Once wasp grubs have been introduced to a swim and failed, you are going to struggle no matter what your next plan of attack is to be.

Collecting grubs involves killing off the adult wasps and then digging out the nest, which can be as large as a football if it's a good one. To do this, poison must be applied to the nest entrance in the daytime and a number of powders that are safe to other wildlife are available from chemists and garden centres. The timing is vital, otherwise you are in for a painful experience. Applied in the daytime, the powder will do its work after all the wasps have returned to the nest at dusk. In fact, a good way to find a nest in the first place is to follow a wasp in the last hour of daylight as it returns home.

Follow the instructions on the packet to the letter and you should be safe but never, and I stress never, attempt to dig out a nest that has not been left powdered overnight – and even then take great care.

Once out of the ground, the nest will look like a paper ball of comb and is known in angling circles as 'cake'. Inside each 'cake' you will find the soft white grubs, about an inch long and as thick as a pencil. Watch out for partly hatched grubs as these young wasps are already well armed and hurt just as much as a fully grown adult.

If you plan to fish the same day the grubs can be picked from the cake and used fresh, otherwise freeze the whole nest as quickly as possible. Grubs left unfrozen will last no more than a day or so, and soon turn a dark brown as they die and rot. They are soft, and need to be fished with great care otherwise they will be thrown off on the cast. Bait up with three or more at a time in the hope that two will remain on the hook. Try a piece of cake, too – its sweetness is loved by big chub.

The cake is also good if scalded with boiling water, chopped up and mixed with cereal groundbait. But be warned: it doesn't work on all waters. I've had some spectacular failures with the stuff on my home River Nene, even when fishing pegs that I knew were stuffed with chub.

● *A sample of prepared hempseed. Note the tiny white shoot which appears as cooking is completed (see p. 98)*

HEMPSEED

A great bait, both as a feeder and on the hook. It is cheap, clean and certainly very effective on its day. Forget the old stories that surround these tiny black seeds; they are not bad for fish; they are not a drug to fish or humans; they do not grow on the bottom of the river, in fact I doubt any seed that has been boiled will grow anywhere; and they do not get roach so preoccupied they refuse all other baits. These old wives' tales are just a few that have grown up around hemp over the years, and maybe led to the banning of it for so long on many waters and by a large number of clubs and associations.

A pint of hemp will keep a swim going all day, and its preparation involves nothing more than an overnight soaking and then a gentle simmering in boiling water until the tiny white shoot emerges from inside the seed. If I am going to use hemp on the hook, I will take out a portion from the main batch just as a few of these shoots begin to appear, as these slightly undercooked grains are easier to keep on the hook. It is a good idea to keep the water in which hemp has been cooked and use it to mix with your cereal. Fish seem to be attracted by this oily substance, although I would not normally use cereal when actually fishing hemp on the hook for roach.

If you are looking for something a little different, add a few spots of colouring to the cooked hemp. I've had good results by feeding bronze – and red-dyed hemp. Of course the actual black shell is not affected, but the tiny white shoot can look really good in a different colour. Hemp also works well as a loose feed and can be very attractive when fished with either a white maggot or caster hookbait.

Chilean hemp is much larger than other grains and is certainly a better hookbait, but getting hold of the stuff is becoming harder every year. Watch out for under-ripe hemp, too – it has a greenish appearance and will do at a pinch, but it is not ideal. The very best hemp is black when cooked, and adding a little bicarbonate of soda to the overnight soak will help this effect.

After cooking, wash the grains in cold water. Hemp can be cooked up in a big batch and then sealed in plastic bags and frozen. I often take mine to the waterside straight from the fridge, using it as a

cooling agent and packing it between my maggot boxes, or in with casters if travelling overnight.

Hemp as a hookbait only seems to work while the water remains warm, and even then it may take an hour for the first bite to come. Many anglers, however, continue to use it as feed right through the season and in winter it certainly seems to be good at attracting chub, maybe because it lies on the bottom and gives off its oils and flavours.

Theories as to why a fish should want to eat a hard-shelled grain are many, and the favourite is that they mistake it for a small water snail. It's possible I suppose, but I'm more inclined to think they simply like the flavour.

TARES

These black seeds are a little smaller than a pea; they go hand-in-hand with hemp and are used as a hookbait when hemp is fed loose. Prepare them in a similar manner to hemp, by soaking overnight and then simmering until the skin is just soft enough to pass a hook through. Don't overcook, and that's easy to do – watch constantly, because a few minutes too long will transform the rather hard tare into a soggy black mess that is next to useless.

A good tare should not be too large – I pick out the smallest I can find – and should be as dark as possible; it should be only just soft enough to get the hook under the skin – I have found an overcooked tare usually results in a lot of missed bites.

A hookbait, that does not really have much to offer as a loose feed but if you must put a few in with hemp, keep them down to an absolute minimum. Like hemp, the tare can be frozen until needed.

SWEETCORN

Another simple bait to obtain and use: you need nothing more than a grocer's shop and a can-opener. Even the packets of frozen corn are fine. Sweetcorn is good for tench, carp and chub but like hempseed, tends to be more effective in summer than later on (see colour photograph on p. 69).

If fished with groundbait, empty the water from the can into the cereal and mash up some grains, too. Another bait that dyes well, and a different colour is often very effective on hard-fished waters where a lot of natural sweetcorn is used. But as with all the seed baits, it is only effective if used in a swim prior to the introduction of maggots.

BREAD

Another classic bait, and one that can be used in so many different ways. It catches everything from the largest carp to the tiniest canal roach, but as with seed baits, bread is best when used as an opener, rather than as a bait to use when others have failed.

Paste

This was the bread bait on which I caught many bream as an inexperienced youngster, though I confess I never use it nowadays. Instead I go every time for either bread punch or flake; both have a lot more life in them and as a result I believe are more attractive. If you want to try paste, just take a few slices of a new loaf, cut off the crust, wet the bread slightly and mould it to a paste. Yes, it is that simple! but be sure to make the paste just soft enough to stay on the hook. If it is too firm a lot of bites will be missed because the hook is shrouded.

Flake

Flake is almost as easy, and certainly takes no advanced preparation. All you need is a fresh loaf from which a pinch of bread can be pulled and attached to a hook. Try to pinch just enough around the hook shank to keep it on. There should be plenty of loose flake left so that it can swell and fall off in tiny pieces, which is the secret of good flake-fishing – it's a sort of automatic groundbaiting.

Punch

This is the real winner these days when it comes to bread fishing (see colour photograph on p. 70). A thick slice of fresh bread is stamped out with a small punch and the hook is then pulled through the bread to extract it from the punch. This produces a small, circular disc of bread that is almost alive in the water. As water soaks in so the punched bread swells. Strangely enough I always used to take bread with me during the summer but never in the winter. Then the punch arrived in the Fens and quickly became a first line of winter attack on many of our waters. But it really is a bait to start with, and once its effectiveness goes off, a switch to maggot or some other bait is called for.

● *A piece of flake is moulded around the hook, but be sure to leave as much loose and fluffy bread as possible*

Punch also has the advantage of being a small fish bait. It can be fished right down the hook range, depending on the size of punch used – a minute piece on a 22 hook is great for tiny fish. Step up to a piece the size of your fingernail and you are in big fish territory.

BLOODWORM AND JOKER

Really match baits, these are known as little 'red men' and are the most natural of all baits. A large part of the diet of coarse fish consists of these bright red little worms. Most stillwaters hold bloodworms, but collecting them is something of an art and a good bloodworm pond will be a closely guarded secret. I much prefer to buy mine from a tackle shop, although it has to be said that these will never be of the same quality as those you find yourself. They are gathered by scraping a thin metal blade through the bottom mud so that worms come up on the blade, folded over the leading edge.

Both bloodworms and jokers bought from tackle shops come in damp peat and folded in newspaper parcels. Kept this way and stored in a not-too-cold fridge they will survive for a couple of days, but after that they soon lose their bright colouring and die.

The joker is a smaller version of the bloodworm, in fact it is the larvae of the gnat (bloodworms are midge larvae). It is found in streams and running water that carries some pollution – sewage outfalls are a good source, and jokers can be scraped up just like bloodworms or gathered in a fine net that is pushed along the bottom after first disturbing the worms by stirring up the silt.

Jokers are used as feed; it is the bloodworm that goes on the hook. They are usually introduced in a firm cereal and often only at the start of fishing, the angler 'filling-in' the swim with ten or more big balls. Response is often immediate despite the commotion. Bloodworms are delicate to use and will not tolerate thick forged hooks, so always use a small one of a fine wire pattern. The barb, too, needs to be a micro one.

On shallow waters where heavy groundbait is not a good idea both worms can be fed almost neat. First, dampen them by spraying them lightly with a plant mist spray filled with water, then add a pinch of dry leam (a light-coloured clay), and the resulting

ball of worms can then be picked out and fed immediately. This will only work in shallow waters because the worms will swim away. The heavy feeding just mentioned is also a way of laying down an artificial bed on the bottom over which the worms will stay, hovering attractively.

Biggest drawback with both bloodworm and joker is the cost. As baits go, buying them can prove expensive and in terms of time and effort, collecting your own is not much better. For the hard-bitten match angler they are essential on difficult waters, but as a pleasure bait they are non-starters and will probably produce more small fish than you really want to catch.

WHEAT

If this book had been written ten or even twenty years earlier, wheat would have been one of the main baits featured. But like so many good things in angling it seemed to fall from favour over the years. In the case of wheat, this was because hempseed was suddenly allowed on so many waters and anglers turned to it as an alternative. Now, after a decade or so of regular hemp bombardments, the fish that many rivers are beginning to produce to the deadly black seed are very much smaller. Maybe it is because the younger fish have grown up with it and see it as part of their natural diet, who knows, but it is a fact that hemp produces fewer exclusively quality fish catches than ever before.

Wheat is a good alternative to try on these hemp-tired venues. It is still a catcher of quality roach and certainly every bit as good as it ever was (see colour photograph on p. 132). To prepare wheat, simply wash it off in cold water and then simmer in hot water until soft. When ready for use it will have swollen to almost double its natural size, and most of the grains will have split open to reveal a whitish inside.

Fish it over loose offerings in the same manner as hemp. It's great as a roach bait and I've taken more than a few bream and chub on it, too. Certainly something to bear in mind as an experiment on your local waters. Like other seed baits it takes an hour or so to get going, but once bites begin they usually provide a big bag. The bites themselves are almost impossible to miss, too.

6
Floats and Rigs

A float has two functions in life: to support the bait and to register a bite. It will do those tasks best if it is matched to prevailing water and weather conditions and is correctly shotted.

The patterns and rigs which have been chosen here are all tried and tested ones, each designed to do a specific job. A range of sizes in each style will send the angler to the waterside well armed to cope with any situation.

The importance of good shotting principles has already been stressed but now is the time to match each one with the float to which it is best suited and to the conditions for which it was designed.

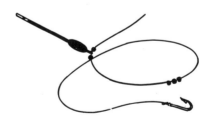

THE AVON

When and Where to Use the Crow-quill Avon

Conditions: Will perform under a wide range of conditions but is best when fished with a back or upstream wind. Can also be made to work if the wind is downstream, but will demand regular mending of the line as a bow forms.

Where: Deep rivers are ideal, but small Avons will work well in swims as shallow as 5ft. Perfect for use when overhanging trees make casting difficult with a waggler.

Suitable for swims ranging from turbulent to almost still.

● *A beautifully made set of crow-quill Avon floats. The pole winders are used to store the delicate floats complete with shots and hook*

Formerly the 'Avon' referred to a float made with a cork body which was usually set high up on a cane stem. As a float for fishing fairly fast and turbulent water it worked well enough, but it was a far cry from the crow-quill version that in match-fishing circles has become known as the 'Topper' in honour of its inventor Mervyn 'Topper' Haskins.

'Topper' designed his float to tackle the deep and often sluggish waters of his local Bristol Avon. The problems facing anglers there are many, but this float has solved them well and has since been adopted on waters of all sorts and sizes and to good effect. First of all, the crow-quill Avon was designed to take a bait through the slow-moving deep water at the correct pace – that is to say, at the speed of the current close to the bottom. This is made difficult by the prevailing upstream wind on the Bristol Avon which causes the water nearer the surface to move much more slowly and in some cases even upstream, against the natural flow.

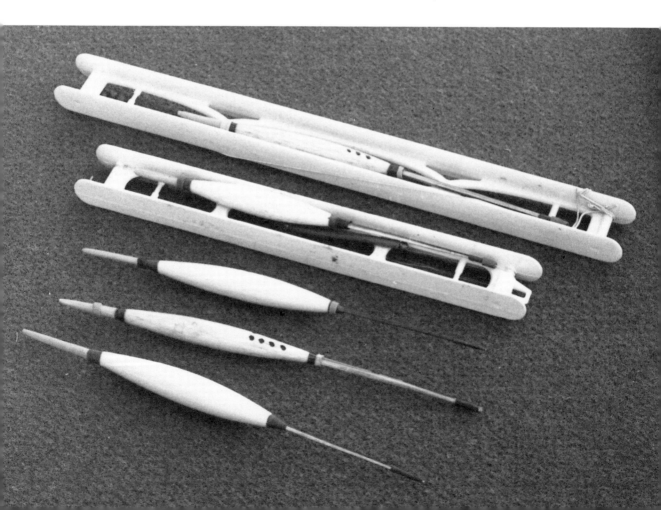

A waggler fished under these conditions will not carry through, because the main bulk of shotting load is centred directly beneath it and the line which sinks below the surface with this float will also be pushed back upstream – just the opposite problem to the one caused by a tricky downstream wind which a waggler is often called upon to deal with.

The Bristol Avon is deep – anywhere from 8 to 15ft is normal – so 'Topper' needed his float to get a bait down fast, but then make it push through naturally. These two requirements come from the bulk of shot the float can carry and the manner in which they are placed. Result is a rather crude-looking set-up, but believe me, it works! In fact I have adopted it to fish several of the deeper sections of my home River Nene and found it superb for anything from small roach to chub.

A range of 'Toppers' will probably carry loads from 8 to 20 BB shots, and as you see from the diagram they go on the line in one big bulk. There is no splitting them down to smaller loads, no spacing out along the line and certainly no substituting the BBs for larger shots. The slight flow acts on the big string of BBs as if it were some sort of underwater sail. The BB works best for this purpose and although I have tried to disprove the theory many times, have always failed and reverted back to the big string of shots.

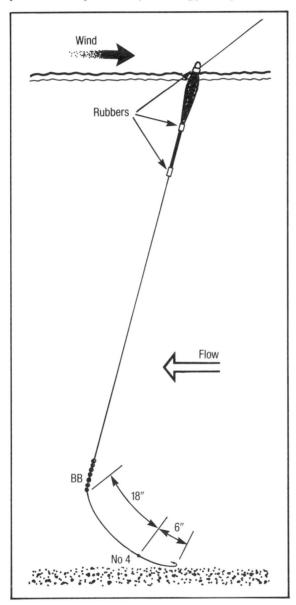

However, one alternative that does work well is a strip of tungsten tubing, but it must be of the same diameter as a conventional BB shot. I position mine by locking the strip in place with a BB at either end. Only other shot used is a tell-tale, and even this one is much larger than usual, normally a size 4, and this can go as close as 6 or 7in from the hook, with the bulk of the string around 18in higher.

Before we get too involved in fishing this strange but brilliant rig, let us look at the float itself. Made from a crow-quill which passes through the balsa or polystyrene body, it is a big, but delicate float. The body is usually left in its natural state, covered only with enough clear varnish to seal it. Paint serves no purpose and will only reduce the carrying capacity.

The quill stem is vulnerable to damage and it is vital to use three rubbers to attach it to the line. One rubber goes on above the body, a second directly below it and the final one on the extreme bottom end of the stem. The body will be fairly long – up to about half the total length of the quill is about right – and is also streamlined; despite its size it will register bites very well.

I store some of my favourite 'Toppers' on pole rig winders. This keeps them safe from damage and I always have a range ready and accurately shotted.

● *A typical Avon float rig which will push through against a wind. The bulk shot deep down will pick up the flow and carry the tackle along. Note the three rubbers used for attachment of the float*

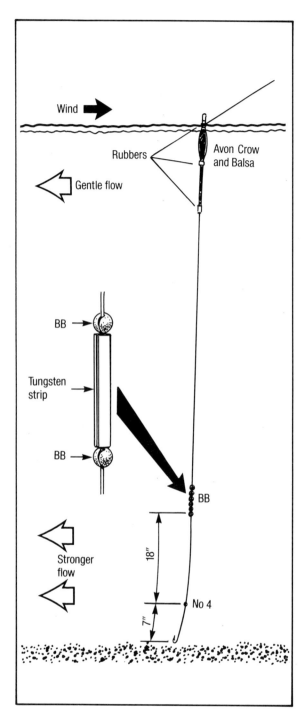

Wind ➡

Rubbers — Avon Crow and Balsa

⬅ Gentle flow

BB →

Tungsten strip →

BB →

BB

Stronger flow ⬅

18"

No 4

7"

● *The usual string of BB shots used for the Avon float can be replaced with a strip of tungsten tubing and then locked in place with shots*

Make sure the line on which they are stored is always shorter than the depth at which the float is likely to be used. This dodge ensures there will be no knot above the float which could break, losing the float as a result, or get jammed in the top ring of the rod. Rigs stored on winders have a loop tied in the line. This is then used to join them to the reel line by means of a tucked half-blood knot.

The Avon can be cast either overarm, or underarm as with the stick float. Cast underarm, the bulk shot streams out in front carrying the float behind and the flight is unbelievable – it is possible to fish at full waggler range with very little casting effort. Being able to to cast it underarm is another reason why this float performs so well on the Bristol Avon: the river has a lot of high banks and overhanging trees, and attempts to cast a waggler all too often end in disaster with the float going no further than the nearest branch. With the Avon float, a low underarm swing gets both the distance and the tree clearance in one. Always remember this float's ability to perform on such swims; using one even when conditions are not ideal can pay dividends.

Conditions which favour the 'Topper' are wideranging. A back, or upstream wind is best, but because of the sheer bulk of shot being used it is possible to control it well even in a downstreamer. It takes a bit of working at, and it is vital to lift the rod regularly to mend line that has formed a bow. Try to do this without upsetting the float's free travel.

All this talk of bulk shot and big tell-tales has probably painted a picture in your mind of a rather insensitive rig. You would be very wrong. Fished in 13ft of water with a no 4 tell-tale and a bulk of say 14 BBs, a bite will still register as if the float has been pulled down a hole. And the fish seem to hang on for a long time – I reckon what happens is that the fish takes the bait and moves away as normal, but because the bulk and the large tell-tale are so close and heavy they start to move and register the bite quickly. Once the downwards move begins, it keeps going for much longer than it would if the shots were placed in a more conventional manner.

Feeding needs thought, too, when fishing the Avon in deep water. The bait is going to be on, or close to the bottom at all times and that is where any feed needs to be, so it is usual to fish in conjunction with groundbait which has been mixed fairly firmly and will break up in the last foot or so.

THE BALSA

When and Where to Fish the Balsa

Conditions: Good wind conditions, either upstream or from behind. Not one to struggle with in a strong downstream gale.

Where: In deep, powerful water the largest patterns are fine but the conventional balsa should not be held back hard. Go instead for the Pacemaker if the bait needs to be checked back. Both patterns are fine on waters that are too deep or powerful for a stick float rig.

The tiny all-balsa patterns are for close-in work with delicate shotting, and should not be expected to cope with anything more.

● *A selection of balsa float patterns. From left: a slim version of the standard balsa; two small floats for close-in work; a single chunky pattern; and a range of five Pacemakers*

Like the crow-quill Avon, the balsa is a float associated with a large amount of shot loading. Generally this is so, but there are smaller versions which will perform under certain conditions and in fact it is worth carrying four styles of balsa: a chunky pattern ranging from five BB to five swan; a medium range of a slimmer but similar pattern from five no 4s to four BB; and a Pacemaker range of four or five floats covering four BB to three swan. The fourth pattern is a shorter and much lighter model that has a limited and very special use; it is a maximum of 3in long and can go down to 1½in, taking anything from two BB down to three no 6 or so.

The big balsa is a simple float. It is a piece of balsa to which a short stem of cane has been fitted. This cane stem is nothing more than a strengthener for the narrowest section of balsa, and should protrude no more than about 1in from the bottom of the body. The top will be fairly thick in order to ride rough water and there may or may not be a pronounced shoulder. Some are a simple cigar shape that tapers down from the thickest, upper section down to the diameter of the stem.

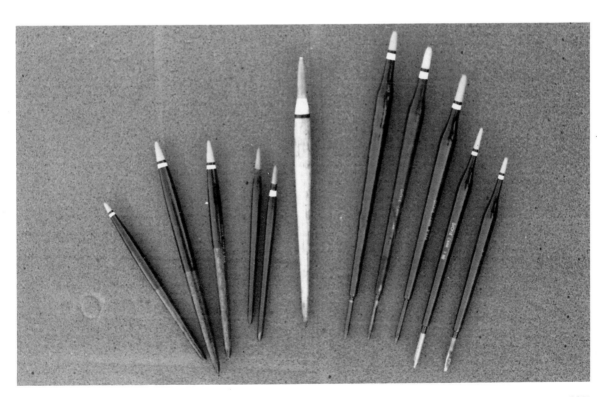

Floats and Rigs

The whole idea is to create a float with maximum stability and buoyancy so it can ride out the downward forces of swirling torrents.

Shotting is not unlike the bulk used for the crow-quill Avon, but the main difference is the use of stabilising shot right next to the stem – this will be anything from a swan down to a AAA. Nothing fancy about the overall shotting pattern, either. A big balsa is used for getting a bait down and keeping it there as it runs through very fast water.

● *Three patterns of balsa float. The large balsa is shotted with a single bulk for getting a bait down quickly in very fast water. The medium balsa has this load broken down for a slightly more attractive drop through the last few feet. The Pacemaker can be shotted very much like a large stick float with a series of decreasing sizes of shot*

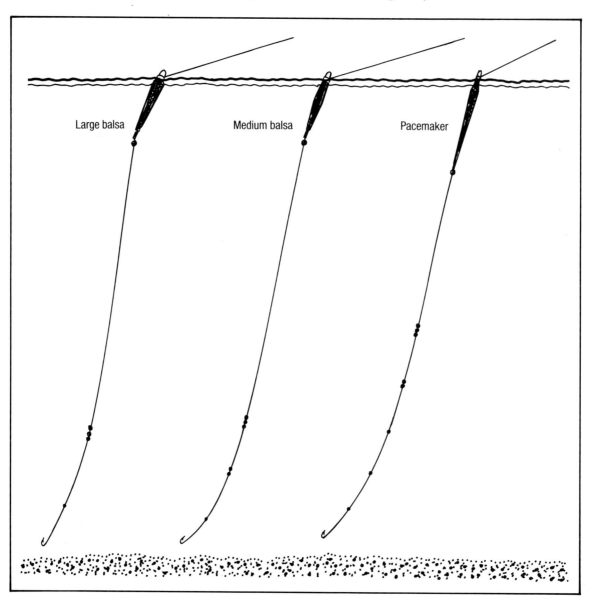

Large balsa   Medium balsa   Pacemaker

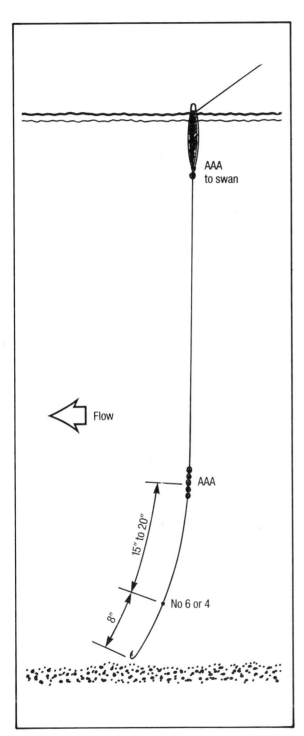

● A heavy balsa can be shotted with a large bulk and just a single tell-tale beneath

It is, of course, fished double rubber and can either be allowed to run through unchecked or held back slightly. Holding back is not really the way to get the best from this shape, however, and it is usual to ease it back, rather than hang on it hard. Overdo the holding back and it will ride up high, and will not be sensitive.

Cast with the underarm swing and restrict its use to the swims for which it was designed.

The smaller range of the balsa can be used for shallower and less powerful swims; it can also have the shot load broken down if required. Like its larger brethren it is limited in so far as holding back is not easy.

A slightly more versatile pattern is the Pacemaker very similar in shape to a conventional balsa but with a finer tip and more pronounced shoulder. Because of this shoulder it holds back better, the flow acting against the angular face of the shoulder to create a downwards push and thus restricting the tendency to ride out of the water.

Shotting, too, is a little more delicate. It can be fished as a bulk, but a stabilising shot at the stem is best followed lower down by a breakdown of the remaining load into gradually reducing amounts and ending with a single small tell-tale.

Casting is again best done underarm; once in the water, ease the Pacemaker through, checking every few feet to cause an attractive lifting of the bait.

This float is a good substitute on swims that have proved a little too turbulent for a conventional stick float, and because of the thinner tip section it does tend to be more sensitive than the full-blown balsa already described. It is a good float for medium-depth waters – say, 5ft down to 9 or 10ft.

I have found that when fished a fair way out, it is best to substitute the stabilising shot for a much smaller one, adding the remaining load to the first bulk below. In flight this has the effect of making the load pull the float along, rather than creating two areas of weight which then tend to spiral along in the air.

Final set of balsas is a very special one and it has caught me a lot of fish under certain conditions. It was first shown to me by Trent specialist Colin Walton who used it very close-in with casters and hempseed for roach and chub. Much smaller than all the other balsas it is really more like the top of a stick float that has had the stem removed. It works

107

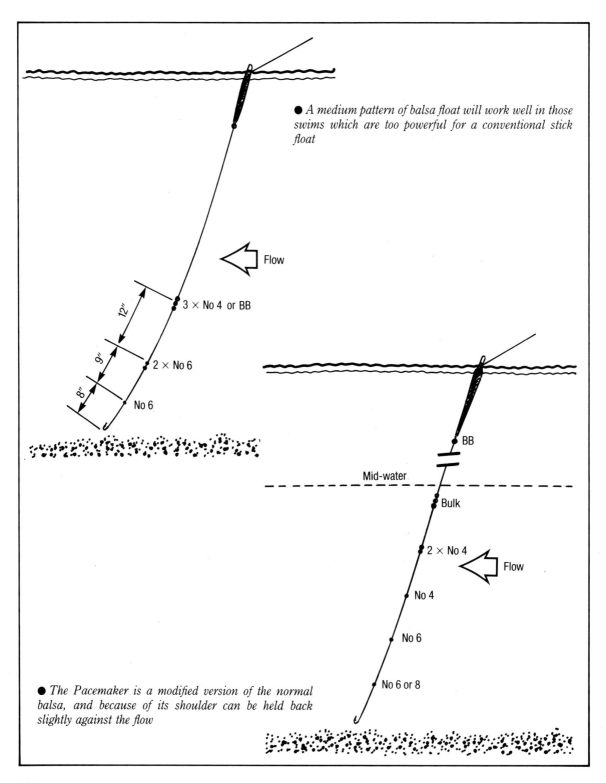

● *A medium pattern of balsa float will work well in those swims which are too powerful for a conventional stick float*

Flow

12"

9"

8"

3 × No 4 or BB

2 × No 6

No 6

BB

Mid-water

Bulk

2 × No 4

Flow

No 4

No 6

No 6 or 8

● *The Pacemaker is a modified version of the normal balsa, and because of its shoulder can be held back slightly against the flow*

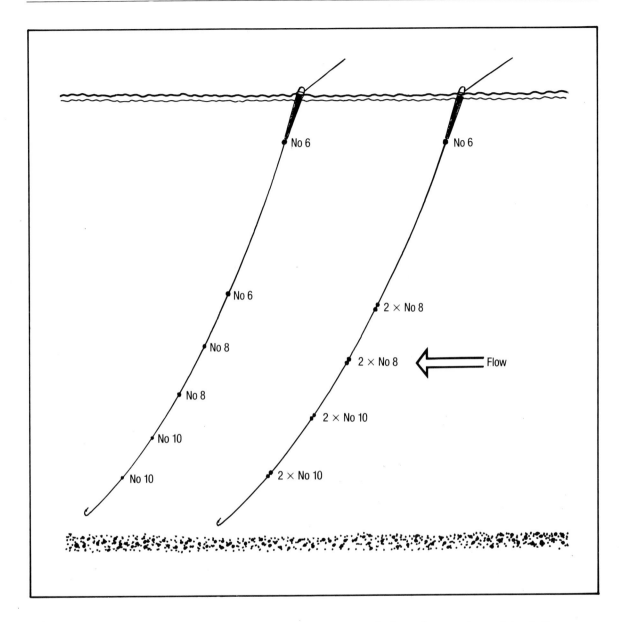

● *Small balsa patterns can be shotted with strings of shot, either used singly or in small bulks*

really well along the margins and in shallow water that still has a little pace.

Fish it on a fine line, and spread the tiny shots down the line. The only exception to this individual shotting is if hemp is being used and shot bites develop, in which case it is a simple matter to double up by reducing the size but increasing the quantity of shots being used.

It is not a float to be held back hard, and anything more than a·check will lift it too high to be effective.

Relate size of float to depth of swim and try to start with the smallest you feel able to manage under prevailing conditions. A simple double rubber attachment is all that's needed and it is a super little float for catching just about anything from chub down to gudgeon. Use it with its limitations in mind, and it will serve you well.

The delicate nature of the float and its shotting make it ideal for catching fish on the edge of the main flow and on swims where loose feeding can be done. Use it only when the swim is sheltered or with a behind or upstream wind. It is not one to struggle along with when the weather and water conditions are unsuitable.

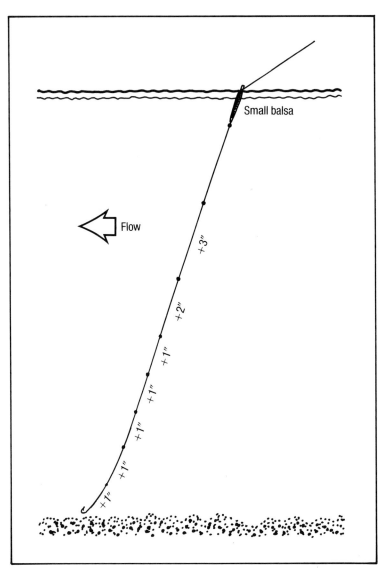

● *A really specialised balsa for shallow-water fishing on the edge of the main flow. Shotting is delicate and spaced down the line*

THE DRINKING-STRAW FLOAT

When and Where to Fish the Straw

Conditions: A favourable wind is best for the straw, but it will cope with blustery weather if you select a large enough size and length.

Where: Canals, rivers and stillwaters will all respond to the right choice of straw float. Go for the insert type on canals, and step up the diameter and size if there is a flow. A very good float for fishing a shallow, far bank shelf where casting range is required but where as little disturbance as possible is essential.

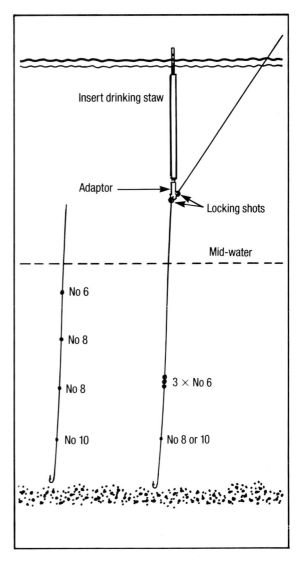

● *Two ways to shot an insert straw float. On the left a slow drop rig, and right, for fish close to the bottom*

Plastic drinking straws make superb floats, and depending on their size can produce a whole range that will cope with anything from a wide Fenland water to a narrow and hard-fished canal. One of my favourites is a standard straw into which a fine insert of peacock has been glued at the tip – a great float for fishing close to the far bank of canals, and because it is so cheap and easy to make I am not unduly worried if I lose a few through casting too close to weeds or bushes.

The plastic straw is already waterproof but a thin coat of varnish (non-cellulose) will make it stiffer and more durable. By adding a second, larger diameter piece of straw to the bottom, a much larger and even more versatile float can be made up. The only other requirement is a short piece of cane in the base to act as a stem.

It is very light and sensitive – because of its hollow nature it will carry a fair amount of shot, yet it will still land lightly on the water, making it ideal for canals, shallow water and in particular when fishing right up on the far bank shelf where there may be fish in only a foot or so of water. With an insert it is also a good float for fishing 'on the drop' when fish are feeding high in the water. In fact the only thing this float will not do is face a fast flow, and even this can be overcome by making up a few from the largest diameter straw you can find.

Drinking straws are probably the nearest thing you will find to true peacock quill and are far superior in every way to a similar float made from sarkandas reed. As wagglers go, it is a float material that could easily see you through a whole season – certainly it

is one that will take a lot of beating for stillwaters and those with just a steady flow. Without the insert, use a balsa plug, and it will ride a flow nicely.

Fish it with an adaptor on its stem and locked in place between shots in the normal waggler fashion. Shooting can be either a bulk of, say, three or four no 6 or a string of small shots spaced out and gradually reducing in size down the line.

As regards selection, all the angler need do is choose a diameter and length best suited to the

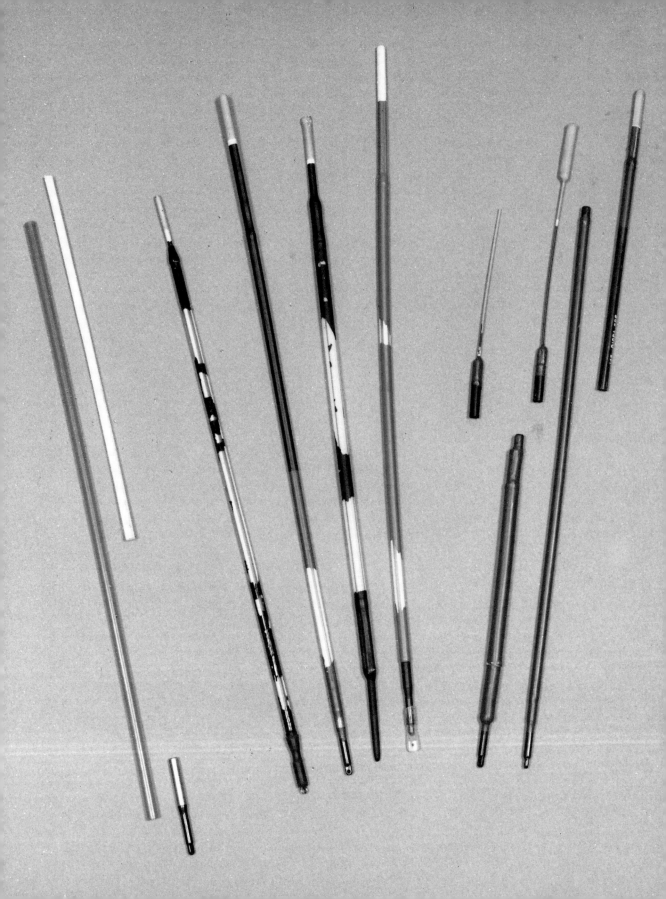

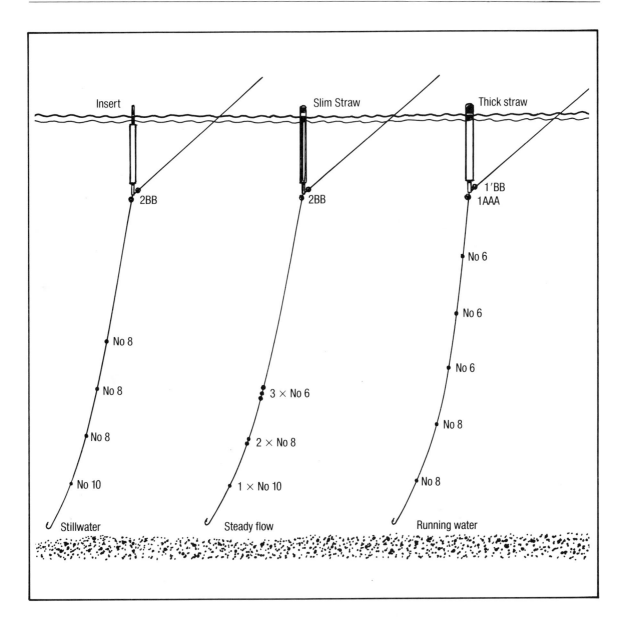

● *Three methods of shotting straw floats according to their thickness and to suit different types of swim*

● *It's surprising what can be done with a packet of drinking straws! These examples were made by former RAF champion Geoff Bibby and have interchangeable tips*

swim being tackled. Stillwaters and light wind conditions will enable a fine insert to be used. Step up on diameter if flow is present and the straw needs to be checked in any way.

I have also made these floats self-cocking and partially self-cocking by pushing a shot or two covered with Araldite inside the bottom of the straw before fixing the stem. It works well, but as with all loaded floats the straw will tend to 'bury' beneath the surface on landing.

CANAL DART

When and Where to Fish the Dart

Conditions: Good to average wind, but will cope with a surface skim.

Where: Canals and small, slow-moving rivers or stillwaters. Range limited to about 12yd. The fine tip makes it difficult to see in poor, broken light such as when fishing opposite thin undergrowth and trees that let light through. Very good when cast tight to the far side of canals which demand good but lightly shotted presentation.

● *A typical shotting pattern for the dart. Bulk of the load is built into the bottom of the float body*

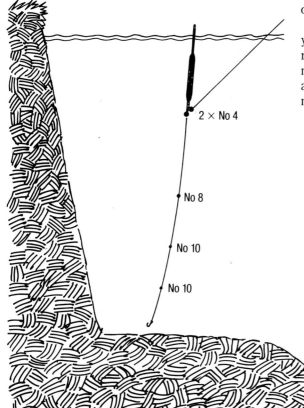

2 × No 4

No 8

No 10

No 10

I do not like loaded floats, but the canal dart – specialised, and rather limited in its use – is nonetheless a float that is certainly worth having handy for the day, and can make all the difference (see colour photograph on p. 17).

Made from a slim balsa body with a very fine cane antenna, it is heavily loaded and casts well, yet needs only a very small amount of shot down the line. The thin antenna is super-sensitive and will register those delicate bites that would probably be missed on a conventional waggler. It also copes reasonably well with wind and surface skim – this is due to the loading which acts a bit like an anchor and gives the angler something to pull back to without moving the tackle too far off course.

A real winner in ideal conditions, the dart is superb for fishing close to the far bank and casts well either overhead or with the sideways technique. But this is not the float with which to tackle big waters – don't use it on anything more than a canal or a Fen drain, that calls for a cast of 10 or 12yd.

My advice is, keep three or four different sizes in your box and use one only when it is called for. It really is for delicate work and waters where the very minimum of shot is used. Fish it with a small hook on a fine line and it is a great catcher of tiny fish. It will not tackle heavy flows or even modest ones.

CANAL WAGGLERS

● *Wagglers with a difference. These are canal greys made from balsa. A useful pattern where delicacy needs to be coupled with good tackle control against a skim*

The term 'waggler' is perhaps a little bit misleading, since these canal floats are only 6in or so in length and not the sort of float you would use on normal waggler waters. The canal waggler comes into its own on narrow fisheries where delicate presentation, coupled with the ability to beat a surface skim are called for.

Balsa is the best material for the canal waggler since it is both light and buoyant: it will land lightly on the water, carry a reasonable amount of shot for its size and remain stable enough to permit line to be buried beneath the surface to cope with skim. Fished bottom end only, the canal waggler is suited to fishing up to 12yd range and in depths of about 6ft, according to the size of float selected.

This pattern is the one which earned the 'canal grey' its name – a simple balsa body and stem that was finished in a matt grey colour and soon became the 'fashion float' on hard-fished canals of the Midlands and North-west. But don't let the name fool you. These floats can work on waters such as

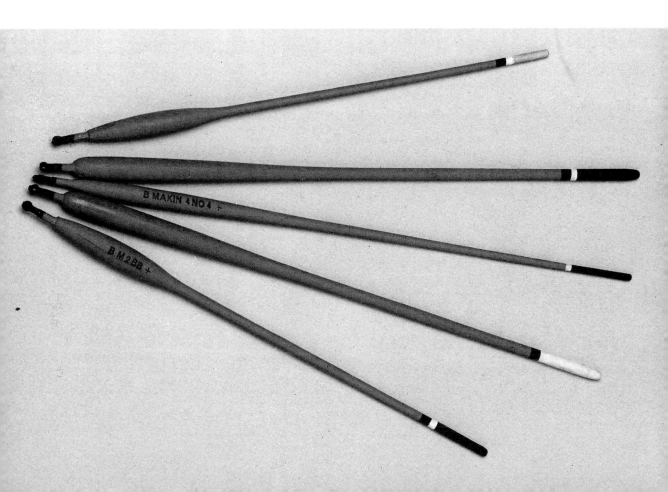

the Fen drains, or for that matter whenever the depth and flow is not too great and fishing is to be at close range.

The float's tip is slender so bite registration is good, but because it is thicker than the one on a 'dart', it allows a little more pressure to be applied for beating the skim. Fish a fine line – 2lb would be the maximum and a 1½lb is better – in order to keep everything supple and to provide good casting qualities. It should be possible to cast this rig by holding the hook length in the left hand and casting with an underarm and upwards sweep of the rod.

As with most hard-fished waters, canals need to be tackled with care and are certainly no place for a lot of shot strung down the line. Typical of the canal greys would be a capacity of between 2BB and 4BB, of which the vast majority would be used as locking

shot. One or two no 8s would go just below mid-depth and then another 8 and a 10 spaced equally between this bulk and the hook. But if conditions get difficult, don't just struggle on. Switch floats, or bring down a little more bulk to give stability. It is always better to fish slightly heavier and get good presentation, than to go for delicacy and get fewer bites because you have less control.

On those awkward days when fishing is very difficult because of a bad skim or a blustery wind, I often switch to a pole but retain the canal waggler, using it in exactly the same manner as with rod and reel – I will therefore have reduced line length to a minimum, yet can still fish at the desired range without reverting to the extra weight and bulk of a longer float.

● *A canal waggler shotted like a scaled down river float. The bulk goes just below mid-depth*

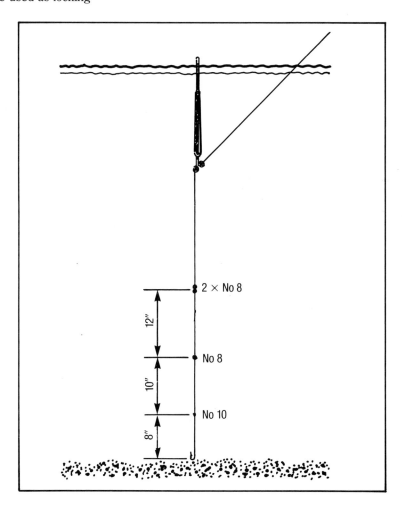

CROW-QUILLS

When and Where to Fish the Crow-quill

Conditions: Best fished in good conditions as a small stick float, or close-in against a slight skim as a reversed quill.

Where: Ponds as a reversed quill, or on shallow and steady flowing rivers as a stick. Use only for close-range fishing, and don't expect too much from this light float.

A number of anglers will be surprised that I include this set of floats in my collection, but on certain days a good crow-quill can still out-fish a lot of its more modern cousins. Its biggest limitation is its lack of size-range – a good one is unlikely to take more than around 3BB. If only crows grew to twice their natural size!

Used double rubber with the thickest end uppermost, it will trot through a steady flow with ease, and is nice to fish with hemp and tares or anywhere that calls for a bit of finesse and very little range. The best quills are the straightest, but with care it is possible to straighten a bent one by warming it gently over a small flame and gradually applying pressure by stroking it between finger and thumb.

The thick end of the quill, being hollow, is buoyant and rides well, working a bit like a small balsa. And if the wind is skimming along making double-rubber fishing difficult, just slip off the top rubber and use it like a small waggler. It will have a limited application

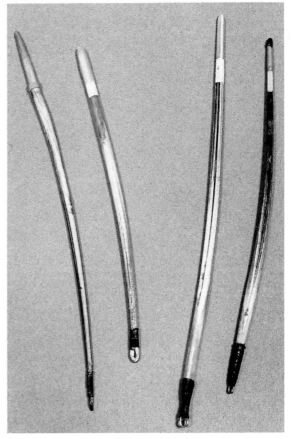

● *Crow-quills make excellent floats suitable for a wide variety of waters*

● *Only the fairly small size of the feather restricts the uses to which the crow-quill can be put*

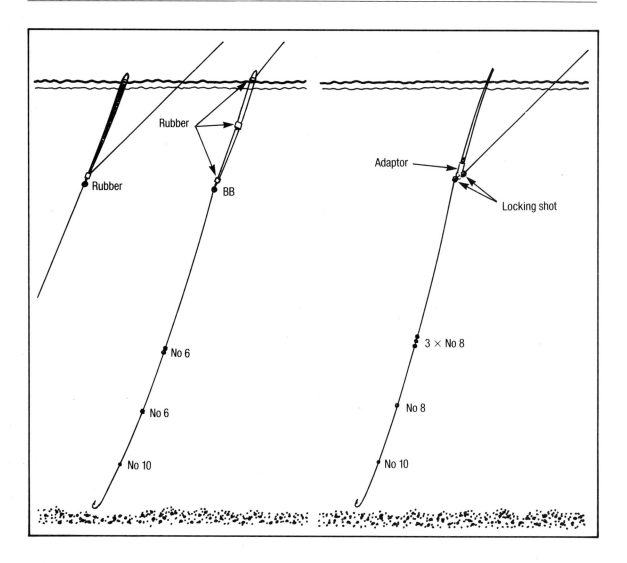

● *Used with the thick end uppermost the crow-quill will work as either a top and bottom pattern, or as an improvised waggler to beat a skim*

● *On a stillwater the reversed quill, attached bottom end only, is a fine float for catching small fish*

used like this, but it is surprising how well that top-end buoyancy holds up.

A crow-quill is also good used the opposite way up, attaching it bottom end only with a small adaptor and a couple of locking shots. With the thick end downwards you now have a fine-tipped waggler, the hollow end acting like a small body beneath the surface. Use it this way for rod-end work with small

fish, and it can be a very efficient little tool and certainly one that is worth the small space it takes up in a well-equipped box.

The crow-quill is usually perfect float material – I have tried the larger goose, seagull and swan and all have fallen by the wayside and are now no longer included in my tackle. However, take care how you rig up the quill, top and bottom – it will not take a lot to break it and it will pay to add a third rubber to stop any bowing effect caused by the slight natural bend of the float.

Fishing top and bottom with a crow-quill is best done by casting it like a stick float. In the reverse situation it becomes a small waggler.

FEEDER FLOAT

When and Where to Fish the Feeder Float

Conditions: Because of its weight it will cope with bad winds.

Where: Will cope with running water but is best suited to still or slow-moving fisheries where long-range loose feeding is required. A good float for fishing across rivers to chub which live under the hulls of boats moored on the far bank.

A rare bird, this one has never really caught on despite a lot of promotional work by former world champion Dave Thomas. At first glance it looks like a conventional bodied waggler, but closer inspection will reveal a hollow body which has a scoop-like opening towards the bottom and a series of small holes near the top. Idea of the feeder float is to fill the body with loose feed such as maggots or casters and then cast just like a normal float. As the rig lands, so the float cocks and the bait trickles out directly over the hook.

Like most anglers, I was a little sceptical when I first saw the rather bulky body of this float. But having tried it several times with some success I now believe it is a pattern that can be a winner under certain conditions. It really comes into its own on those tricky waters that demand long-range fishing but will not tolerate groundbait and as a result have to be fed with something like sticky maggots.

To use the feeder facility it is just a case of holding the float and pouring bait down inside the body. It doesn't spill out because as the cast begins the float remains in the tip-down position and in flight the body leads, thus pushing the feed back inside the hollow. Once in the water however, the body cocks and the bait empties out. The smaller holes at the top end of the body are there only to let trapped air escape. Without them, the float would not settle properly. Even with the holes I have noticed that at times the float still settles a little high, and can only assume this is because some air is left inside. The feed does not seem to affect the float in any way and there is no riding up as the contents empty.

● *A feeder float with its hollow body and scoop-like opening towards the bottom – a clever idea which allows loose feed to be introduced at very long range*

Casting must be accurate, otherwise you end up feeding all over the swim. But that shortcoming apart, it is a good method – especially for fish such as the Nene's far-bank chub population. Actual cast needs to be a fairly smooth lob rather than a jabby throw, because the total load is well in excess of that imposed by even the largest 'normal' float. If there is one drawback it is that the float is a little slow to use because of the time taken in loading it with bait, and the extra care called for in making the cast.

Commercial patterns of the float are still to be found in a few tackle shops, but otherwise it is a case of making your own: carefully drill out a piece of balsa to form a tube and then glue a top and bottom in place and form to the usual body shape, remembering to form both the exit scoop and air holes.

● *A simple rig for the feeder float. Most of the loading is used as locking shot so that the bait falls slowly in with the loose feed*

The feeder float is particularly good in a facing wind, and the usual effect is to bring fish up in the water with the result that bites come very quickly. Best shotting with which to cash in on the constant stream of falling loose feed is a very light string of shot – no 8s and 10s. It pays to step up line strength a little – one of 2½lb to 3lb is safest, coupled with a softish-actioned rod. The adaptor also needs to be a firm fit in order to take the considerable casting loads imposed upon it.

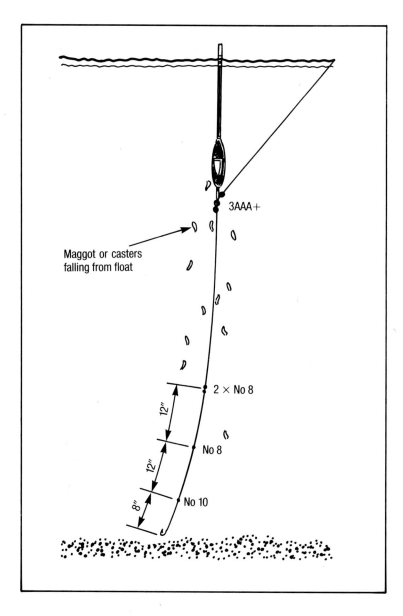

3AAA+

Maggot or casters falling from float

2 × No 8

No 8

No 10

12"

12"

8"

INSERT WAGGLER

When and Where to Fish the Insert Waggler

Conditions: Reasonable wind; not a brilliant float in a bad downstream wind if the insert is very slim. Good float for beating a surface skim if line is well sunk.

Where: Any stillwater or slow-moving river where bite detection is critical. Not a float for fast waters, but will cope with reasonable flows if allowed to run through unchecked.

The insert waggler is possibly one of the most widely used floats available today yet it can only be used effectively on certain types of water. It is not really a float for water that runs hard, and unless you have particularly good eyesight it is not the one for fishing at very long range. But used correctly, it is a superb invention, combining a considerable number of qualities from other floats.

The 'insert' can be used on almost any pattern of waggler and my favourite is a straight peacock quill with another thinner piece acting as the insert. This peacock insert is very light and does not affect the overall balance of the float. A cane or plastic insert of the same diameter displaces exactly the same amount of water and therefore registers a bite with the same amount of sensitivity. But when it comes to casting ability, I'll take the double peacock every time.

Idea of this thin tip is to give the best possible bite registration, and it is ideal for showing bites that come 'on-the-drop' – that is to say a fish intercepts a slow-falling bait before it reaches full depth. This 'on-the-drop' feature is only one of the insert's uses. It will work equally well when fishing the bottom of still, or very slow-moving water. On running water it will go through without trouble but only if allowed to travel unchecked and if there is no part of the tackle actually dragging the bottom.

Another insert type of waggler is the stepped down version; this can be made from a series of quills, gradually reducing in diameter – the thickest

● *Limited scope, but still a great float, the insert waggler has a number of special qualities*

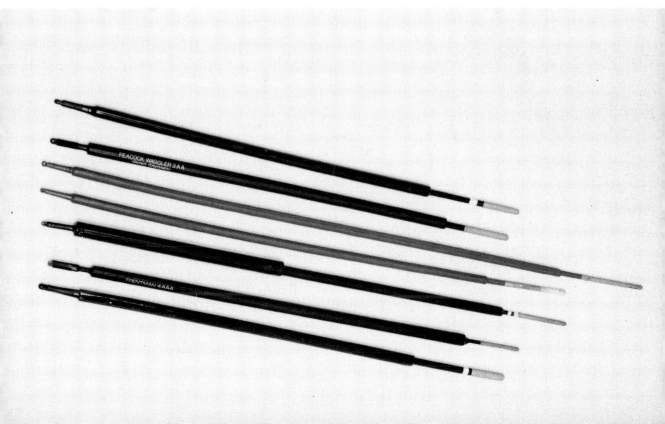

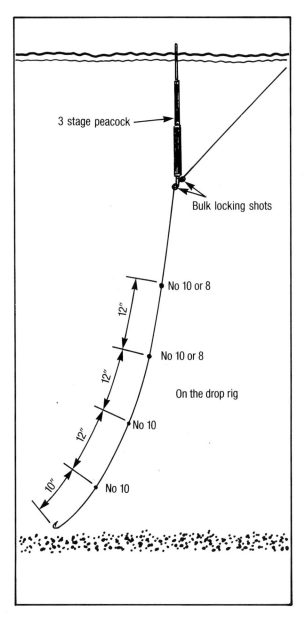

3 stage peacock

Bulk locking shots

No 10 or 8

12"

No 10 or 8

12"

On the drop rig

No 10

12"

10"

No 10

● *Shotting is kept down to small single shots strung down the line. This will give good bite registration and a slow fall to the bait – two of the pattern's best qualities*

quill – usually peacock – is used at the float's base, then reducing progressively until the slimmest at the tip. Qualities of the stepped waggler include very good stability, and the ability to perform well in a downstream wind: stability is given by the bulky peacock in the base of the float acting like a body; and the wind-beating effect comes from the slimmer section being used nearest the surface where skim is going to be strongest.

I have made these floats with up to four different diameters and a total of over a foot long. They take time to make but are well worth the effort – and if you are really clever, you can make the tip inserts interchangeable to provide a whole set of floats in one.

The whole principle of an insert is to provide as delicate a bite registration as possible, but you get nothing free in this world and as diameter reduces, so will the float's ability to cope with current, drag and poor visibility. With these drawbacks in mind, you may find that your first-choice insert creates all sorts of problems – however, a change up to one half as thick again is often all that's needed to deal with the conditions, and you shouldn't lose too much in the way of bite registration.

Shotting can be done in many different ways, but of course for a slow-falling, 'on-the-drop' rig it is usually nothing more than a bulk at the float, followed by a string of several tiny and individually spaced shot down the line. I have always hammered home the need to adopt the below mid-water rule as a means of stopping tangles – however, the insert is one of the floats where I will often string out shot all the way down the line in a similar manner as for those used with a stick float.

Length of the insert is also of some importance. Too long and it will be very unstable in the water: too short, and in anything but the best of conditions it will not work well. A ripple will upset it to the degree where bites are difficult to detect (other than those that pull the whole float from view). Go for something 1in–2in long, according to the overall dimensions of the float – and don't be afraid to have a fair amount showing. This is not a float that can be dotted right down to only a fraction above the surface.

Something to watch for with the insert is the number of fish that can come off soon after the strike. Often, especially on waters where there is a fair number of hand-sized skimmer bream, a good bite shows, the strike is rapid and a fish is felt, only for it to part company a fraction of a second later. I believe this is due to the float's sensitive nature causing the strike to be made too early, before the soft-mouthed fish has taken in the bait and hook properly. What happens is the hook just nicks the very edge of the fish's lip and fails to gain a firm hold.

The cure is simple: delay the strike – and this is best done by taking off a small shot to allow more of the insert to show. The delay will then be automatic because it will take a little longer for your brain to register the fact that the float is going under. Alternatively, if you have the self-control, leave everything as it is but make yourself slow down a bit, either by leaving a little slack line or by counting off a second or two in your mind before striking. If you have an interchangeable insert, a third course of action is to switch to a slightly longer one, while leaving the shotting unchanged.

As already explained, the reason for the insert waggler's excellent bite registration is its very small displacement of water – the smaller the area displaced, the more sensitive the float. While this is fine at close range, it does create a few problems when trying to see clearly a fine tip at a considerable distance.

Answer is a hollow tip, which to my knowledge was first marketed back in the early 1980s by Sundridge Tackle. Principle is very much the same as a conventional insert, but the tip looks a bit like a piece of plastic drinking straw with a hole cut in the side. The outside diameter of the hollow tip is around 4mm but because it is already full of water a biting fish feels no more resistance than with a bristle or insert tip. But from the angler's point of view, the 4mm is of course very much easier to see at range.

I have used this float to very good effect on Ferry Meadows Lakes at Peterborough where long-range float fishing for bream can be great fun. The problem we faced in the early days was one of bite detection – the bream were large, but often bites were nothing more than a very tiny movement of a conventional float. We tried fine inserts and they worked, but by the end of a day we all left with very sore eyes. Enter the hollow tip, and all the troubles were solved in one. Bites were registering the same as on a small insert but we could see them much easier.

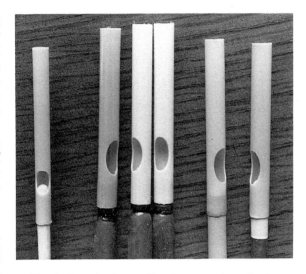

● *The hollow tip float will take over when the insert becomes useless due to extreme range at which it becomes difficult to see easily. These hollow tips are made from a light plastic and have a hole cut in the side to allow water to flow in and out*

You can prove the theory yourself with a little simple mathematics.

When a bite moves a solid tip insert, it displaces water equal to the area through a section of the insert. That is to say, a 2mm diameter insert displaces: Pi(3.142) x the radius of the insert squared. That is, 3.142x1 squared, the answer to which is 3.142sq mm. Now take a 4mm diameter hollow tip with a wall thickness of say .25mm. The outside diameter has an area of 3.142x2 squared, giving an area of 12.48sq mm. But from that we now subtract the inside, hollow section which is already full of water and therefore displaces nothing. This inside area is calculated as: 3.142 x 1.75 squared, equalling 9.62sq mm. Subtract this from 12.48 and the answer is 2.89sq mm. From that you can see that although we have a much greater area of tip to look at, the effect on a biting fish is almost the same as with a much finer tip.

Casting is not upset by the hollow tip because the side openings allow the water to run out immediately a strike is made. Keep a few hollow tips handy and use them when a finer tip is difficult to see. They suffer the same drawbacks, however, as a bristle or insert in a flow, in that they cannot be held back or the bait allowed to drag hard along the bottom.

THE MISSILE

When and Where to Fish the Missile

Conditions: Such is the bulk of this float that it takes a lot to reduce its effectiveness. A large missile allows line to be sunk easily, but it is at its best with a back wind and nothing more than a ripple on the surface.
Where: Big waters and in particular deep ones. Flow must be only slight and the rivers of the Fens – the lower Nene, Welland and Great Ouse – are classics. It is also a good float for lakes which hold good heads of bream or other large fish which tend to stay well out.

As the name suggests, this float is a weapon for tackling big waters where long-distance casting is the order – 50 or 60yd is possible, and in many ways it is a good substitute for a leger and one that has found many friends on the wide, wind-swept waters of the Welland, Witham and lower Great Ouse. It is a big float first popularised by Coventry anglers, and in particular the great Billy Lane – it was the Coventry team who perfected the method for the 1967 National Championship on the Great Ouse Relief Channel, a venue that until then had been dominated by the leger. Unfortunately for Coventry and many others in the event, the 'Channel' fished very badly, producing an almost endless string of dry keepnets.

I was captain of the Peterborough DAA team in that match and like most of the others taking part, had nothing to show at the end of five hours' graft. The only fish I saw all day was a small skimmer bream that rolled over on the surface in front of me and died. But such was the impact Coventry's idea made on me that day, that I soon got cracking on making my own missiles and was later to return to the Channel and find out just how good the float was.

A true missile is made from a long peacock stem on a balsa body. This body carries a considerable load in its base and it is this that provides much of its considerable casting power. Commercial missiles are not always loaded correctly – if indeed at all – and you may be forced into making up your own. A fairly thick piece of peacock of at least 1ft long, and a large balsa body is needed to provide the load-carrying capacity.

Loading can be in the form of a brass stem or the bottom half of an Arlesey bomb. The bomb makes a nice streamlined shape to the body's bottom, but take care when you drill it to take the stem. A good idea is to make up four or five floats of the same dimensions but with different loadings in the body.

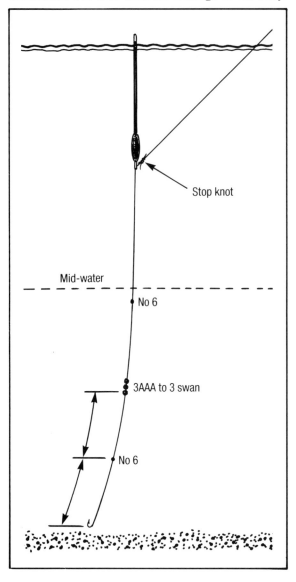

● *The correct way to fish a missile is as a slider. The no 6 shot placed just below half depth is a stop on which the float rests during casting. A good means of tying the stop is shown in the section dealing with sliding floats later in this chapter*

● Missiles – the big brothers of the floatbox and the tool for casting very long distances. Invented by the late, world champion Billy Lane for the Great Ouse Relief Channel

Such a set will enable you to fish with varying amounts of shot down the line, thus giving a choice of fall rates so that fish may be taken on the drop. The more loading that goes into the body the further the float will cast, but you do have to throw them very high into the air to get maximum range.

Billy Lane often fished his missile as a slider, and even on shallow waters he insisted that no locking shots were used. I could never understand this idea until I tried holding it in place with two shots. All I achieved was a spectacular crack-off where the float was locked. A situation, Billy explained to me soon afterwards, which was caused by the tremendous force exerted on the line in one place by the float.

The correct manner to fish a missile is with a stop-knot (see p. 140). This will allow the float to rest above the bulk shot during casting and whilst giving the maximum range possible, reduces the risk of breakage considerably. It goes without saying that a good line is needed, and one that sinks well. I use a minimum of 2½lb breaking strain, and even then it must be in perfect condition if it is to cope. The rod needs a bit of backbone, too, but it must not be too tippy. Striking is easy despite the range. This is because the sliding effect permits you to pull through the float and contact the fish before having to move the considerable bulk of the big balsa body and a lot of loading.

Strike with a sweeping followthrough to ensure you pick up all the line quickly. And when casting it is important that all line is sunk quickly to reduce bowing because of the long range. The trick is to overcast, stick the rod tip in the water and wind back quickly to the required fishing spot.

Shotting is simple. A bulk of between three AAA and three swan and a single no 6, or four tell-tale. By keeping the bulk well away from the hook you are likely to get fish on the way down; these will show a bite as several inches of peacock sticking out of the water.

Although I have sung the praises of this float, it is not one often used these days; this may be because the waters where it ruled twenty years ago have declined or because swim feeder tactics have been perfected – if nothing else, these are less demanding. For pleasure fishing though, the missile is a most enjoyable and satisfying method and one that can bring rich rewards on days when the leger should, but doesn't, produce.

THE STRAIGHT PEACOCK

When and Where to Fish a Straight Peacock Waggler

Conditions: Will cope with most conditions depending on the thickness of quill used. Will tackle running water that is made difficult by a downstream wind.
Where: Use it almost anywhere, the only limitation being the amount of shot it can carry. Use thick floats to fish fast running water, leaving plenty of tip showing so that it can be checked slightly. Thinner floats are best for slow or still waters.

If I had to pick just one float pattern with which to fish for a whole season it would be the straight peacock. Given a wide enough selection of quills it is possible to tackle just about any water you care to choose with a reasonable chance of success. A thick-topped 'straight' is ideal for running through a fast swim, while the opposite end of a full peacock tail quill would be well suited to a small water such as a canal.

So what makes this such a super float? For a start, it casts really well; it is light and very buoyant, taking a good shot load for its size; and as quills go the peacock is also tough – some in my box have survived for years, calling for nothing more than a few spots of fresh paint at the end of a season. It is one of the most versatile floats, and also one of the cheapest and easiest to make yourself, a full quill producing at least three good wagglers of varying thickness which are suitable for different types of water. Another good thing is that it is easy to master, providing a few basic rules are followed. First of these is to get the shotting correctly balanced.

The peacock is going to be locked on 'bottom end only' by using an adaptor between some fairly large shots. This locking shot bunch is going to be around three-quarters of the total loading – any less and you will begin to struggle with casting, either for range or accuracy. The only exception is when a really large shot load is used down the line, in much the same manner as when fishing a crow-quill Avon. Used like this, the float would be locked with two very tiny shots and the bulk shot used as the casting

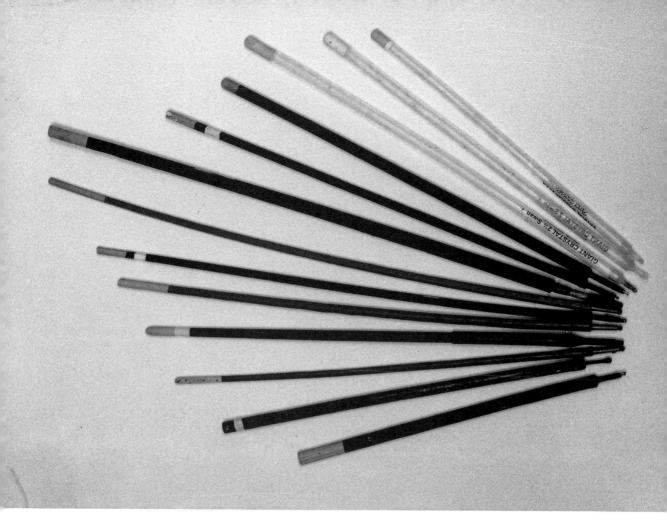

weight, pulling everything behind it through the air.

But let us first take a float made from the very thickest end of a quill. Here we are talking about a diameter of perhaps 5 or 6mm, maybe even more – such a thick-topped float will not be very sensitive and so it does have some very strict limitations. But this lack of sensitivity can be used to advantage in order to fish a fast-moving swim that cannot be tackled with a 'top and bottom' pattern of float, perhaps because of a very bad downstream wind.

Our float is going to carry three-and-a-half swan shots – but by all means consider bigger ones if conditions demand them. The larger the load the more control you will have, but continue to apply the balancing rule whenever possible. So the float – a 5mm diameter specimen of some 20cm long – is fixed to the line by an adaptor and locked in place by the equivalent of close to three swan, leaving the other half-swan to go down the line.

Locking floats in place with one very large shot

● One of the most simple of all floats is the straight peacock. Used in different thicknesses it will cope with most waters. On the top of the picture are three Drennan Crystals – clear plastic floats which perform just like peacock quills

such as a swan usually results in problems with them sliding about, losing your carefully set depth as a result. So fix a swan either side of the float and then make up the rest by adding a AAA and then a BB beneath the float and a BB above the other swan. The total is now three swan. How the remaining shot is spaced depends on the depth of swim, the current and how we wish to present the bait.

For a straightforward run-through, taking fish at any depth from mid-water to the bottom, nothing will beat a string of evenly spaced shots that gradually decrease in size as they approach the hook. Variations on this theme can be made by pulling more of the string down to form a bulk, below

127

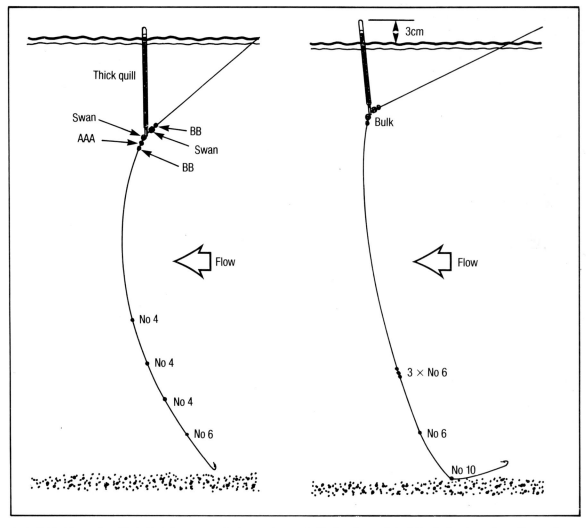

● *A thick piece of quill shotted for use on fast running water. A large amount of shot is used around the float and then single shots strung out along the last few feet*

● *By leaving a lot of float showing above the surface a peacock can be made to drag a bait along the bottom. The only shot that actually touches the bed is a no 10*

which are perhaps two or three single small shots.

However, we have to consider what effect running water will have on this float if it is checked. Even with such a thick top, a fast flow acting against a peacock held back hard will quickly pull it under. So we can only control the tackle's travel down the swim to a limited degree, and this degree will depend firstly on the diameter of our float – the thicker the top the more holding back it will take – and secondly on the amount of top left showing above the water.

It may sound very crude, but try fishing this float in a strong flow with a good 3cm sticking out. With practice and concentration you will be able to check its progress by applying pressure to the line at the spool until the tip all but vanishes. Get this control right and you will make the under-loaded float run through slower than the current with just a little tip still showing. By varying the amount of under-shotting applied to a float you will be able to arrive at a compromise between sensitivity and control. A similar principle can be applied to this float in order

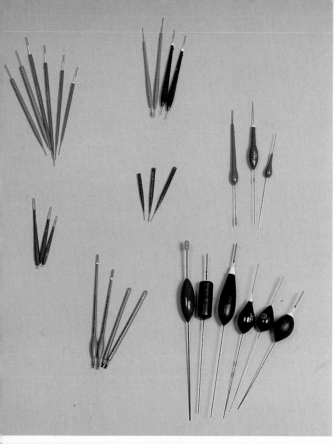

● *Seven patterns of pole float which will cover most situations. From top left: balsa bristle, tapered balsa bristle; centre left: canal balsa, flat top, bodied bristle, pole waggler, German style (Chapter 7)*

● *(pp130–1) A dreamy stretch of water, but choosing a swim needs to be done with care (Chapter 8)*

● *Plastic winders are used to store complete sets of pole tackle. Mark each one with details of hook size, line and bottom strength and total length of line (Chapter 7)*

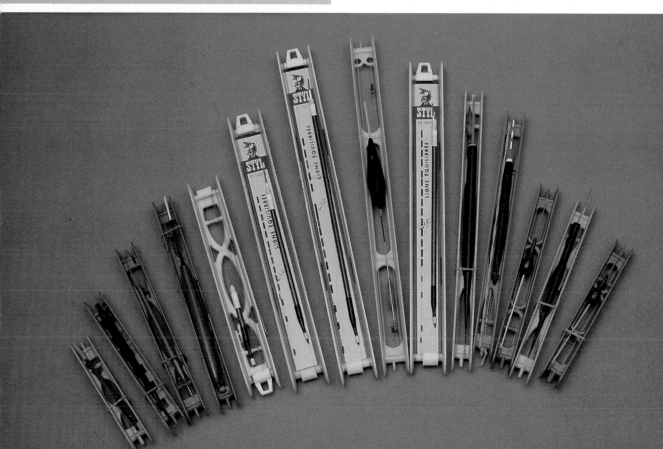

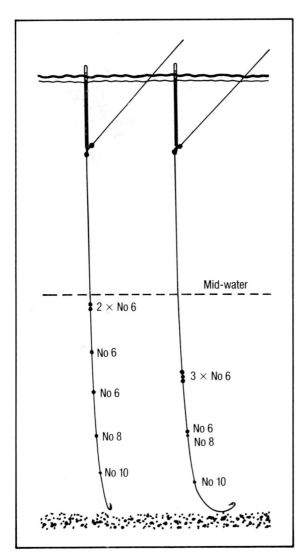

Mid-water

2 × No 6

No 6

No 6

No 8

No 10

3 × No 6

No 6
No 8

No 10

● *More conventional sizes of peacock waggler can be used to tackle the slower waters such as the rivers Nene, Welland, Cam and stillwaters. Shotting can vary a lot but these two basic patterns will give a choice of either a medium fall rate (left) or a bait which is stable near the bottom*

● *Superb roach like these are what could be expected with baits such as wheat, tares, flake or even sweetcorn (Chapter 5)*

● *A gallery of spectators can ruin your match unless they stay well back and off the skyline. The high hedge in this picture will at least provide some background cover (Chapter 8)*

to get it to pull a bait along the bottom. But try this with a slim-tipped float in a flowing river and you will fail every time.

If you under-load a thick quill which has been set to fish overdepth with a very small shot – say, a no 8 or 10 – as a tell-tale which is allowed to drag along the bottom, the float will bounce along merrily. You will, however, have to learn to distinguish between movements caused by the dragging shot, and a bite – it is something you have to experience for yourself rather than be taught. And you may need to alter the tell-tale size until one is found that will not cause too much of a breaking effect.

Obviously it is a good idea always to go for the slimmest float possible, one just capable of coping with prevailing flow conditions and the amount of slowing down that needs to be done in order to get bites.

Moving down the thickness scale, a good quill for average flows – such as would be found on lowland rivers like the Nene, Welland and Witham – might come from the middle of a quill. It will carry between three and six AAAs and have a tip of around 3mm diameter. But as when selecting any float, you should firstly decide on the amount of shot required to do the job and then find a float to match. In fact this is the manner in which I always tackle up. On goes the adaptor, locked by the bulk of my shot. Down the line the required shotting pattern is arranged, and finally the float needed to carry my choice.

Same principle is applied with regard to most of the load being used to lock the float. For example, a four AAA choice gets three AAA as locking shot; the rest will be used to catch fish on or very close to the bottom – I am thinking of a typical middle-Nene swim of 9 or 10ft that will hold a reasonable head of skimmer bream and small roach.

If roach are the dominant species it would be advisable to start by loose feeding and fishing a fairly spaced-out rig that would fall slowly through the last 2 or 3ft of water. If this fails to work well enough and odd skimmers are encountered, it will pay to add a few inches to the depth setting and alter the shotting to give a steadier presentation close to the bottom. Do this by pulling some of the spaced shot down to form a bulk – try the altered rig for a while, and if skimmers come faster go for a little groundbait to keep them tight to the bottom and feeding.

In order to get the best from this rig, should there be anything but a perfect wind, it is vital that as much line as possible is sunk beneath the surface, so cast beyond the fishing area and wind back a few fast turns on the reel.

One thing to bear in mind after all this talk of tip thickness is that the larger the float's diameter, the less effect a tell-tale shot will have in registering a bite. It follows, therefore, that you always try to use the largest one possible. A good example is a 4mm thick quill with a no 10 as a tell-tale – remove the tell-tale and you would struggle to see any difference it has made to the float. Substitute that 10 for, say, a 6 or even a 4 and a difference would register. Again, be prepared to change to suit the day. And the closer a shot is to the hook, the more sensitive will be the bite registration – but it is all a case of judging just how tolerant the fish are going to be of a shot close to their intended dinner.

The final straight peacock, without entering into the realm of insert patterns, is one with a tip of perhaps 2mm diameter. Now that is a slim float and it will work very much in the same manner as an insert, but because it lacks the bulk lower down, its stem will carry less shot and be slightly more unstable. A fine-tipped straight peacock is a super float for close-in work or for tackling the larger canals and small, slow rivers. They cast well enough for a 2AAA model to cope with 12 to 15yd easily in good conditions, and in shallow water they can be cast to land without too much splash.

So with these three floats made from a single quill, we are able to tackle a host of totally different waters and conditions. At this stage I make no apology for overlooking similar floats made from sarkandas reed which in my opinion is very much a second-rate material. It is heavier than peacock and as a result carries less shot for a given size; it does not cast as well and is notoriously difficult to paint – even after a lot of work with glasspaper to prepare the surface I find it still peels very easily. For the commercial floatmaker it is much easier, and probably cheaper, to produce a sarkandas float that looks every bit as good as a peacock. Only when you fish the two materials side by side will you appreciate the considerable difference.

BODIED PEACOCK

When and Where to Use the Bodied Peacock

Conditions: A good float to combat bad wind conditions because of the considerable amount of bulk shot it carries. Works well when fish are being caught near the bottom in conjunction with groundbait.

Where: Wide and windy waters that are fairly deep. Will be a good choice if small fish are a problem – the use of big bulk of shot will get a bait through them before it can be damaged.

The next step up the scale from the straight peacock is the bodied version. Basically the roles of the two patterns are similar, except that the bodied style is best used on slower waters where wind, rather than current, is the problem. With a body it is obvious the float will carry a greater shot load, but one other characteristic is its ability to remain stable in rough conditions (see colour photograph on p. 88).

To some degree modern rod designs have made bodied floats less popular and certainly not as essential as they were in the early years of glassfibre – today there are few waters that cannot at least be covered with a straight peacock. So the body is there only to provide stability and extra load-carrying capacity that may be needed for a specific purpose other than sheer casting performance.

One thing I can never understand is why so many inexperienced anglers opt for a short-stemmed bodied waggler to tackle a slow-moving water that has a downstream wind blowing along it. That situation is more suited to a longer, but similar load-carrying straight. Length in the float's stem is essential if line is to be buried to prevent bowing and drag. The extra stability of a body can help, too, by giving you something to pull back to.

Most commercially produced bodied wagglers have fairly bulbous body shapes. A really effective pattern, however, is a peacock to which a slender balsa body has been formed at the base – it is really little more than a swelling, but it does give the float superb stability. Casting qualities are also good because of the streamlined shape.

There is little difference between fishing a body and a straight, but striking will need to be carried out with more of a sweeping followthrough in order to

● *Bodies added to peacock quills will add considerably to the stability and increase the shot-carrying capacity in order to cope with strong winds*

● *Striking while fishing a big bodied float needs to be done in a downstream, sweeping arc to reduce resistance created by wind and flow*

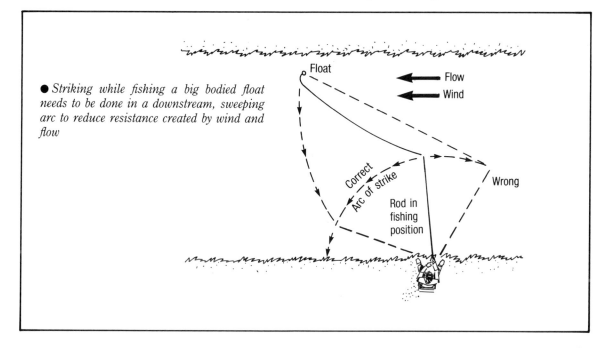

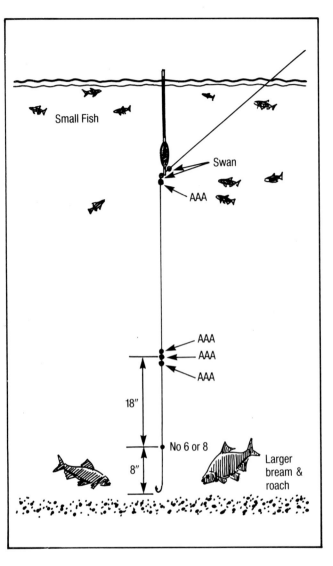

Small Fish

Swan

AAA

AAA
AAA
AAA

18″

No 6 or 8

8″

Larger
bream &
roach

● *The bodied peacock lends itself well to the use of a big bulk of shot in order to get a bait through small fish feeding high in the water*

get the bulk of a body moving effectively and to make positive contact with the fish. Striking upstream is not advised because then you have to overcome the pressure of water pushing against the body *and* against the line – which no matter how well you are fishing, will have formed some sort of bow. To strike correctly the rod is swept sideways, bringing the tip *downstream* in an arc. If you do it in the opposite direction – moving the rod upstream – the line has to be moved much further before contact is made.

Like the straight peacock, the bodied version is fished bottom only by means of an adaptor and locking shot. But because of the considerable load it carries it is a good pattern to use when there is need for a bait to be got down quickly. I can think of a number of situations when this is likely. The swim may be deep and fish are being found only in the bottom few inches. Wasting time with a slow drop is stupid in such a case – bulk is what is called for, and because the body gives so much load capacity there is still weight to spare to add at the float and so three-quarters of the total can be used for that purpose.

Small surface-feeding fish such as bleak are sometimes a problem. They grab a maggot as it falls and either get hooked themselves or just ruin the bait intended for better fish feeding deeper. Adding a big bulk well down the line may speed the descent sufficiently to keep them at bay.

A big bulk load close to the bottom can also help a waggler perform just as it does in the case of the crow-quill Avon. A large lump of shot, well down near the bottom, is going to remain very stable and act like a drogue, slowing everything down to the natural pace of the current rather than letting surface skim take over.

When I was fishing with the Peterborough DAA team in the Captain Morgan Cup knockout competition, we had two very good seasons during which we developed a certain method of fishing a stretch of our water where most of our home rounds were staged. It was a good venue, called Orton Downstream, just above the town. The water varied from 6 to 11ft deep and was packed with fish – roach, chub and a very big head of bream ranging in size from 4lb each to the more usual 8oz, to 1lb 'skimmers'. Weights were required all through the team since the result was decided on total weight and not points.

Fished with a slowly falling bait, a lot of small fish would be taken and a weight of 5lb or so was all you could expect. (Groundbait was part of the secret, too. What we used was a float, either a thick peacock with a slimmer insert top or more usually a bodied waggler, that would take a load of between three and four swan, maybe even more at times. We could reach anywhere on the river with this float – at least once we had mastered the knack of casting with a big bulk down the line. A bulk of three or more AAA would go on 18in or so from the hook, and beneath that a no 6 as tell-tale; all the remaining load was used to lock the float.

It was crude but it remained stable – an essential requirement if the larger skimmer bream were to be fooled – and the small fish didn't get a look-in on the way down. Result was, we got in a lot more effective fishing time before the opposition realised what was happening.

Groundbaiting was heavy and if the opposition happened to cotton on to our bulky float style, they still fell foul of this trick. And although we fed a lot, the skimmers didn't go off after two or three hours as was so often the case: we knew why! This prolonged feeding was because what we put in contained very little feed; also, its colour seemed to appeal to the fish on that stretch. Our mix was nearly pure, riddled peat! The only food value in it was the small amount of white cereal that was added to make it bind up fairly stiffly, and a good supply of squatts and a few casters.

I tell this story to show that by combining a certain float's qualities with a feeding plan it is possible to control the manner in which a swim responds. In the case of our plan it worked like a dream for a couple of seasons and we won a place in the Irish final – but got beaten at home the next year by a crack ABC team. We thought we had read the conditions right and went for the same groundbait and bulk shot attack. Most of the ABC men fished much lighter rigs for chub and except for one good bream weight they all found 'em, or at least the smaller fish which we had completely neglected until it was too late.

We had overlooked the change our river undergoes every autumn – which came a week or two earlier than expected. Our groundbaiting, which had won so much for us, killed our chance completely. That, too, goes to show that it never pays to become too obsessed with one method.

BLEAK FLOATS

When and Where to Fish the Bleak Float

Conditions: Do not affect this float too much, mainly because it is fished at such short range.

Where: Whenever surface fish are the target, in particular bleak or any tiny fish that need to be caught very quickly in order to build a weight. Will suit all waters, the only limitation being the distance it can be cast efficiently.

Bleak fishing belongs to the really competitive match angler and is scorned by many of his opponents – mostly by those who are unable to do it well. But nobody will ever convince me that being able to catch three, four or even five fish a minute is not a skill. I've seen some very good anglers really struggle trying to make up a weight of these tiny surface feeders just because they lacked the basic knowledge of how to keep fishing smoothly for long periods.

The float is a very important part of effective bleaking, but you will need to add the right hook and bait to it, too, along with a set-up on the bank which you know the way around blindfolded. Bait needs to be a smallish hook maggot, preferably an old one that is tough and will withstand catching half-a-dozen fish before bursting. Hook pattern is either barbless or micro barb with a long shank for rapid removal.

But bleak fishing is an art in itself, and all I intend to deal with here are a few float alternatives. What is needed is a short float that has no edges, stems or bristles that can tangle. I developed a very simple little float of about 3cm long, a piece of balsa with the ends shaped to a blunt point over which fairly long rubbers are attached. This is where care is needed: the rubbers must overhang the ends of the float by 4 or 5mm so there is no chance of line tangling between where it leaves the rubber and the float's tip.

Casting weight, if the float itself is not sufficient, is in the form of two identically sized shots – one at each end of the float and pushed down inside the overhanging rubbers. By placing them at both ends the float doesn't cock, but instead rests flat along the surface. A bite just tows the float along and you lift – not strike – into the fish.

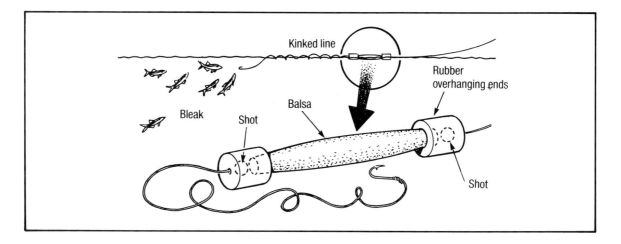

● *A complete bleak fishing rig. Note the shots used at opposite ends of the float to give extra casting weight without causing the float to cock*

Although what we have made is truly a float it is not the first thing that indicates a bite. To make this, kink the line beneath the float by pulling it between two tightly pinched fingernails – the resulting spirals, after having a little grease applied, sit right out of the water in a series of loops that make ideal, resistance-free indicators. I won a lot of matches like that with weights of around 14lb from the Nene – some in matches of only four hours' duration.

Another 'float' that works well is a length of old floating fly-fishing line. All you do is tie in about 10cm of fly line about 18in from the hook. This thick line gives weight for casting but offers little resistance to the bleak.

Bleak respond to the splash of tackle going in. So with this in mind, always 'cast' the tackle down hard to make it plop as it lands – if a big weight is on, the bleak come rushing from nowhere. Further evidence of this splash effect was demonstrated to me by Italian international Milo Columbo during an invitation event in Ireland. He showed me it was possible to catch surface fish with a bare, red-coloured hook just by making the tackle splash as it hit the surface – and the fish he demonstrated on were roach from a hard-fished water!

For my bleak floats I prefer balsa to pieces of quill because the wood has that little extra weight. I did try some harder, heavier woods such as lignum but found they didn't perform so effectively.

THE SLIDERS

When and Where to Use the Slider

Conditions: Will work under most conditions and with some advantage when there is a difficult skim on a deep water. A balsa fished as a slider will cope with running water but cannot be held back hard.

Where: Deep water or anywhere which makes fishing with a fixed float difficult, such as beneath overhanging trees or with a high bank behind. Very good for fishing at long range when a large fixed float results in a lot of missed bites because striking is not effective.

One of the most under-used floats – or more correctly, methods – is the slider. Ask ten anglers when they would use a slider and nine will say when the water depth is deeper than their rod length. Such a statement is not wrong of course, but the effectiveness of a slider goes a long way beyond that.

We will look at both the 'bottom end only' slider and the 'top and bottom' float used in running water. Both work on the principle of being able to slide freely along the line until stopped by a special knot. There is even a commercially made stop available which works very well, but I admit to being a bit old-fashioned and stick to a knot I know works well enough, and which can be repeated easily on any spool I own.

In order for the knot to work, the eye in the float

must be used instead of the more usual adaptor. A good tip with a waggler-style slider is to attach a small swivel to the bottom eye and use that to take the line. But in every case the eye or swivel must be small, otherwise the stop-knot will pass through and the float will then continue its passage along the line unchecked. The eye must be a complete circle, too. A simple U-bend of wire whipped to the stem soon results in jamming, and even line breakage. The swivel, of course, provides a really good eye and also gives the float that bit more freedom to hang freely during casting and while the slide is taking place.

So, having sorted out the mechanics of the float, we can now turn to the conditions in which it can work for you and act as a bonus. In deep water a slider makes casting easier by placing the weight of the float and the bulk shot all close together, rather than having float and shot anything up to 15ft or so apart. Fishing under overhanging trees or below high banks, both of which can make casting a fixed float difficult – if not impossible – is much easier with a slider because again, the float sits near the bulk shot; it can even be cast underarm like an Avon or stick float.

Where a lot of load is needed to reach a distant deep swim the slider enables an effective strike to be made, because the line actually passes through the float – otherwise it would have to move the float's whole mass which would absorb much of the strike's effectiveness. When there is a bad down-stream wind and a bow forms in the line a strike will be more direct by working round this bow, through the float and down to the hook, again without having to move the float, too.

Light sliders do not work well and I suggest the best pattern for a sliding waggler is one with a good body to it. The bulk and buoyancy of this body ensures the float remains stable and is less inclined to be pulled off the required position as line sinks through the slider ring.

Another good tip is not to just let the float sit on the bulk shot but instead place a stop-shot a foot or so above it – this little stop-shot need only be just so large as not to go through the float eye. Idea is it separates the float and bulk and in doing so prevents the possibility of tangling in flight.

The actual slider knot is easy enough to tie but even a perfectly tied one will not work well if clipped

● *Two typical sliding floats. The eyes whipped to their stems are very small to prevent the stop knot passing through*

wrongly. Use a fairly fine and supple line for making the knot – 2lb is about the maximum for use with a match rod – and leave both ends about 3cm long. Cut them shorter and they become too stiff to pass easily through the tip ring of your rod. Fancy shotting is out, too. Go for a bulk with just one or two single tell-tales below.

When you first start slider fishing you may worry about how and if the shot has pulled through to fish correctly. But don't panic – if everything has been done as I've outlined it will work. To satifsy yourself, watch the float as it lands on the water and you may be able to see the line making a little wake as it speeds down through the ring. The float will not

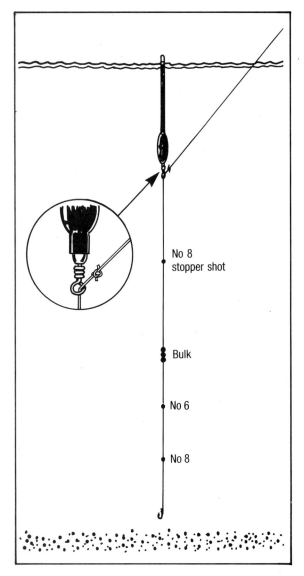

No 8
stopper shot

Bulk

No 6

No 8

● *A typical slider rig. Note the stop shot on which the float can rest during casting. The stop knot above the float cannot pass through the eye, or in the case of the float shown the small swivel*

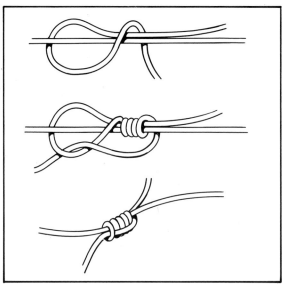

● *The slider knot. Use a fine line of around 2lb breaking strain and leave the loose ends long. Pull it just tight enough so that it can be moved along the line but will not slip*

cock properly for a few seconds, the time taken for the weight to sink fully and begin to take control. Delicately shotted, you may even be able to spot the next stage as the float tip dips a fraction more as the tell-tales reach their positions, too.

Should you tangle on the cast the effect will probably be noticed very quickly – possibly in a more dramatic fashion than when fishing a fixed rig. What usually happens is the float cocks immediately because shot has wrapped itself round the stem.

My advice is: fish a slider when you think it will serve a purpose. You will catch some fish and confidence will grow.

The 'top and bottom' slider is really a balsa with an extra ring set at the top; it is this top eye that needs to have a small diameter since it is where the stop-knot will rest. These eyes are set out at a 90-degree angle to the float's body, and it is vital that they are in line with each other to ensure that line runs through quickly and unhindered. Fish it on running water just like a conventional balsa, but don't hold it back. The bulk will, however, permit a bait to be dragged along the bottom without any problem.

Only other shot will be a tell-tale no 4 some 25cm above the hook, and a stop-shot – say a 6 – above the bulk.

Finally, a mention in passing of the various other inventions that are passed off as sliders. Most have some form of offset eye that locks the float when the line is tightened. I have never found a need for this sort of complication, and cannot think of any situation where they would work better than the stop-knot method.

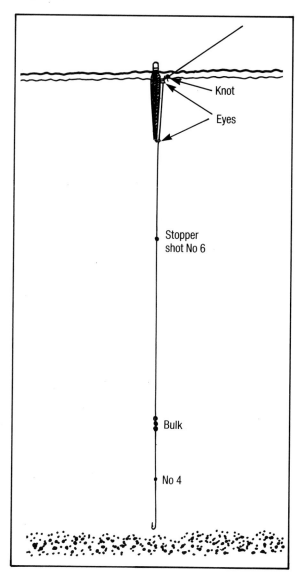

● *The top and bottom slider is a simple rig calling for a big bulk of shot and a single tell tale*

THE CONVENTIONAL STICK FLOAT

When and Where to Use the Stick Float

Conditions: Best with a back or upstream wind. Can be used with a wind blowing downstream but control will be difficult and presentation less effective.
Where: Running water that is not turbulent. Speed of the flow is not a problem. Good float for catching fish at all depths and in particular 'on the drop' if correctly shotted. A good float for swims of 6 to 8ft deep but greater depths can be tackled with larger models.

Stick float fishing is an art that few anglers have fully mastered. It demands total concentration and a lot of hard work if the float's potential is to be fully realised. Get a stick float working as it was intended and it is a pleasure to fish; get it wrong, and it will quickly become a nightmare of missed bites, tangles and frustration.

If you want to see a stick fished properly go along to the River Trent and watch one of the local stars fish a match when the river is in form and carrying just a little extra water. Worked through a swim well, the stick will almost talk, constantly checking the bait just a fraction, before moving downstream, almost inch by inch. A running water method, the stick is at its best in good conditions, that is to say when the wind is blowing either from behind or in an upstream direction. It can be used with a down-stream wind too, but it takes a lot more skill in order to make it perform at its best (see colour photograph on pp. 16 and 87).

Basic principle of a stick float is to use a dense material for a stem and a light, buoyant wood for the upper section. The dense stem acts in a manner which causes the stick to pivot, when held back, at a point some two-thirds up its length. This action makes the bait swing forwards ahead of the float and rise slightly in the water. The contrasting densities of the two materials also help stop the float riding out of the water when it is checked.

The stick in all its forms is fished 'double rubber' and works best on a light line of 2lb or below. It is a delicate method calling for a degree of care in placing shot, and also in casting if tangles are not to be a problem.

The traditional stick float is one made with the upper one-third of balsa, beneath which is a cane stem. The whole thing has a nice streamlined shape and if correctly dimensioned should just begin to cock even before a shot is added. Such a shape will be the one to use when the flow is even and without turbulence and fishing range is up to about two or three rod-lengths out. A stick float is at its best, however, when fished close-up – one rod-length being ideal.

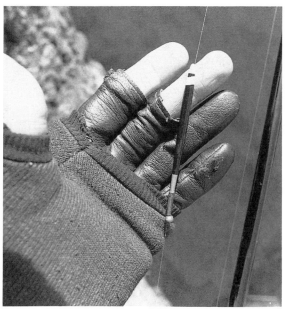

● *The correct way to rig a stick float. Note the bottom rubber overhangs the stem and has a shot pushed against it to act as a marker and for extra stability*

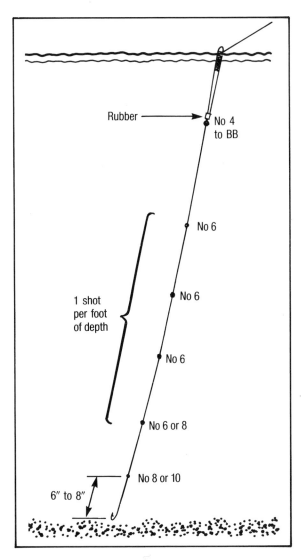

● *A good starting rig for the stick float. Work on one shot per foot of depth as a guide*

For a normal swim as just described the stick will be shotted with a string of small shots – no 6 are about right. A general rule is one shot for every foot of depth, but be prepared to switch floats according to conditions. Use a thin band of silicon rubber at the top of the float, if possible in a contrasting colour to the actual top so that it is easier to spot any lift bites that may occur. At the base, fit a 10mm-long piece of black silicon, making sure it overhangs the bottom of the float so that there is less chance of a tangle.

Directly beneath the stick goes a shot, both as a marker/stop and to give a rig a little more stability. Next, string out a row of no 6 or 8 shot, according to the power of the flow, using at least one for every foot of depth. The final shot, some six to eight inches from the hook, will be either an 8 or a 10, the smaller shot being used in clear water or a swim that is lacking in pace.

Casting underarm will put the float directly in front of you, so 'mend' line immediately to bring it all in a nice straight line upstream of the float. Now the work begins: it is a good idea to fish this method standing up but as low down as possible, and ideally right on the water's edge. By standing you will be

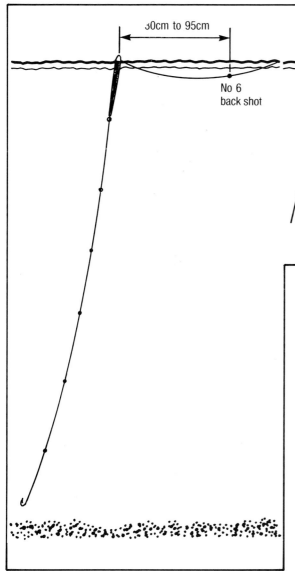

● *A small shot pinched to the line above the float will help combat a difficult wind*

● *(right) In extremely poor conditions a large shot, up to a AAA, can be pitched above the float and held out of the water by keeping the rod tip high and the line tight*

able to concentrate better and have more control over the proceedings.

Use a fixed spool reel with the bale arm open, and control line as it runs off with a finger on the spool. Alternatively, a closed face with the pick-up pin disengaged can be used in the same manner. It can be a help if the left hand is used just above the reel to further control the line, feeding it out as required.

On the strike take care not to 'bump fish off' when closing the bale arm. If your fixed spool pick-up rotates in the right direction you can trap line with the index finger and eliminate the bump effect. With a closed face there is less chance of losing fish because the pin does not create a shock as it engages. A third option is a centre pin and it is this reel that many stick float experts will use, simply because of the excellent control and feeling of direct contact it provides.

Once the float is in the water and moving downstream you can ease back on it, causing a slight pause, at which stage the bait is being swung forwards and upwards slightly. It is now, or when the float is released again, that bites usually occur. The trick is not to overdo this checking operation. Done right, the float will do nothing more than pause but if it rides up, then it is either a poorly balanced stick or you are hanging on too hard.

This is the traditional stick method, but do not be afraid to run a float through completely unchecked – this can often work on days when checking brings nothing. Alternatively try adding an extra shot so

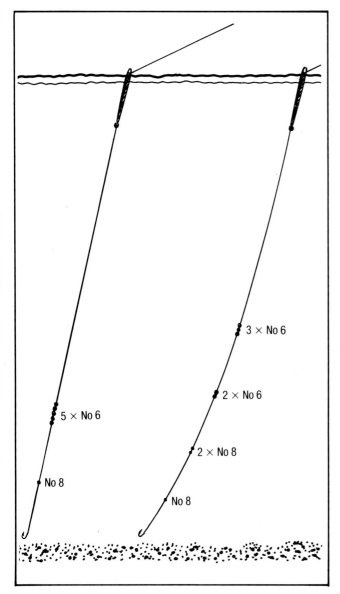

3 × No 6

2 × No 6

5 × No 6

2 × No 8

No 8

No 8

● *Two alternative shotting patterns to the conventional string of single shots. The big bulk will give stable presentation but no rise-and-fall effect*

that when not checked the float just sinks and a check causes it to just show above the surface. By very careful line pressure you should now be able to ease the bait right along the swim at a rate slower than the flow – a good method when the water is cold and coloured.

Remember what we said about feeding, too. The system is to feed and then cast into it, not the other way around.

Although the stick is a method to use in good conditions, there will be times when you will be forced into trying it when there is a bad wind pushing downriver. The trick here is to backshot, that is, to add another shot ABOVE the float. Such a shot is there to sink the line in much the same manner as the extra length of a waggler does. A no 6 placed 30cm to 45cm up is usually right, but again be prepared to experiment.

If things get really bad, or you just want to exert some real control, try adding a really big shot – say a AAA – 45cm above the float. But instead of letting this extra weight sink, you actually hold it out of the water by rod-tip support. In such a case you are holding back to the shot, supporting it in the air by raising the rod and gradually allowing line to peel off the reel, while still keeping this shot suspended.

It's a great idea and if nothing else, will help teach you good stick float control. You may even want to try it when conditions are good so that it's something you have confidence in at a later date. Only drawback it has, of course, is when it comes to casting – but distance is something you don't need anyway in a gale.

While on the subject of conditions it is worth looking at other stick float shotting methods. The traditional 'shirt button' string of individual shots is fine under good conditions, but if things get hard, there is nothing wrong in pulling them together to form a single bulk – or moving them into three or four gradually reducing bulks. For example, a float carrying ten no 6 shots and an 8 could have the pattern altered to give four 6s, then three, two and one, followed by the 8 as a tell-tale. By pulling everything down nearer the hook the even rise and fall of the bait is lost, but a more stable presentation will be achieved. These patterns also work well in heavy water or in swims that have limited fishing distance, such as can be caused by pegging that is too close.

WIRE-STEMMED STICK FLOATS

> ### When and Where to Fish the Wire-stemmed Stick Float
> **Conditions:** Similar to the conventional stick float. Favourable, upstream or back wind is best but back shotting can help cope with downstream skims.
> **Where:** Swims that are too turbulent for the conventional stick.

The wire-stemmed stick float comes into its own in swims that are too turbulent for a conventional stick of cane and balsa. As the name suggests, it has had its cane bottom replaced by a thin length of wire to reduce volume so that it offers less of an area on which the turbulent water can act; the float can therefore ride along without being bounced around or pulled under.

Something to watch for with the wire stem is that you can actually fix it to your line efficiently – because the wire is so small in diameter you may find none of your usual float rubbers are small enough. The answer is to use pieces of the silicon tubing used for pole floats. The more thoughtful manufacturers of stick floats go to the trouble of fixing a short piece of plastic material to the base of the stem to make up the diameter enough for it to take a standard float rubber.

The overall shape of the wire-stemmed float will not have such an even taper as the cane and balsa, and if only a rubber at the top and bottom is used, there may be a bow effect created by the line not being able to follow the float's contour closely. The answer is always to use a third rubber at the top of the stem, directly beneath the balsa body – overlook this rubber and you are sure to get a lot of nasty tangles.

Wire stems do not cast as far as the cane- or lignum-stemmed sticks but usually the sort of range at which a wire is fished creates no problem.

Shotting can be much the same as for any other stick, but don't get too much bulk high up in the water otherwise the advantages of a slim stem will be offset by water pressures reacting against shots. The half-depth rule is applied to this float as often as possible, and my favourite pattern is a series of

● *Wire-stemmed stick floats, good patterns to use on turbulent waters where a normal stick float cannot cope*

reducing bulks rather than a string of single shot. As with all stick floats, the opening shotting pattern is unlikely to remain in position throughout the session As bites slow, or you lose contact with the fish for any reason, the tactic is to start moving shots around – put more length between hook to tell-tale shot, perhaps; break down the lower shots into smaller sizes, or slide the whole lot into one big bulk. The permutations are endless, and by moving them in this way it is possible to make the bait perform in a variety of ways before you even consider altering depth.

What must go hand in hand with all this shot-changing is good reasoning: think out every move and try to imagine what a new pattern will achieve in

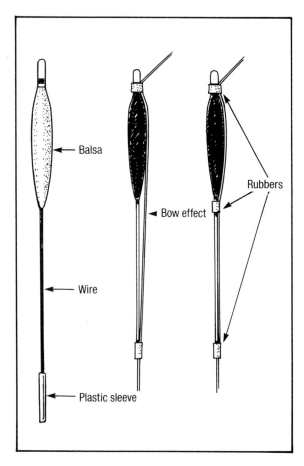

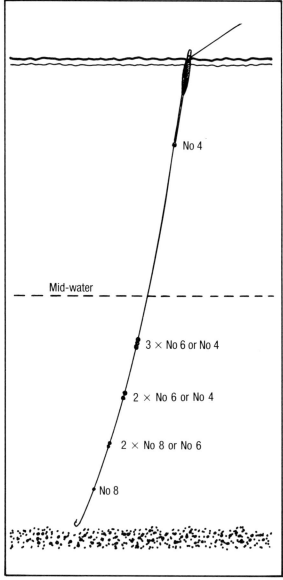

● *A simple wire-stemmed stick float with a plastic sleeve at the bottom of the wire to make attachment to the line easier*

● *Use three rubbers for attachment so that there is no bow effect caused by line passing over the body*

the way of different presentation. But never be afraid to change – if you are not catching fish a new plan costs nothing and is always worth a try.

Having worked your way through the possible shot changes, the next stage is to try giving the bait to the fish at a different speed. A straight run-through unchecked has not worked; easing back in traditional stick float fashion has picked up the odd fish or two, but nothing regular. Now really holding back hard – even so much so that the float is not allowed to move downstream at all – is worth a try. Fish will often take a static bait while refusing all others, especially in very cold conditions. In such situations it may call for an extra foot on the depth, too, in order to keep the bait close to the bottom.

Should you begin with a wire-stemmed stick only to find it cannot cope, then the next move should be to a full balsa or Pacemaker with the shot bulked and the whole rig allowed to run through unchecked.

● *A good pattern for the wire-stemmed stick float is a series of decreasing bulks, starting just below half depth*

THE CHUBBER

When and Where to Use the Chubber

Conditions: Best with an upstream wind or with one that is from behind. Can also be cast a long way against the wind but will not perform well when there is a bad downstreamer blowing.

Where: On those swims that are too powerful for the stick, balsa or Pacemaker. Very good on turbulent and very fast swims where long casting is required. Good for fishing big baits intended for fish such as chub.

In the smaller sizes is a good pattern for fast, weedy and shallow waters.

The bulkiest float in my box is the chubber and it is one that rarely sees the light of day, probably more because of the area in which I live than anything else. It's a float for those big powerful waters that need a lot of bulk to get a bait down and also a float that is buoyant enough to ride through the boils without being pulled around.

It's a good float, too, for big baits. Fishing luncheon meat on one can be really exciting at venues such as Thrumpton on the Trent. Here the usual attack is a giant feeder for the big head of chub and barbel. That's fine for match days, but having to feed upwards of a gallon of maggots a time is not really one for pleasure fishing, and the luncheon meat and float is a very productive alternative.

Big bread-flake baits, wasp grub or lobworms, all are great with this float. And because of the heavy shot-loading it is easy to put very soft baits out a long way without fear of throwing them off on the cast.

Tackle will need to be stepped up a bit, too. A 3lb line is about right, coupled to the sort of rod you would want for big wagglers – those with a bit of beef in them but not too tippy. A range of chubbers from about two swan, up to maybe five or six, is going to cope with most waters.

Traditionally made from either a cork or balsa body with a very short cane stem, and a tip (in the case of the cork body) either of quill or balsa let into it – the balsa version has the body extended to include the tip, too. The cane stem is there only for attachment purposes and does little to influence the

● *Big and bulky, these chubbers are capable of riding very fast and turbulent waters. The clear ones are of hollow plastic and the dark ones of balsa*

way the float works. I say the traditional way of making these floats only because the latest ones are plastic. In the case of the Drennan 'Loafers' which are really a form of chubber, this material is clear and helps reduce fish-scaring shadow in shallow water.

Double rubber attachment goes without saying but be sure the rubbers are up to the job. Silicon is best and the bottom piece needs to be a good 10mm long and fixed to overhang the stem a little to help prevent wrap-over tangles.

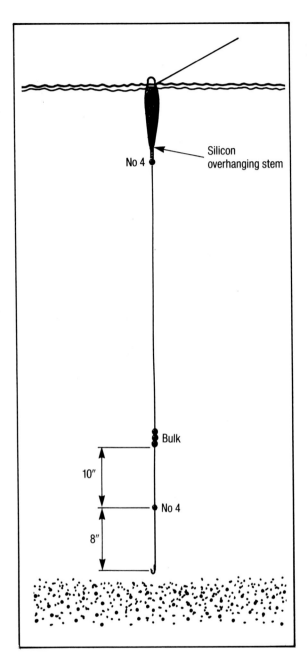

Silicon
overhanging stem

No 4

Bulk

10″

No 4

8″

● *Chubbers need a simple shotting pattern of a single bulk with a tell-tale beneath. Use strong silicon rubber for attachment*

Shotting needs nothing fancy. It's a big bulk about 45cm from the hook and a tell-tale no 4 halfway between it and the hook. A small shot can go beneath the float stem to act as an insurance against slipping on the strike but keep it small, a BB at most.

Casting is easy: use an underarm swing just like the one used for the Avon or stick float, but for extra distance keep the rod high and throw the rig in a big arc. Once in the water, mend your line and then let the whole outfit run through unchecked. In the right sort of swim a bite is not difficult to see – despite the float's bulk it usually vanishes as if it has dropped down a hole. Maybe this is because the sheer speed of flow forces a fish to grab a bait and make off with it without having time to hesitate.

Another situation in which I have found chubbers to be ideal, is when stalking chub on small backwaters of the Nene and on areas of the upper Welland. These swims are shallow but full of pace and I usually go armed only with a trout bag carrying a few bits and pieces of shot, spare floats and hooks, a landing net and a pair of polarising glasses.

There is nothing fancy about fishing this way. A small chubber of perhaps two swan, a big hook and a bait to match is all I need. Once a chub is spotted I swing the rig across and well upstream, letting it run down so that it passes right in front of the fish. Reaction is often immediate: a fish can be seen taking the bait – a second or two pause, strike and you are in.

The float in this case is a means of support for the bait rather than an indicator. Try it, it's terrific fun for a change and because of the chubber's short profile it can be fished right through weedy swims and in places where other patterns would fail.

For very deep swims a sliding version of the chubber may be needed. This is an identical float but with two fine wire and small diameter eyes set in the side as on the conventional top and bottom slider.

Carry a range of chubbers but don't expect to use them too often. They are very specialised and intended to be used only on waters already described. They have no place on slow-moving rivers. Fished at the wrong location they will cause nothing but trouble and produce very little in the way of fish.

Remember too that large diameter rubbers will be needed to fit the bulky tips of this float pattern. Silicone tube is best able to cope with the stress produced by constantly striking.

THE ZOOMER

When and Where to Use the Zoomer

Conditions: Limit its use to days when there is only a gentle wind blowing upstream and ideally from slightly behind. Flow must not be too strong.
Where: On wide waters where long casting is needed. Ideal depth is 8 to 10ft. A very good float where bream demand good presentation of a bait, either slowed down against the flow or made to lift attractively off the bottom.

The zoomer is probably one of the most misunderstood floats ever invented. Used wrongly, as it too often is, it is next to useless. Get it right, on the right day and under the right set of conditions and it can be deadly, even to a degree where it will out-fish a good leger angler on a bream water. Ivan Marks, the international from Leicester, is credited as its inventor, or at least the angler who first popularised it on the lower Welland in the days when we used to catch a lot of fish there.

Now as most match anglers know, the natural Welland from Spalding up to just below Deeping was dredged many years ago to form what appears to be a wide man-made water. For most of this length the old river bed followed the middle to far bank of the new profile, and it was in this slightly deeper area that most of the river's bream lived. Depth was around 8 or 9ft and to reach it demanded long casting. I say 'was' in all this only because more recent dredging has again altered much of the river. I suspect, too, that it will never return to its former glory. Like so many of the eastern area rivers it has suffered badly over the years, and the latest problem is the regular visits by seals that swim up from the Wash and then stay for months on end to enjoy the easy feeding a shoal of bream or roach can provide.

But enough of this depressing talk. The zoomer is a float that may just be right for a water similar to the old Welland. But to make it work, conditions have to be right and the zoomer is a float that only comes out of the box a few times a season.

Made from a balsa body, it is loaded with either a brass stem, or has weight let into it with a 3mm cane

● *Classic examples of the zoomer, a terrific float when conditions are right*

149

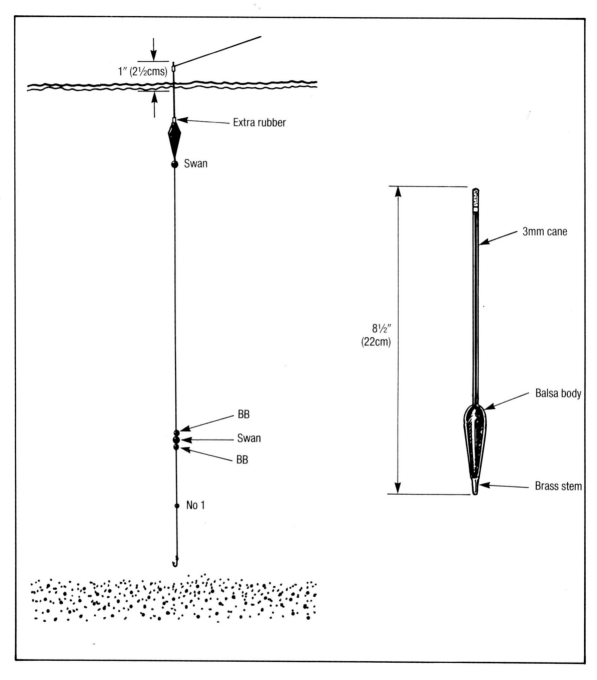

1" (2½cms)

Extra rubber

Swan

BB

Swan

BB

No 1

8½"
(22cm)

3mm cane

Balsa body

Brass stem

● *The zoomer correctly rigged with a swan shot under the stem. About an inch is left showing above the surface so that it can be seen easily at distance*

● *(right) Correct dimensions and materials are essential if a zoomer is to work well*

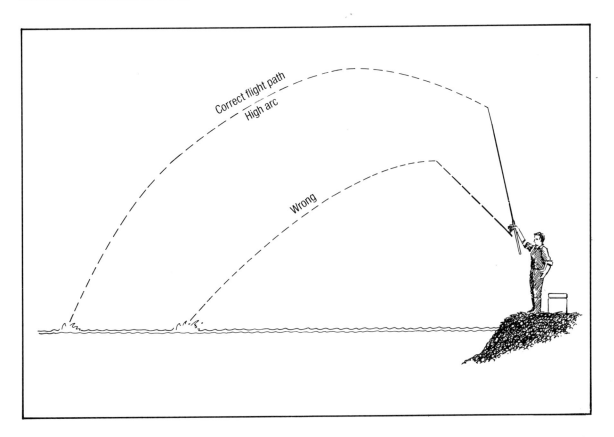

The zoomer is cast high into the air in order to obtain the long range for which it was designed

stem that brings the total length to around 22cm. It looks like a waggler type of float but the differences begin here for it is fished 'top and bottom' just like a stick float. Attached like this it is easy to see why its use is restricted to the right conditions – that is, with a wind blowing upstream and slightly from behind and with only a modest flow.

In addition to the loading built into the float it will carry a further two and a half swan or more. A swan goes beneath the stem and then one and a half swan somewhere below half depth. The actual position of this bulk will need to be altered to suit how fish are coming – if they are found to be feeding on the drop, then keep it high up. If bites come only after everything has settled, then gradually move it down towards the hook until the optimum setting is achieved. Below this bulk is a single shot – Ivan usually suggested a no 1 or thereabouts, so that a fish intercepting the bait is forced to move a shot big enough to have a considerable effect on the float, bearing in mind you are fishing at long range and will need to be able to see the reaction.

Having got a zoomer set in this manner, the cast needs to be a high lob to set it flying 30yd or more in a wide arc. As it settles, the loading and top shot will take control quickly, followed by the bulk and finally the tell-tale no 1, pulling the cane stem down to leave an inch showing. Yes, an inch – you'll need a fair amount out of the water to see it. If of course the stem stays out higher – strike! A fish has intercepted you on the way down.

With the conditions as described there will be no problem with a bow forming in the line, other than perhaps a small one upstream of the float. You can now make the float work for you by raising the rod tip every so often. This movement causes the bow to increase slightly and also to raise the float an inch or more out of the water. What happens now is the bait lifts attractively and often results in another bite.

151

From this you will see it is possible either to hold a bait very still, and certainly hold it back against a gentle flow, or to cause it to rise and fall almost by the inch.

If you decide to make your own zoomers – and you may have to, because I don't know of any commercial ones that meet with Ivan's original specification – don't make the mistake of building in too much load so that the swan is not needed below the stem. If you do, the result will be a float that does not cast too well and will tend to 'bury' on landing.

Like so many good floats, the zoomer is intended for one set of conditions. Use it in any other and you are losing all the advantages and may even be handicapped yourself. With the zoomer it helps to use a long rod; mine is always a 13-footer, but one of 14ft would allow even more control when trying to create the slight lift and check using the line bow.

7
Pole Fishing

Pole fishing is a method that many top float anglers said would never catch on in Britain. Once regarded as only for tiddler-snatching continentals, it was not considered worthwhile on our fish-rich rivers. But with greater involvement in world championship events – and more than a few thrashings as a result – a few poles began to appear back home. The first ones were pretty horrible. Made from fibre glass, they were floppy, heavy and not long enough. Carbon came on the scene and lengths increased, coupled with a considerable reduction in diameter and much stiffer actions. The method is still not the answer to every float fishing problem, but it is yet another tool vital to the goal of becoming an all-round float angler.

Pole Fishing

The biggest advantages a pole offers over conventional tactics are better presentation, more sensitive bite registration and in the case of match angling, more speed. The pole to buy is the stiffest, slimmest and longest you can afford. It should be a 'take-apart' rather than telescopic, except in the case of the top three sections which can be telescopic to good advantage. The joints must come apart smoothly and a new model may need some work doing on it to ensure this is so. A very careful and gentle rub-down with fine wet-and-dry paper is the best way to remove any high spots, but do take great care not to overdo it.

A choice of tips is handy; one with an internal elastic system rigged up, the other a very fine 'flick tip' for speed fishing, usually with full length lines. Simplest way to fix a line to a flick tip is via a small ring whipped to the top, but removal is not always easy, although some anglers have developed quick-release knots for the job.

Instead of a full eye on the tip, mine have been kitted out with a simple modification in the form of a U-shaped piece of fine but stiff wire. The legs of the 'eye' are left long – about 12mm – with only one actually whipped in place. The other leg is left lying alongside the pole. On each rig is a 15mm length of suitably sized silicon tube and an end loop. The loop goes into the U of the eye and the silicon is then slipped over the whole thing to hold down the loose leg and keep the rig in place. Removal is quick and simple.

An alternative – first shown to me by former world champion Ian Heaps – is to keep two pieces of silicon on each rig: a small diameter piece about 12mm long goes on first, followed by a second, slightly larger diameter piece some 5mm long. The rig is fixed to the tip with the larger diameter silicon about 30cm back from the extreme tip. The rig's line is now spiralled around the joint several times until it reaches the tip. Now push the second piece of silicon on so that it just protrudes. No knots are needed, yet the whole thing stays put no matter how hard you pull. The spiralling creates resistance to take pressure off the silicon, and also prevents the bowing effect that would otherwise occur when the pole was bent.

An internal elastic system is vital for the other section, and it pays to buy a spare top and second joint so that more than one strength of elastic can be

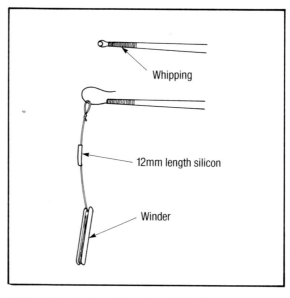

● The flick tip of a pole needs to include some means of attaching the line. A very small eye can be used or alternatively one with only a single leg whipped down. The other leg lies alongside and is held down with silicon tubing once the line is attached

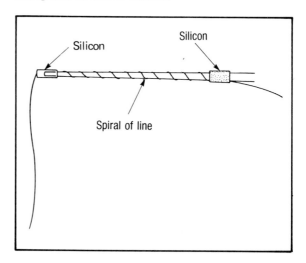

● A tip without an eye can have line attached by two rubbers and the line wound round in a spiral

● British anglers joined the locals on this lake near Paris for a Sunday morning pole-fishing session. The pole is one of the fastest growing methods in Britain and one that should be a part of every float angler's armoury

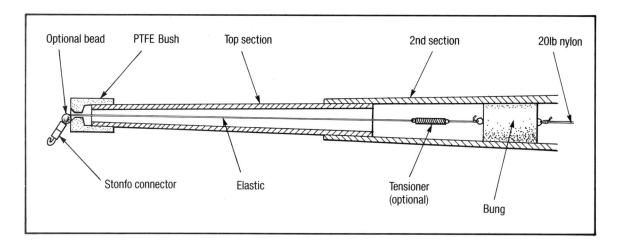

Optional bead PTFE Bush Top section   2nd section   20lb nylon

Stonfo connector Elastic   Tensioner (optional) Bung

● *The two top sections of a pole fitted with internal elastic*

made up at a time and carried as a spare. Setting up an elastic rig takes a little time and care if all is to operate correctly and efficiently. The elastic needs to be suited to the fish likely to be caught though a medium grade is usually about right and by adjusting the tension it will cope well with most situations. The more tension put into it, the stronger it becomes.

At the tip a PTFE bush is essential to enable the elastic to run smoothly. These bushes are available in tackle shops and come in either external fitting for small diameter tips or internal for larger bores. Do not glue them in place, but find one that is a tight fit and can just be pushed on firmly – you can build up the pole's diameter by whipping the tip for a short distance.

Elastic is best used through the top two sections, which can be taken apart and folded down alongside each other for ease of transport. It may even be possible to get them both inside the next joint in the normal manner. At the bush end it is best to use a tiny connector called a 'Stonfo' fitting, which is fastened to the elastic and provides a quick and easy way of attaching rigs by means of the notch and retaining sleeve.

At the other end, some form of bung is needed inside the pole to anchor the elastic. I've used everything from pieces of tapered dowel to balsa float bodies, but the one that works best is the 'Uni-Bung', a tapered, hollow nylon bung which can be cut with a razor blade to suit almost any pole on the

market. The elastic is tied to this bung through an eye at one end; at the other there needs to be a length of 20lb nylon which protrudes from the joint and can be used to assist removal.

When everything is fitted, the elastic should have just enough tension to ensure it returns smoothly inside the pole after a fish has been landed. In wet weather, however, some sticking may occur and adjustment then becomes necessary: having removed the 'Stonfo', the adjustment can be made by retying, although this is not always easy on the bankside – a far better option is to use a tensioner inside the pole. This invention is just a short piece of plastic with a small, open eye at each end, through which the elastic is threaded. More tension can be applied by winding a few extra turns of elastic around the plastic stem.

Having got the pole in order, now we can look at the actual floats which will be needed. The shops are packed with a wide assortment of shapes and sizes,

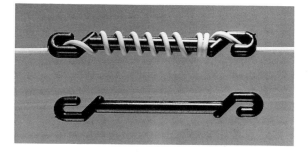

● *A small and simple plastic hook like this makes elastic tensioning easy work*

● *Two fine stillwater rudd, the result of selecting a swim wisely (Chapter 8)*

● *(below left) Leicester match ace Stan Piecha with a specimen perch. Many anglers fear the prickly dorsal fin, but handled with confidence there is no danger of injury (Chapter 9)*

● *(below right) A classic example of using a landing net safely. Placed across the knees it will catch any fish that is dropped accidentally (Chapter 8)*

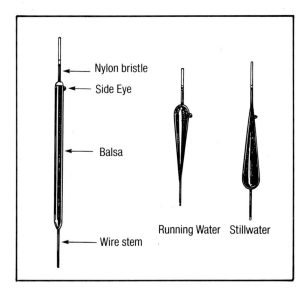

- Nylon bristle
- Side Eye
- Balsa
- Wire stem

Running Water   Stillwater

● *The basic straight balsa bristle float is a good example of what is required in a pole float. Body shapes vary according to whether the float has been designed for running or stillwater*

but unless you are a collector there is no need for half of them. About six or seven patterns will be sufficient, and even then a few of them will only come out a few times a year.

A good pole float for most uses will have a top bristle of either fine wire, nylon or cane. A small eye is fitted to the side of the body and there is likely to be a stem of wire, thin cane or fibre glass. The eye is there so that a top rubber can be eliminated because air trapped by one would completely upset the shotting of these delicate floats. The eye also helps the float retain an upright position in the water.

Sorting out the correct float shape for each job is easy enough if you apply the same principles as those used for other floats. That is to say, bulk near the tip will suggest a float for running water. Bulk at the bottom, such as with a waggler, is best suited to slow or still water. A good all-round pattern is a simple straight-bodied balsa with a side eye and bristle, but of course there will be limitations to what it can do.

● *The vital moment when the scales tell their story. Even at this stage matches can be won or lost through careless handling and inaccurate weighing (Chapter 8)*

POLE FISHING MADE EASIER

Casting

A pole float is not cast by an overhead action except by some of the continentals, who seem to do it with great skill and enthusiasm when fishing a long line.

With the more usual short line rig, the drill is to bait the hook, flick the tackle into the water and assemble the remaining joints as they are pushed out over the water. While doing this, tangles can be prevented by keeping the float on the water surface. It is only when you get three metres or so of line and tackle drifting about in the air that problems begin.

Feed the pole out, keeping the tip as close to the surface as possible and the float will stay on the surface. Once at full length the pole can be raised, and the rig placed correctly if any adjustment is needed. Often pushing out as described is all that is required.

With a long line rig, drop the hook in at the water's edge, hold the pole with both hands and swing it slightly out and briskly upwards so that the float and weight fly out in what starts as an arc moving upwards. When it reaches full distance the pole is already coming back towards the water surface. This movement works a bit like feathering line off a reel. Timing everything correctly is the part which takes a little practice.

Breaking down

Breaking the pole down so that the hook is level with your hand can be made easier by using a marker of some description on the pole at the appropriate section. Special brightly coloured rubber rings are sold for this purpose; these also have the advantage of a tiny eye moulded into them, used to hold the hook when the rig is not being used. However, an elastic band or a strip of white sticky tape will work just as well. Set your marker just above the joint to be broken down – when it is felt in the left hand as the pole is fed backwards, you know it is time to begin the unshipping process.

The breakdown joint must always come apart freely and with no hint of sticking. A good pole angler will already have worked on these joints to ensure they are free-fitting, but an extra little insurance trick is to fit them together carefully and

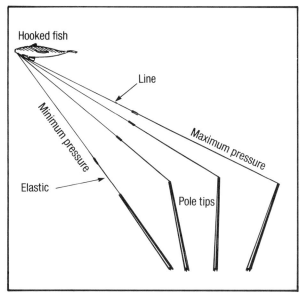

The diagram labels: Hooked fish, Line, Minimum pressure, Maximum pressure, Elastic, Pole tips

● *The amount of pressure applied to a fish can be increased by increasing the angle between elastic and pole tip*

then bind a couple of turns of tape over the male joint at the point where it protrudes from the female. This will now act as a stop and eliminate any chance of sticking due to joints being forced together too firmly.

Elastic

Elastic must operate efficiently from inside the pole and be correctly tensioned so that it retracts fully every time. Keep it as friction-free as possible by adding a few spots of one of the special lubricating substances made for the purpose. A good, cheap alternative is a few spots of washing-up liquid.

The amount of pressure applied to a hooked fish can be varied when using elastic by the angle at

● *A set of special rests bolted to a tackle box is the best method of supporting a long pole but take care when you stand up as there is a danger of the box being tipped over by the weight of the pole*

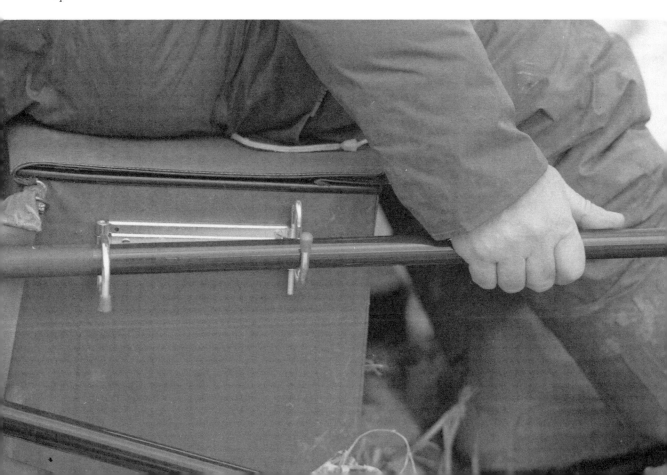

which it is allowed to pull over the tip bush. For the most friction-free pull the pole is pointed directly at the fish so that there is no angle formed at all. As more pressure is required, so the pole is made to form a gradually increasing angle by moving it away from the fish or raising it. As the angle increases, so does the amount of friction created by the elastic moving over the bush's surfaces and like this it is possible to effectively double the pressure being applied. You can try it for yourself by holding the top sections in one hand while pulling elastic straight out. Now try the same thing while forming angles of increasing steepness – you should feel a considerable difference.

Check elastic regularly for signs of wear or perishing. The slightest damage will reduce its breaking strain dramatically and sooner or later cost you dearly in a lost fish and tackle.

Pole rests

Conventional rod rests are not usually up to the task of supporting a long pole, and by far the best is a pair of rests that are attached to the seat box. The forward rest of this type has an upwards-facing U, while the rear one is the other way up so that the pole butt sits beneath it, the butt kept in place by the weight of the pole trying to pull the tip downwards. These rests are very good, but be sure to get one that is broad enough to spread the considerable load that is going to be applied to a very small area of pole where it crosses the rest. A badly designed, narrow metal rest can easily result in a section cracking or breaking completely.

Used in these double rests a pole will be supported very rigidly, but take care not to stand up when a long pole is in position as the seat box will probably tip over and the whole lot will end up in the river!

A rear roller rest can be employed too, so that breaking down sections can be done as smoothly as possible. It may be made from two rubber rollers set at a vee, or a vee of what looks like two paint rollers. It should be set well back from the fishing position and to the right side of the seat box, at a height which will allow it to accept the pole butt as it is passed backwards prior to breaking down. With such a rest it is possible to feed back a very long length in one go without any hint of jerking.

Safety

Carbon is a good conductor of electricity and as poles continue to grow in length, so does the danger posed by overhead power lines. Already several deaths and some very nasty injuries have occured as a result of poles touching wires, so *always* check before fishing that you are nowhere near any such danger.

Canals and other artificial waterways are the worst places for power lines. Some canals run along high ground with dense bushes behind the towpath, and such undergrowth can hide power lines which stretch across lowland meadows. Again, *check* before pushing a pole through any growth which could hide lines from your view.

Electrical storms are dangerous, and it is best not to fish a long pole while one is passing over. Take special care on open, flat areas where a raised pole will be the most obvious earthing point for a storm.

Poles are a potential danger if used carelessly on busy canals. Boats, as we all know, are a bit of a nuisance, but never try to save time by raising a pole to let a boat pass beneath it. It's a trick a lot of canal regulars use, but the danger of a hook catching a member of the boat's crew is very real and such incidents do nothing to enhance angling's image.

Take care, too, when pushing a long pole backwards suddenly. Towpath users seem to have a nasty habit of being in the wrong place at the wrong time and the first you know of their presence is a sickening crack when they step on a section.

For the same reason it is best to support sections of pole not in use off the ground, either by setting them on a couple of rests or by using a vertical support made for the job – this comes in the form of an aluminium or plastic tube with a stake at one end. The stake goes in the ground, providing a 'pot' into which the pole can sit.

Carrying poles to and from the waterside also needs a little care, and they are protected by a plastic tube or some form of case to prevent breakage.

Many poles are broken through joints jamming together. Prevention is simply a case of keeping them clean and free from grit – should a joint get muddy during a session, dip it in the water and wipe it clean.

Be careful not to let a joint slide into the water. Carbon does not float, so recovery usually involves a diving display – not a good idea in the middle of winter. Sloping banks are the worst for this type of loss and it is a good idea to use the keepnet top as a holding area for detached joints. Mine are slipped off and allowed to sit inside the net top – the water also gives the ferrule a quick wash at the same time.

POLE FLOATS

Pole floats need to be shotted up at home and stored on winders marked with all the relevant information (see colour photographs on p. 129). Mark the winders with details of line-breaking strain, hook size, bottom strength and overall length. A good means of fastening everything to the winder is with either one of the commercially available elasticated hooks, or by using a piece of pole elastic tied in a loop and passed through the line loop before hooking over the end peg of the winder.

All this shotting up and preparing winders is a time-consuming task but one that can be made easier by using a French invention which looks like some form of plastic shuttle cock. The idea is, that the device has a neutral density in water and so does not affect the balance of any float to which it might be attached. The float to be shotted is fitted into a small slot at the top, locked in place with a little lever and then lowered into a bucket of water.

An estimated shot load is placed on the flat pan surface which is beneath the float's stem, adding or subtracting weight until the correct load is achieved. Everything is now removed from the water, the float released and fixed to the required length of line, after which the shot used for balancing is also attached. It's an idea that saves hours of work and calls for very little in return other than a check that all air bubbles have been shaken off before balancing is completed.

● *This device makes pole float shotting simple. The float is set in the top clip and the whole thing allowed to float in a bucket of water. Shots are added to the flat surface of the holder until the correct balance is achieved*

The straight balsa bristle

When and Where to Use the Straight Balsa Bristle

Conditions: A good all-round pole float that will cope with fairly difficult wind conditions if used in a large enough size.

Where: Still or running water, but on fast-running water it will be difficult to control if held back hard. Fine on slow-running water and can be fished either with weight in a bulk or strung out for a slow-falling effect.

First float to look at is the simple balsa bristle. On waters like those in the east of England it is a float that could see you through most of the season, and a range of sizes to cope with varying depths of water and flows is all that is required. The body (as the name suggests) is of balsa, a straight one taking up most of the float's length apart from the bristle and wire stem.

The bristle is fine but some variation in both thickness and colour does help to deal with varying degrees of light intensity. A good idea, if possible, is to use those floats which have interchangeable tips so that fewer rigs need to be carried around. Shotting can vary from a simple olivette and a tell-tale to a string of shot, or a series of, say, three gradually increasing bulks. The bulk or single olivette is the easiest to use and it will usually bring some sort of response.

Another handy rig – and one you can adapt to suit many of the stillwater pole floats – is with styl leads strung down the line. These give the rig a slow-falling character and are very good for fishing on the drop. Lead laws restrict the largest legal size to a no 12 (equal to the permitted .06g) and in order to fasten these tiny leads a special tool is required – buy one where you obtain your styl leads. Each styl has a tiny slot cut along its length and this must be facing out from the tool when it picks one up. Easiest way to do this is to place a few styls on the container lid and tap it carefully with your finger: they will jump and land with the slot facing downwards, making them easy to pick up correctly. Now lay the line in the slot and pinch the tool together to fold the lead over the line. The only conventional shot used is a tiny tell-tale.

Length of line above the float is usually kept to a minimum when presentation is the most important thing under consideration. A good rule is a length between one and two metres, but for really delicate stuff go down to no more than half a metre.

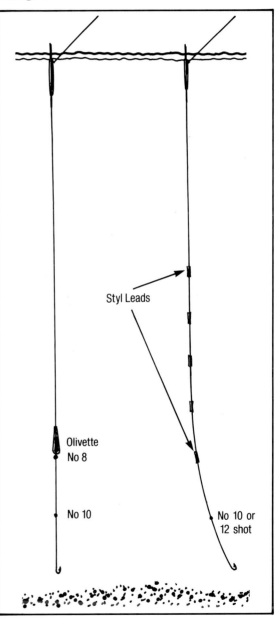

Styl Leads

Olivette
No 8

No 10

No 10 or
12 shot

● *Two very effective methods of loading a straight balsa bristle. The single olivette will work under most conditions while the string of styl leads give a slow-falling effect*

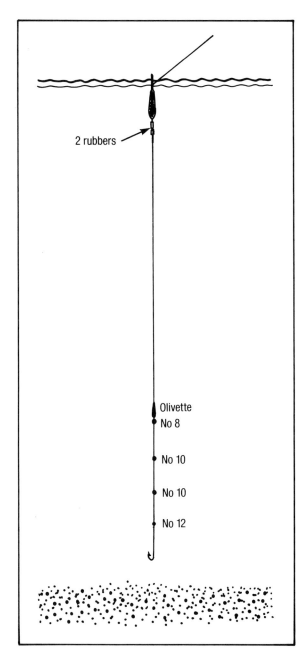

2 rubbers

Olivette
No 8

No 10

No 10

No 12

● *A tapered balsa bristle rigged with an olivette and small shots will work well in stillwater and rough conditions*

Tapered balsa bristle

When and Where to Use the Tapered Bristle

Conditions: Able to cope with a choppy surface and difficult wind. But don't be afraid to use a large pattern if conditions and depth demand it.
Where: Stillwaters. Not a float to cope with flow, but one that is a stage above the straight bristle when it comes to stability.

A close relative to the straight balsa, this one will provide a greater weight-carrying rig and is very stable. It is a stillwater float but one that can tackle rough conditions, the low bulk of its body keeping it steady when the water is choppy. Size can range from very small, taking nothing more than, say, three no 6s, up to the equivalent of a couple of swan.

Best rig is a short line for good control, and an olivette which takes up most of the bulk. This weight low down gives more stability, while two or three shots beneath act as a tell-tale and final slow drop. Shot everything down so that only the bristle is above the surface. Bites are easy to spot, showing either as a lift or a complete disappearance of the float.

Because of the bulbous nature of the body, it pays to add a second piece of rubber tubing to the stem directly beneath it; this will ensure there is no bow of line from body to stem which may result in a tangle. As with all floats that have wire stems, the longer the wire the more stable they become, the wire acting in the same way as bulk locking shot does on large wagglers.

With this float, and for that matter any other, the size must be matched to water depth. As depth increases, so you will need a bigger size if control is not to be lost. Also remember that the longer a pole the larger the float may need to be.

Canal special balsa

When and Where to Use the Special Canal Balsa

Conditions: Will work under any conditions other than a fast flow, but only because it is fished on a short line.
Where: Shallow waters such as canals and particularly effective where there is overhanging vegetation.

This handy little float is one you will probably have to make yourself, but you will be able to knock up half a dozen or more from odd pieces of balsa or even the remains of old broken floats. Only 3–4cm long, these are used for fishing very shallow water right under the far bank or beneath overhanging trees where it would be impossible to cast a float with rod and reel.

A simple cigar-shape of balsa, at its thickest point some 5mm diameter and tapering from a blunt bottom to a tip that, unlike most pole floats, doesn't have a bristle. The bottom has an eye, which can be made by straightening out an eyed hook of about size 10. The barb of the hook helps keep the eye from pulling out of the soft balsa but it still pays to glue it in place.

Fishing this float calls for a short line with no more than about half a metre from float to tip. Although it is a rig intended for water with a depth of only a metre or even less, it will cope with greater depths if the size is increased accordingly. Setting up this float is very simple, too: attach it through the bottom eye only and then lock it in place with two shots, which also make up most of the total load – a no 6 or 8, and another 8 or even a 10 as a tell-tale.

This rig was one first shown to me for a national championship on the Oxford canal, designed for fishing casters right under the far bank bushes where a lot of carp and chub lived. With the very short line it was a simple matter to push the tackle across and under the foliage – the fish were not bite-shy and a take was more of a mad dash than a bite in the true sense. And this super little float was still sensitive enough to register a bite from the water's population of tiny gudgeon.

We didn't do very well in that particular national, but it is a float that now stays with my pole tackle all season and has caught fish on several shallow waters of the Fens.

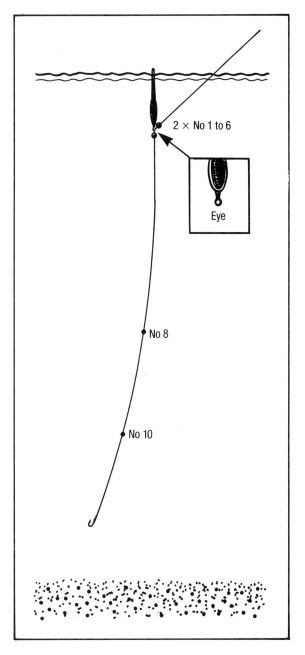

● *The canal special balsa has a base eye made from a straightened out hook glued in place*

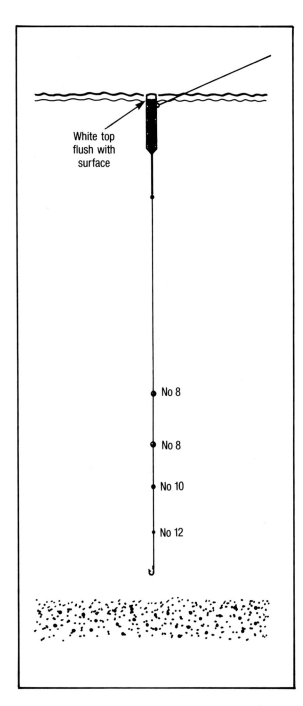

White top
flush with
surface

No 8

No 8

No 10

No 12

● *The flat top pole float is always shotted so that its top is flush with the surface*

The flat top

When and Where to Fish the Flat Top

Conditions: Works really well in a skim by remaining stable and not riding out if correctly dotted right down.
Where: Canals, still or slow-moving waters that are shallow and when small fish are the target.

Make up several short lines of, say, three, four and five metres in total length and fitted out with flat top patterns, and with these three winders you will be well armed for tackling shallow, close-in swims that hold small fish such as gudgeon. Usually made from balsa with a short wire stem and a side eye, this float demands very careful shotting, and even the size of bait and hook must be taken into account.

Reason for this delicate shotting is that the float must be dotted right down so that it just holds up in the surface film. Add an extra maggot, or step up the hook size to a size bigger and a forged instead of fine wire pattern, and the whole thing vanishes beneath the surface. Which shows how sensitive it can be if rigged correctly. Actual shotting is via a string of evenly spaced tiny shots, size 8, 10 or even 12 is usual. Mine are set in an even spacing down to a 12 which goes on as the tell-tale some 8cm from the hook, even closer if bloodworm fishing.

The float is usually painted black or any dark colour and the very tip – just the flat top face and not the side – is painted white. What makes this float so different from the bristled types is that it does not ride out of the water much when held back against a skim.

An alternative, but very similar float, is one made from a short piece of peacock quill with a fine wire stem glued into the bottom. It works just like the balsa version, but tends to have a greater load-carrying capacity for a given length compared to balsa.

These floats are made with an overall length of as little as 3cm up to around 6cm – such a range is more than enough.

166

The bodied bristle

When and Where to Fish the Bodied Bristle

Conditions: Best in good conditions, but will work if there is a little skim or ripple.

Where: Anywhere that fish are hard to catch. Best in stillwaters; will not work in a flow of any strength because if held back it will ride out of the water.

This float is one that allows you to move the bait around in a very attractive fashion, and typifies the skill and ingenuity of the continental anglers who devised it for their hard-fished waters where every bite has to be worked for. The rather strange body shape is topped by a bristle and the usual side eye. The body is of balsa; because of the bulbous shape at the bottom and its narrow neck, the pole tip can be used to make the bait lift just a fraction off the bottom. This movement often earns a bite, if only from a small fish.

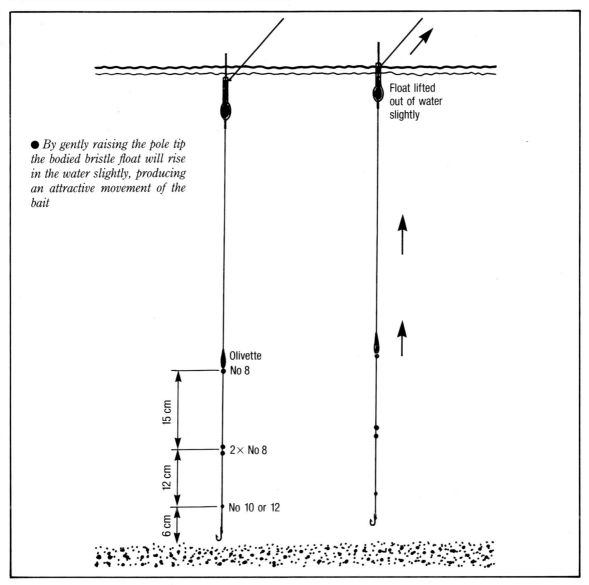

● *By gently raising the pole tip the bodied bristle float will rise in the water slightly, producing an attractive movement of the bait*

Float lifted
out of water
slightly

Olivette
No 8

15 cm

2× No 8

12 cm

No 10 or 12

6 cm

Shotting is a single olivette and stop-shot that will pull the float down to well along the neck. Below this olivette is a second shotting of a pair of no 8s or 10s according to the float's size. Finally a 10 or 12 goes on to just set the bristle – this can be as close as 6cm from the hook, with the other shot spaced 12cm and then the olivette a further 15cm higher.

The rig is fished on a fairly short line so that the pole tip can be used to control lift accurately. By easing the tip upwards and then lowering it again, the bait – which is fished just on the bottom – rises and falls back to its position. This is a deadly method on hard waters, and one that comes into its own with bloodworm baits.

A range of sizes is all that is needed to cope with increasing depths and pole lengths. The shotting rig is always the same, and the hook set to sit just on the bottom. Very accurate plumbing is essential if this method is to work at its best.

German-style float

> ### When and Where to Fish the German Pole Float
>
> **Conditions:** Don't worry too much about conditions. If the float is large enough it will work no matter how fast the flow or how strong the wind. The only limitation is being able to hold a long pole still enough.
> **Where:** Great on the big, deep and powerful rivers. Try it in flood conditions that are too much for ordinary floats. The same, but smaller patterns are good for average flows where holding back is required.

This monster is a long way from the other floats we have looked at for pole work – in the largest sizes it is likely to be mistaken for a pike float. Even so, it is one which has enjoyed a lot of good bags under difficult conditions. I first used one in Germany to fish the massive River Wasser. That river makes the Trent look like a stream and the flow tears along at a fast walking pace. It's deep too . . . and packed with bream.

There are three body-shapes: a sort of fat-looking Avon shape; a simple cylindrical pattern with a flat top and bottom, or what is almost a perfect sphere. All three are designed to be held back hard against the flow and to carry the largest olivettes – a typical German float in this range will take the equivalent of about four swan or more.

It is the body-shape that holds the secret of why these floats work so well. The idea is to present a flat, or angular surface to the flow so that when the float is held back, water pressure pushing against it acts in a downwards fashion and thus prevents the float riding out. It looks a crude float and there is certainly nothing delicate about the manner in which it is shotted.

It is fished on a long line, ideally so that fish can be swung to hand or netted without having to break down the pole. But I have fished it with a little compromise so that I needed to knock down only the last two or three joints from an 11m pole. This reduces the distance it can run through the swim, but makes it much easier to handle until confidence is gained in going the full length.

Casting is a sort of upwards flick of the pole tip which causes the considerable weight of the olivette to fly out and drag the float behind it. Strike in an upwards direction too, in order not to have to pull the big float upstream against the flow which it has been designed to resist.

I have described this float as a monster, but in fact the spherical version can be found in much smaller sizes and even in miniature will work in the same way. Again, it is a case of balancing weight to flow.

These big floats have proved very effective on the prolific waters of Northern Ireland such as the Bann where very heavy bags are often taken, fishing so that roach of over half a pound are swung to hand. It's hard work and takes a brave angler to do it. To say nothing about needing a good pole to take the strain.

To use the biggest floats safely tackle will need stepping up beyond that normally associated with pole fishing. Don't be afraid to use lines in excess of 4lb breaking strain. This style is crude by normal standards and needs tackling with confidence.

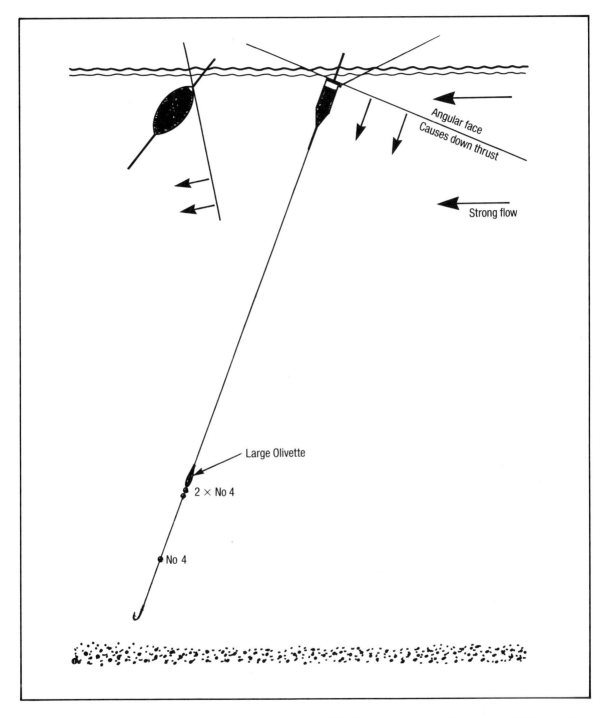

Angular face
Causes down thrust

Strong flow

Large Olivette

2 × No 4

No 4

● *The German style pole float can be held back hard against the flow due to water pressure acting on the angular faces formed by the body*

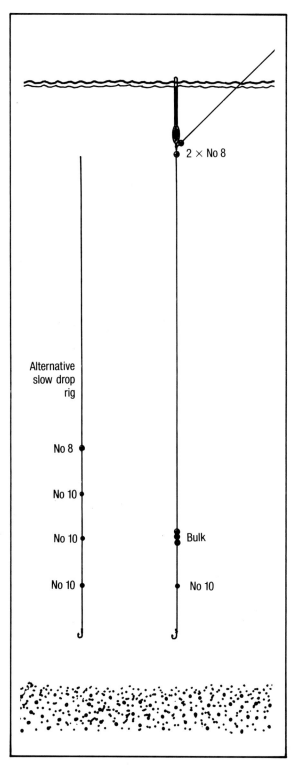

2 × No 8

Alternative
slow drop
rig

No 8

No 10

No 10   Bulk

No 10   No 10

The pole waggler

When and Where to Fish the Pole Waggler

Conditions: Skimming or blustery winds that make top and bottom bristles difficult to use.
Where: Still or very slow waters.

I like to have a few small wagglers set up on pole winders for those days when a top and bottom bristle does not seem to be right. There is nothing special about them, they are just small by normal waggler standards. Use them to cope with a blustery or skimming wind on stillwater, and again just match the float size to pole length and depth. If you are struggling with a certain float it is odds on it is too small. There are no rules to this game other than those limiting your own ability to control your tackle.

Don't leave too much line above the float – a metre is probably the most you should want – and then only if conditions are good. The float itself has a small balsa body and a stem of the same material. There is no bristle and the tip is usually no thinner than 3mm in order that it can be fished on a tight line without pulling under too quickly. Don't try to hold it back should there be a flow, but use the length and bottom only attachment to sink line.

Shotting is simple enough and can be varied between either a simple string of shots, or a bunch and tell-tale depending on how fish are feeding. If the water is warm and you expect some fish to be well off the bottom, string out the shot; otherwise go for the more simple bulk, locking the float in place with a couple of no 8s.

● *The pole waggler can be rigged either with a bulk or string of shot. It is the float to tackle a skimming wind*

8
Practical Skills and Match Fishing

Watercraft – the ability to spot a good swim and recognise what lures fish to the same areas year after year – is just as important as being able to cast well. Properly mastered it can add to the chances of regular success for the pleasure fisher and give the match angler the best return from a given peg. Understanding the effects that wind and weather have on fish location is also important.

Playing and landing fish on fine tackle needs skill but, like so many things in fishing, can be tackled by applying some basic rules.

Then comes the ultimate challenge – match fishing – the sport where float fishing skills can decide so much. Tactics and how to outwit your opponents are going to need some consideration.

CHOOSING A SWIM

Rivers

Good float fishing skills, perfect bait and the best tackle available will still not catch fish if used in the wrong place. Finding the best swim is just as much a part of the float angler's craft as being able to work a stick float through it inch by inch. Unfortunately, learning to spot a possible hot spot is not easy – it is a skill that comes with experience over several seasons (see colour photograph on p. 157).

Local knowledge is one vital ingredient to be put into the mixture which helps ensure a reasonable level of consistency. Use your ears, and listen to tackle-shop gossip. Use your tongue and ask your regular dealer what is being caught locally and where. Use your eyes, read local and national angling papers for more information on what, how and where fish are being caught. Armed with information, you are some way towards putting fish into your own net.

Early-season hot spots tend to reappear year after year, as do others at the back end of a season. A shoal of bream, for example, may take up a regular residence every February. These reoccurrences are more than just coincidence. The fish turn up in the same old places because it suits them to be there. Maybe a warm water outfall raises the temperature a little, or possibly there is a clean gravel bed over which freshly spawned fish congregate to clean up. A rich bloodworm-filled patch of silt or a sheltered spot away from floodwater are just some other possibilities.

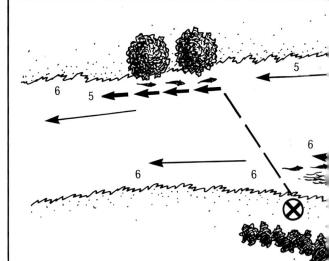

● *A summer river showing the best places to fish from and where fish are likely to be in relation to flow and bankside features*

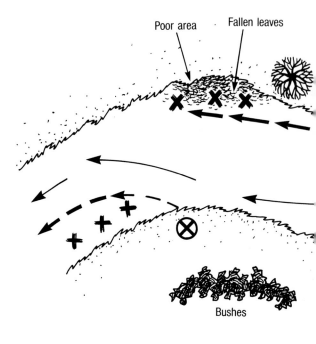

Poor area   Fallen leaves

Bushes

● *In winter fish will move away from their summer haunts and the angler needs to choose a swim with great care*

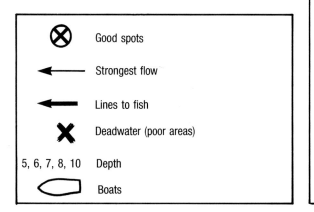

⊗	Good spots
←	Strongest flow
◄	Lines to fish
✗	Deadwater (poor areas)
5, 6, 7, 8, 10	Depth
⬓	Boats

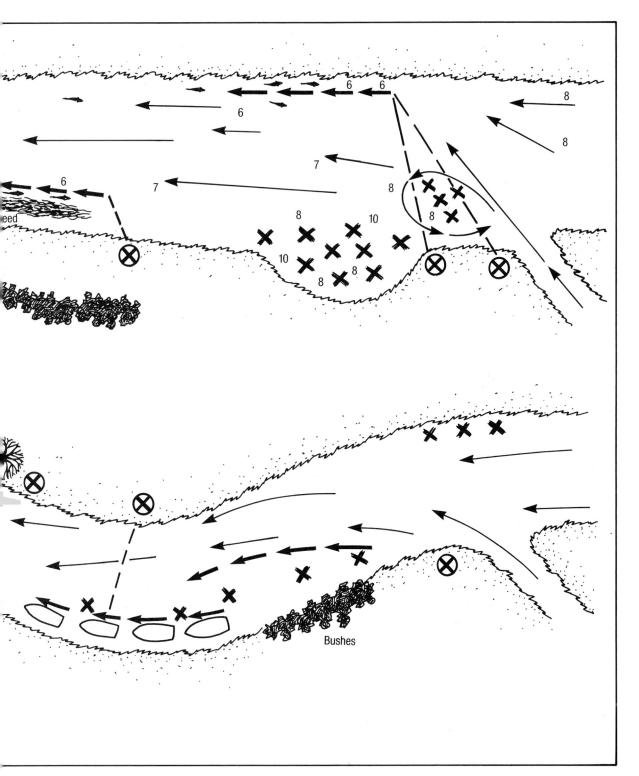

Large concentrations of fish move around in order to find new feeding grounds rich enough to sustain their needs, but a diary recording where, when and how you made good catches is a worthwhile thing to keep and can go a long way towards revealing any possible pattern of migration.

At the early part of the season it is no good returning to the swims that fished well in the closing months of the previous year. Since those cold days of winter the river and its population will have undergone many changes. Water temperature will have risen and adult fish spawned, both these factors causing massive migrations during the spring.

By June the swims to look for are those over clean gravel, or at least ones with some extra flow. This faster water will hold a higher oxygen content and fish will stay with it for most of the summer. So start your season on a river by fishing swims just below locks or weirs and fish the fastest flow – it's surprising how even sluggish fish such as bream will turn up there.

Having located a good area, try narrowing the choice down by considering other factors that may add to your chances of success. An overhanging tree on the opposite bank may be a good chub haunt – select a spot upstream of it so a float can be run down with the current right under its branches. Check out what is on your bank, too. A few bushes behind will help to break up your outline so fish are less likely to be scared off by a silhouette standing out against the skyline; weed at the edge of a swim can also shield an angler from view, as well as perhaps providing fish with shelter from bright sunshine and predators.

During the warmer months of summer the still, dead-looking pools are not usually good places to fish. They will be full of winter debris washed down by floods and oxygen levels will be low, so there is unlikely to be much in the way of natural food.

Even a good swim can be wasted if it is fished wrongly. In the Nene Championship, the angler above me had drawn a real 'flyer' on the downstream point of a backwater. A nice flow was pushing out from it and moving across the river to create a current along the far bank. My neighbour chose to cast upstream of the backwater into some dead water. He caught very little and found it difficult to keep his line out of the flow which was now trying to drag his tackle back towards him. Result was a badly

presented bait that would have been most unattractive even if there had been fish to catch.

The backwater's current was carrying a lot of food and acted as a natural holding area. All I needed to do was cast across and let my float trot along in the flow. It worked, and I picked off fish right through the match, and won with over 10lb of roach. However, the swim above should have been the winner, not mine – chances like that are ones you have to make the most of while you can.

Depth is less important than many anglers believe. The deepest is rarely the best until winter and even then not always the one to go for. It is when conditions have been settled for some time that fish will be keen to feed and will go searching away from their usual haunts. These are the times when everyone seems to get in on some action. Fish don't like changes – a sudden downpour, a slight frost after a mild spell, or even a bright day after a fortnight of dull, overcast skies will often be enough to take the edge off sport for a while.

When you think you have found a possible swim, put your kit down carefully, keep off the skyline and go for a walk a few swims either side of your probable pitch. It's just possible you may see a patch of slightly more coloured water punctuated by tiny bubbles, both of which may be signs of a feeding bream shoal.

A pair of polarising glasses will also help spot cruising chub under the bushes, or perhaps a submerged weed-bed that can be fished down to. The real secret is not to rush into the first spot that's vacant. If it is empty because anglers have walked on beyond, then there may be a good reason. Time spent investigating is a sound investment.

As winter sets in, so fish begin to move back to old haunts. Now the deeper, slower areas will be more attractive – but don't rush to extremes. Start off by trying a day in a deeper-than-average swim, but not the deepest. If trees have not yet lost their leaves they will still be fish-holding features. But beware the first falls of autumn, a river full of leaves is a nightmare, and one that does not fish at its best.

When floods arrive, it is time to move to the sheltered spots in bays or on the inside of bends. Small inlets that are not big enough to consider under normal conditions may now hold a lot of fish.

Rows of boats moored up for the winter seem to hold an attraction for chub which have moved down

● *A good fish caught under freezing conditions. The biggest problem at the time was preventing line freezing in the rod rings (Chapter 9)*

● *Sun shining on the water can be the cause of eye strain. Use an eye shade and polarising glasses to reduce glare (Chapter 9)*

from beneath trees now bare of foliage. Go for the ones with black-bottomed hulls – it is these darker craft that often have the biggest head of residents beneath them. Maybe the darkness gives fish a greater feeling of safety and camouflage.

Stillwaters

Stillwaters are often the hardest to choose well – big waters in particular can have whole areas almost devoid of fish for no obvious reason. One theory is that wind blowing across the surface produces contrasting temperature layers. Think back to your school days and you may remember that temperature also changes the density of water. At 39.2°F it is at its heaviest: depending on whether the surface is warmer or colder than that temperature, so the deepest part of a lake will be either the warmest or coldest, too. So you will see on a really cold day the best bet is likely to be the deepest.

However, it is not always as simple as that. Think back to those wonderful days when you have gone to your favourite lake and found a calm swim with the wind blowing off your back – casting and feeding were very simple and presentation was perfect. Strangely, results didn't quite match up. Then on the next visit you were forced into fishing the only spot vacant. It was facing right into the wind; the surface was rippled and the wind made feeding just that bit harder – you also needed an extra AAA shot to help keep presentation, even at best, merely average. You caught all day long (see colour photograph on p. 178).

There is a scientific reason for this into-the-wind side being favoured by fish. Wind currents cause a layer of water called the *thermocline* to tilt as it is pushed across a lake. This layer can cause quite drastic temperature changes within a matter of feet and the result is, fish may follow it to where it suits them best.

Another reason and one more easily understood, is that food will be blown across to the shore into which wind is blowing. The wave action also churns up the bottom and creates colour into which fish will move, and this often brings them in close to the bank where you can fish with ease despite the breeze in your face.

During summer, a feeder stream running into a lake is a good spot because the water will be rich in oxygen and has possibly been a spawning ground. Sandy shallows nearby will be other areas to fish in early season. Go for swims with plenty of rich green weed – but steer well clear of them once frost kills off the growth and decay sets in. The rotting material will give off gases that are not tolerated by fish.

Many species of fish love to feed along the edge of ledges and slopes. If, by careful plumbing, or even by chatting to the local diving club, it is possible to find such a place you could be in for a real treat. Bream are great lovers of slopes and steep drop-offs, maybe because they can feed from them without having to stand almost on their heads, as they are forced to do on a flat bed.

General rules

When trying to decide which swim is the best on a given stretch of water, a good tip is to think like a fish. Ask yourself where you would want to live if you were swimming around down there. Take into account possible sources of food, available cover to shield you from predators, water temperature and how varying depths will affect it. There may be some fresh oxygen supplies in running water during warm weather, but watch out for streams and inlets entering a fishery – some feeder streams can be very good, others may be carrying hidden pollution.

Avoid swims near inlets during winter when surface water is likely to be very cold. And in the case of fisheries close to roads, a lot of anti-freeze salt is sure to have found its way in.

A real winter banker is a warm water outfall from an industrial site – but again, the content needs to be of an acceptable standard. One of the best sources is a power station which uses water for its cooling towers, but avoid these areas on days when nothing is being pumped in, they are often hopeless. Having become accustomed to an artificially high temperature, fish will be in no mood to feed after being hit by a sudden chill.

Weedy waters that have been treated chemically to kill off growth, will fish badly for a week or two after spraying has been done. However, a dredger working through a water can be a bonus. The colour and fresh bottom created by such work is a sure place to find a lot of feeding fish, and the closer you get to the dredger the better it can be.

● *A nice sheltered swim on a stillwater but the angler may not be in the best spot. The far bank, where there is a ripple, is probably the most productive area*

PLAYING FISH

'Keep the rod up and don't give a fish any slack': this is about all the old angling books ever advised on the subject of playing fish – fine in principle, and the angler who applies it will not go far wrong. But there is so much more that can be done in order to be consistently successful in coping with big fish on the small hooks and ultra-fine lines demanded by many of today's waters.

Keeping the rod up would certainly ensure the tip did its job of buffering the shocks created by a fish diving for freedom. The tight line principle is one that must be applied too, for any slack given will almost certainly result in the hook coming free, with obvious results.

A lot of fish are lost because many anglers find it necessary to move the rod from side to side, applying all sorts of different pressures at an assortment of angles. Now this performance may look very impressive, but all it achieves is to loosen the hook-hold by turning it slightly every time the rod angle is changed.

A far better tactic is to strike, then with the rod at the same angle throughout, apply a constant pressure until the fish is ready for netting. There are exceptions, of course – when a fish has to be allowed to run to prevent breakage, or the rod angle has to be altered to steer a catch away from some obstruction such as a weed-bed or tree-root.

Knowing how much pressure is being applied to a hooked fish is something you should find out. Do this

● *The rod can be kept low but the angle should be constant and never with the tip pointing directly at the fish. A sideways pull is a good method of drawing a hooked fish away from the shoal.*

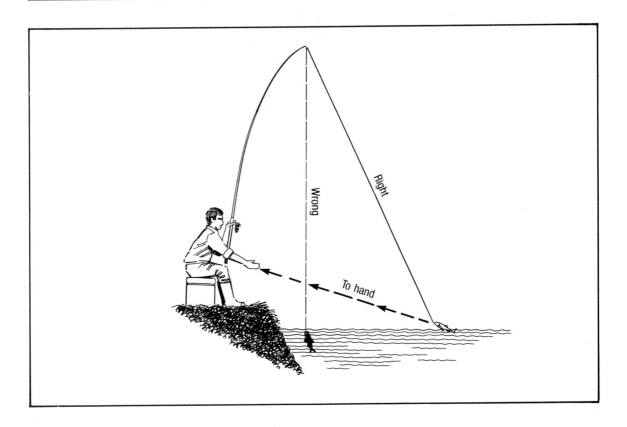

by threading up a line with a spring balance attached to the end; then get a helper to hold the balance while you gradually apply pressure by raising the rod. When you feel the rod is taking a full loading, and that the curve it forms is a little beyond what you would expect to see when maximum force is being used against a fish, get your helper to read off the spring balance. With an average 13ft match rod the indicator is unlikely to read more than 12oz.

Armed with this knowledge you will now have some idea just how little pressure you are actually applying when the rod takes a dangerous-looking curve. This type of constant pressure is unlikely to cause a hook to pull out or the line to break, except one with an ultra-fine bottom.

What *can* cause breakage is a sudden load, a shock which the line cannot absorb quickly enough. This can be demonstrated by your helper now holding the line and giving it a sudden jerk while the rod is held at 60° to the horizontal – the result will probably be line breakage. (If you decide to try either of these tests, be sure to do them with a line

● *Swinging a fish to hand is done by starting the lift while the fish is still well out. It should not be lifted directly upwards as a dead weight*

of low breaking strain, otherwise the breakage might be more expensive than you had planned!)

Like so much of float fishing technique, the key is to do everything smoothly and without any sudden changes. Take your time, and above all, don't panic. You must be in full control of the situation and know exactly what you will achieve by carrying out an action.

With fish that can be swung in 'to hand', the rules all apply. The strike is made, the fish is moved away from the catching area by steering it with the rod, and then while it is still beyond the rod tip, an upward and controlled sweep lifts it clear of the water at a shallow angle. By doing it this way you will be using the momentum of the moving fish to help lift it from the water. What should not be done is to play the fish right to the bank and to a complete

● *A dangerous moment as a fish reaches the net. This is a time to stay calm and as still as possible. Any sudden movement may cause the fish to panic and bolt away*

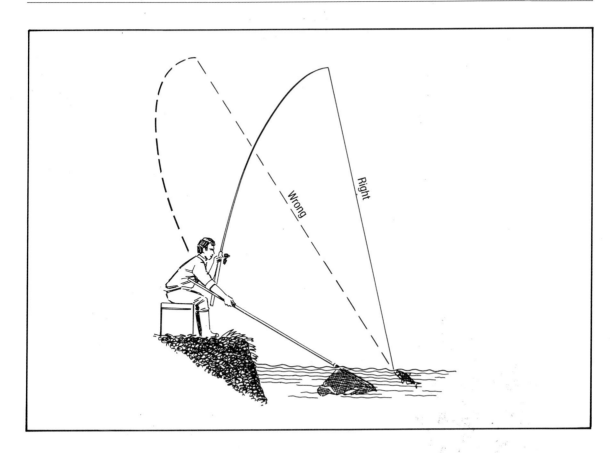

standstill, and then lift it from a dead weight. If you are forced to the standstill situation the fish should probably have been netted anyway.

Done correctly, a fish – say, a 3oz roach – can be lifted at just the right spot so that the length of line from the rod tip is that which is required to bring the fish straight to your hand. All this sounds complicated but once you gain the confidence to do it correctly it will become second nature. One other 'don't': don't look around while you are playing a fish. From the moment a fish is struck to the time it goes into the keepnet is a period when total concentration is required. It is best to keep an eye on the fish at all times, although you could take a glance at the rod tip if you are unsure how hard you are working the tackle.

Landing fish that are well above the hook-length's breaking strain is no real problem because the rod, if correctly matched to the line, is taking most of the strain by absorbing the impact of sudden shocks (as was found in the spring balance experiment).

● *When netting a fish the rod should not be moved too far backwards. Sink the net and draw the fish over in a controlled manner and do not be tempted to over-reach*

Reel drags and clutches offer another safeguard, but they should not be relied upon too much; constant winding against the clutch will also result in a badly kinked line. A better plan is to find a setting close to the maximum load a line will take, and then play fish from the reel handle. But in order to do this the reel must be in good order and backwind freely.

When a sizeable fish is hooked on fine gear it is best to let it have some of its own way, at least throughout the first rush. But while staying well within the safety limits imposed by the frailness of the tackle, make it nonetheless earn every inch of line by keeping the pressure on.

Once you have an idea what has been hooked, then is the time to begin exerting more control. In the case of open water, free from snags, you should be in the driving seat immediately. The fish may want to run: if so, let it, but against resistance at all times. While it is out in open water it can come to little harm and that is the best place to take the sting from its fight.

With the rod at a constant angle, line will eventually be gained and the fish will be forced to come back towards you. Stay calm, and above all quiet. Don't bang about on the bank for this will not only scare off other fish in the swim, it will possibly panic the one that's on your hook.

The landing net should already be in the water, put there long before you even knew it would be required. Keep it still and only reach for it when you are absolutely sure the fish is beaten. The net should be well sunk and the fish drawn over it – on no account chase around as if trying to catch some form of aquatic butterfly; to do so is asking for a lot of trouble.

Once in the net the fish is yours, but don't be tempted to lift even a one-pounder with the net handle fully extended. The best method is to keep net and fish in the water, with the rim just clear of the surface. Lay the rod in its rest and use your right hand to pull the handle backwards, passing it over your left until the net rim can be grasped (see colour photograph on p. 157).

Place the net across your knees and lift the fish so that the hook can be removed. Do the whole operation over the net so should the fish be dropped it will not come to any harm by falling on a hard bank. If it is an exceptionally big or strong specimen leave it in the net, remove the hook and then tip the landing net straight over into the keepnet.

Throughout the time it has taken to beat your fish it should have been played beneath the surface. Letting it thrash around on the surface is going to do nothing for your chances of more fish and may even increase the possibility of the one you've got being lost.

Bream are said to be poor fighters, and this may be true if compared with the more spectacular species such as chub, carp and tench. But they are still powerful swimmers and should not be under-estimated. Play them carefully until ready for the net, at which point draw them to the surface where their flat shape forces them to roll sideways. Once in this position keep them that way, and use a backwards movement of the rod to draw them towards the net. Over-reaching with the net or too

much of a backwards movement with the rod should be avoided, as both considerably reduce the amount of control you have over the situation.

Most fish are easy to handle when close to the net provided they have been played correctly. One little dodge that seems to work well with most species is to keep their head right on the surface – it works especially well with chub, which never seem to give up if allowed to see where they are heading. Get the head – that is to say, the mouth and eyes – above water and they can be drawn right over the net.

Throughout the time it takes to play any fish the angler should be in control, making the rod work towards steering the catch towards the net, and also avoiding any possible escape routes such as sub-merged roots and snags.

In order to do this well, it is vital to understand the reaction of a fish to pressure being applied down the line. If a strong fish is hooked and the rod is kept high, the usual reaction is for it to pull directly against the resistance it feels. That is to say, it will head downwards. Apply the same amount of pressure, but with the rod kept low and to the side and the fish is more likely to rise very close to the surface. This reaction can be used to good advantag to get fish around obstacles.

It goes without saying that every fish should be played with care. However, do not overdo the care to a degree where the fish is allowed to swim around under so little pressure that the hook hold is loosened and eventually pulls free. Just think of those hard days, when every bite has to be worked for. You hook a fish after waiting ages and then proceed to play it with great care, applying just enough pressure to keep it moving. Result is often a lost fish, yet on the good days when it is a fish a cast, fewer fish seem to come adrift despite the extra speed and power under which they are played – or because of it: confidence must come into all this somewhere. Believe in your own ability and tackle, and play every fish positively. It's surprising how much you can get away with.

Getting someone else to net your fish is also something to be wary of. In the case of very big fish such as giant carp then a helper is fine, but for the average sort of fish you should be able to do your own netting. At least that way you are in total control and know exactly what is going on and just when the fish is ready.

JOINING THE MATCH SCENE

Taking part in matches is a fine way in which to improve your angling skills and to learn from other anglers around you. In return, match fishing will demand a lot of time, patience, effort and no small amount of cash before it is prepared to give up all its secrets. And if you are thinking of competition as a means to make some quick financial killing, then forget it. Very few, maybe only a handful of anglers every year, actually make a profit at the end of a season. Open events are expensive affairs and although you will probably want to try your hand against the stars at some stage, it is best not to dive in headlong at the deep end.

Having spent a few seasons perfecting the basic techniques that enable you to fish most types of swim with some degree of success, the first stage on the match-fishing route is to join a couple of small local clubs. A works or pub club is a fine starting point from where you can progress at the right rate. The ideal club would be one that fishes a lot of events on waters nearby. It should have regular entries of around twenty or thirty, and if possible have a few good anglers among its members whose skills will be the foundation on which your learning will be based.

Avoid the big money clubs and those that stage a lot of outings. Large cash prizes often attract sharks who see newcomers as nothing more than 'pools fodder' from whom they can extract easy money. Club outings are fine for a change, but in the early days it is better to stay local for most of the time, to gain the skills and knowledge required to tackle the waters you fish most. Having mastered those, then it is time to take on new and more distant challenges.

Find a club by watching local newspaper reports and asking around among friends or maybe your local tackle dealer as to which they think would be suitable. Don't, however, be tempted to join an outfit where the membership consists entirely of novice anglers. It might be a club where you will win some matches, but at this early stage learning is more important than winning. Aim for a club in which

● *A match in progress. Joining a club is a good way in which to improve your overall skills, but don't expect instant success*

you think you should finish up about in the middle in the results. It may even pay to watch a few matches organised by your proposed new club before signing on. That way you will be able to judge the standard and the friendliness of its members.

This learning period is going to cost money in the form of club and entry fees and buying bait, so it is essential that maximum benefit is gained from every match. To this end keep a diary of your results – a simple notebook will do nicely, with a page devoted to each event. List things such as venue, date, water and weather conditions; then make a note of your peg, its number and as much detail as possible such as depth, snags, where you caught fish and how. The more detail you get down the better, for in a month you will have forgotten much of the vital detail that might make all the difference next time.

Take down as much information as you can from others in the match, too. Find out where the winners drew, and what they caught, and how. Most tell the truth if they are approached properly and know that you will return the compliment when your day arrives. Don't, however, expect the winner to come to you first. You want the information and you must go out and get it.

A good many years ago I was approached in this manner by an angler I hardly knew except by sight. One weekend I had won two matches, and on Monday evening the doorbell rang and there stood Terry, who was later to become a good friend. 'Can you spare me an hour, please?' was his opening request. 'I fished both the matches at the weekend and would love to know your secret,' he added.

Terry came in and soon learned that there was no secret. My tackle box, and in particular the float box, underwent close scrutiny during which questions began to pour forth. Now Terry had been fishing for years, but had not progressed very far. During the regular meetings which followed, it became obvious that he had the enthusiasm and desire to improve. He asked the questions, I provided the answers and in so doing actually learned a lot myself because I had to think more carefully about what had been happening during the four or five hours of every match. All Terry needed was some fine tuning and a little encouragement.

Terry went on to earn a place in the Peterborough national team, so he certainly won his share of matches, and has gone on to help others. The moral

is: don't be afraid to ask, and don't be put off by stories that 'old so-and-so doesn't tell anyone anything'. Ask for yourself: you've nothing to lose.

Having joined a club, the next stage is to prepare for your first event which we shall assume is on a stretch of a local river. Tackle for match fishing is going to take a lot of rough treatment and should be checked over carefully well before the big day. There is no excuse for failure due to tackle problems. The angler who: 'would have won if my line hadn't kept breaking' didn't deserve to win anyway – his line should have been checked and replaced long ago.

Bait must be the best available, but don't make the mistake of going 'over tinned', that is to say with so much variety you baffle yourself. If maggots and squatts with groundbait look a good bet, then make them your main attack. By all means carry an alternative such as casters and worms just in case you draw that real flyer of a bream peg. We all take more than we need, but in match fishing especially it is better to have a little too much than not enough. Prepare it well, riddling off all the rubbish, dead maggots or debris that is unwanted. The aim is to get everything as near perfect as possible prior to the start so that every second of the match is used to maximum effect.

Having paid your entry you can perhaps indulge in the pools – but only if you want to. Never feel obliged to enter an optional pool; they are run for the benefit of the more professional match angler, and at this early stage it may be best just to enter a section pool or one of the smaller main pools. Payout will vary from match to match, but a good one will hand out the total amount taken. Percentage deductions for expenses are not to be encouraged and in any case should not occur at club level.

In a main pool the first places – perhaps down to fifth – will take a share, and in the sections it may be the winner or the first two in each section that collect. A good section pool idea is one run over every ten pegs, with just the best weight from each ten taking a prize. These sort of pools give you something to fish for, even if drawn in a bad area.

● *A nice catch of bream taken on the pole by journalist Keith Elliot*

Having got the preliminaries over, the next stage is the draw – the most important element so far. The draw ticket will bear your peg number and will probably have a space for your name and weight. Fill it in and keep it safe.

Now we can run through a typical match and consider how plans can be laid. We've drawn peg 20 – right in the middle of the match of forty anglers. It's an average sort of area, but one from which it is possible to win, given a little luck. Walk down the bank, keeping well back from the water's edge and clear of all the tackle that will now be scattered around. Stop to talk if you think it will be of benefit but don't be misled at this late stage. All you are doing now is gathering information that may come in handy should your opening plan fail.

Arriving at your peg it looks good. There is a nice colour to the water and some fully leaved trees opposite provide cover which may hold a chub or three. On your bank there is an interesting weed-bed stretching downstream, while the middle of the river looks clear of obstruction.

Set your kit down a moment and take a breather, spending time to study the swim more closely. You may spot movement under the trees or perhaps the weed-bed suggests fish activity. With a little over forty minutes to go, begin to assemble the tackle you are likely to need. But get it in the right order: position your box squarely and firmly; nets are assembled and placed and the bait-stand erected; almost the last things to go together are the rods.

Before tackling up the rods, think over the tactics you now believe will win. Every match should be approached with a target weight in mind – if the winner is going to need 30lb of chub and the next ten are likely to catch over 10lb of roach, there is little point in fishing for 3lb of bleak. Conversely a match on a hard water may be won with 3lb, in which case that is the weight to plan for.

Homework has taken you this far. It won't always be right, but at least your plan will provide a starting point from which you can deviate if things don't work out.

Two minutes to go. You have every possible requirement within reach and if plumbing the depth is permitted before the 'off', you will have done it thoroughly and now know what the bottom contour is like: depth on the edge of the weed-bed is 9ft, the middle shelves gently down to 12ft and then upwards to a ledge of 3ft, some 6ft out from the far bank, right beneath the trees.

Flow is steady and we have set up three rods: a light stick float rig which will be run down along the edge of the weed-bed. A three-AAA waggler with a medium insert for the middle, and a two-swan peacock with no insert for the far shelf. The stick has been rigged with single shot spread down the line and finished with a 22 fine wire hook. The insert waggler hook is a 20, fine wire. Bulk of the load is used as locking shot but there is a bulk of four no 6 just below mid-depth and then two 8s and a 10 spread down the remaining lower half. Finally the straight peacock has all but a no 8 and no 10 tell-tale used as locking shot around the float to permit easy casting across the twenty-five yards of river to within a very short distance of the far bank. Hook is a forged 20.

Target weight today is 12lb, the match held here the previous weekend having produced a couple of 10lb nets of roach, skimmer bream and chub and a winning 11½lb made up of roach, a couple of 2lb bream and a chub of about the same size. Average catch through the match was around 6lb so everyone should be on for a few fish and with a fairly even chance of making the frame. From this information it is obvious that a bonus fish or two is going to be needed to lift the winners beyond reach of the 'also-rans'.

The starting whistle blows, and a shaky hand tries to bait a maggot on the stick float rig but then decides to feed first. That is the first mistake. That clear stretch of water just beyond the weed might be unfishable because of an underwater snag – feeding there will do nothing but put fish out of reach.

Don't feed anything yet, but instead have a cast beyond the weeds with the stick float and see what happens. As yet you are not fishing seriously – though watch what is happening around you and try to get the angler either side, and in particular the one upstream, to show their hand first. In this case the one above has gone straight down the middle with a waggler and has begun feeding there with

● The wife in winning mood! Pauline Haines, a former ladies national champion, with a match catch of Nene roach and a 'bonus' chub. Local knowledge and a planned target weight played major parts in her success

188

loose maggots fired from a catapult. Downstream a similar situation is developing.

Now it is your turn to make a move. If you simply follow the line of feed taken by your neighbours, you might have to share the available fish three ways; instead, start with the inside line and the stick. This gives you a clear run, and fish on that line are not being pulled up or down by anglers feeding nearby.

At this stage there is one important thing to remember: the inside line is likely to die long before the five hours is over and the middle line, if left unfed, may prove to be lacking in fish by the time you are forced to go over with the insert rig. So this is the next stage in our plan. A regular feeding of small balls of groundbait laced with squatts goes in just beyond the line chosen by your upstream rival.

Finally, fire a couple of dozen maggots right in among the trees opposite so that there is a trickle of bait moving slowly along that shallow ledge. Keep adding a regular dozen or so throughout the match, thus holding any chub that may be there and preventing them from being pulled away by regular feed coming from upstream.

The stick is going through unchecked but as yet nothing in the way of a bite, despite half-a-dozen maggots going in just before every cast. The angler above has struck and missed two bites, and the man below has three roach.

Then comes your first bite, a nice roach of 3oz, quickly followed by four more and a small skimmer. Keep the feed going in at half-a-dozen maggots before every cast. Both sides are catching too, but you are ahead by a couple of fish with forty minutes gone. The middle line has been fed constantly, but as yet is unfished.

Bites slow on the inside and then you lose a good fish. Your hook length shows signs of slime so it is likely to have been a bream. Tactic now is to add 6in to the depth you have set the float at, and instead of running through unchecked hold it back hard, easing it downstream in a series of pauses. It works! A bream of 1lb comes on the first cast, and straight afterwards another. Your upstream opponent has landed one of close on 2lb, so things are beginning to look promising.

The tree-line is still being fed with loose maggots and the groundbait plan for the middle has also continued.

After those two bream the inside line has died completely and your upstream man has had another two bream of 1lb each. Now is the time to discard the stick and go for the middle waggler rig. It works too, with an immediate response from a 1½lb bream and three skimmers of 8oz apiece. This could be a big weight match after all.

Three hours gone and the bankside grapevine has brought a visit by two anglers from the far end who have not been catching and have abandoned their swims to watch the action in your area. This is good and bad news. The good news is that you are one of the few in the leading pack. Bad news is their appearance on the skyline which might just put your swim off the boil. If they decide to stay, ask them to sit upstream of you and to get down the bank as much as possible.

As experience grows you will find it is possible to direct your 'gallery' where you want it according to how you place tackle on the bank behind (see colour photograph on p. 132). By leaving a neat gap in the surrounding kit you invite them to sit exactly where they can do least harm. Try it, it works.

Just as the wanderers arrive your upstream threat hooks another bream – the attraction is too much and they pass you by to watch the struggle. It appears to be a bigger fish and after ten minutes he is still playing it, but has gained a lot of line. Meanwhile you have taken two more fish of 12oz each and a run of roach in the 2oz class.

● *A match plan using three different lines of attack. Plan A will take fish early in the match. Plan B takes a line just beyond that of the anglers on either side. Final move is to Plan C where a bonus chub or two may swing the result in the closing stages*

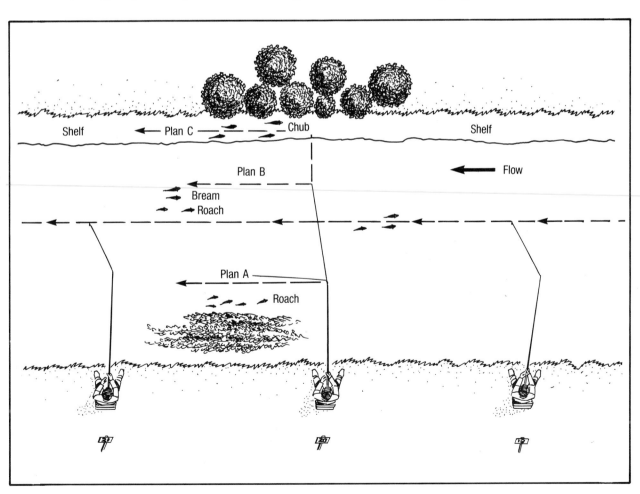

Disaster upstream, the fish was a three-pounder, foul-hooked in the tail and after nearly fifteen minutes it has pulled free right in the middle of the river. A blank thirty minutes follows for the unfortunate angler, during which time you take three more small roach but no bream. He tries the inside line to keep in touch, realising the bream have been scared off by the one which broke free. But constantly landing and netting fish has destroyed the chance of the inside producing any amount of fish at this late stage.

You are left with a decision to make. A quick run-through for ten minutes on your original inside line might prove worthwhile, the scared fish possibly having headed for cover. But scared fish are hard to catch and it is not going to be a good plan to waste too much time there.

An hour to go, you're just ahead according to the gallery and there is everything to fish for. Now you play the master card. That far-side shelf has remained untouched except for a constant trickle of loose feed. A switch to the straight waggler is called for in the hope of a couple of bonus chub to put you beyond reach.

A dozen maggots go over again and the tackle is cast right against the bank. The double maggot brings nothing for fifteen minutes so a drop down to a single offering is tried. Response is immediate – the float doesn't even settle before sliding away. Strike, with the rod low to keep line from catching the branches, and begin moving the fish, a chub, out into open water. The secret with this far-shelf fishing is to get a hooked fish away as quickly and as quietly as possible so as not to upset the others.

Men on either side see what is happening but until now they have not fed across to their stretch of the ledge and unless you make a mistake the resident shoal is unlikely to move away. First chub is close to 2lb, and then one of a 1lb comes with ten minutes left. Seconds remain, but time for one more cast. Over you go and a bite comes just as the whistle sounds. Another chub, which because it was hooked prior to the whistle you can continue to play. Fifteen minutes is the usual 'after whistle' time allowed, but you take just three minutes to add another 1½lb to your total.

At this stage it is nice to sit back and anticipate for a moment all the congratulations. Far better plan, however, is to pack away all your kit so that it is safe

from the dozens of feet that will follow the scales down the bank. On days when you haven't done so well it may pay to offer to weigh in. It's a good means of seeing exactly what is caught, by whom and from where (see colour photograph on p. 158). But be warned: leaving your peg before the scales arrive can mean disqualification in open events and major championships.

Today it will be best to pack up and be sure to clear the bankside of those hook packets you dropped during the heat of battle. Leaving litter at any swim is a crime, in matches it results in your disqualification. The scales arrive from upstream, having weighed the next man at 8½lb. That's the best weight so far, with three more in the 6lb bracket. Make sure the scales are at zero - they have a habit of adjusting themselves, especially after weighing in a decent catch. It's up to you, the competitor, to see that your fish are weighed accurately. Watch especially, if you need more than one weigh, that the totals are added together correctly.

Watch carefully that the scales are used properly. Dial scales used without a tripod should always be held by means of the wire ring at the top – never allow a scalesman to hold the dial with both hands cupped around the sides, which can cause havoc with the workings and a weight inaccurate by several ounces. Everything is ready now for your fish. Pull out the bank-stick and unscrew it from the net before setting off with your catch. That way you won't poke someone's eye out with it when they crowd forward to see your fish. Get well back from the water's edge, too. Many a match has been lost through a big fish rolling back into the water prior to weighing.

The scales can weigh 10lb in one go and your first load takes the indicator past the mark. Don't be talked into leaving it that way in the hope the scales go a little beyond capacity. Take a big fish off and accept the reading, in this case just 9lb. You're in front and still have another weight to go. Second weigh is 4½lb, giving you a total of 13½lb and your first win with the new club.

Today, everything went to plan and you were

● *A handy-sized match fish is swung to hand, saving valuable seconds that would be wasted with the landing net*

helped on the way by an unfortunate incident which ruined the chances of the man above. Next time you may not be so lucky, but even so, going with a carefully thought-out plan will often carry you through. On this occasion the plan was to open an account on the inside and then follow fish across the river. The lost bream on the inside and the upstream angler hooking one soon afterwards were the signals that suggested it was time to change. Then that foul-hooked fish acted as a second prompt and you were home and dry.

Match fishing is a gamble in many ways. The trick is to be able to load the odds as much in your favour as possible. Follow the flock and fish like all the others and it will be the best man who wins every time, at least on even pegs. What you are looking for is the right method to begin with and one that leaves some options open if things go wrong.

For example, it is no good drawing a swim that produces bream only every so often and then fishing for them in a positive manner – you may find out too late that they aren't going to feed at all on the day. Far better to start cautiously and build up, reading the signs as you go and changing to meet situations as they develop. The vast majority of matches are won by anglers who fish the same method all through, rather than having to chop and change constantly.

Club membership is a good way to make friends,

and as you get more into the match scene you may want to form a small match group of your own. This is a fine way to speed up the learning process since a group of, say, four or five dedicated anglers will gather information and experience at four or five times the rate of a solo angler. Some of the strongest match teams of all time have started as such small match groups, and they have produced some really outstanding individuals.

Having enjoyed a bit of success at club level, the natural progression is to the open scene. However, fewer mistakes are made here, and those that are cost dearly. The difference in ability level is staggering, and a good club angler is likely to be well out of his depth on the open circuit for some time. Those that can afford the wait and financial outlay may find it pays off in the long term, if only by making them better for the experience.

Match fishing is like all other forms of the sport in that it is supposed to be enjoyable. Winning is nice, but it should not become an obsession and if competition gets to you so that you worry when things go wrong and get upset by a bad run, then pack it in and go back to 'pleasure' fishing. The world of the match angler should be fun and exciting. It will be tough at times and punctuated by disappointments, but take it as it comes and remember bad runs have to end some time. It's all a case of believing in yourself and your skills.

9

Trouble Shooting

This final chapter discusses those annoying problems that seem to have a habit of occurring when least expected. Most of these can, however, be solved by a little adjustment either to the rig, tackle or technique. The questions are a selection of the most common ones which have arisen during conversations with anglers of all ages and degrees of experience.

TACKLE

Line breakages

Q: What is the cause of line suddenly breaking during use?

A: There are many answers to this question but usually it has become damaged either by mis-use or by some fault in the other tackle being used.

If you slide shots around without opening them slightly first it will cause damage very easily, and at the first sign of any rough spot it must be changed. Watch out that line doesn't catch on rod-rest heads, too, or around spool buttons and other protruding items of kit. Standing on line left lying about is another sure way to ruin it.

A cracked rod ring or a bale arm roller that has become grooved is very dangerous to line. Make regular checks with a magnifying glass and at the first sign of wear, replace the offending item. If you are constantly winding against the reel clutch it will put twists into the line, and that will reduce its strength, too.

Never leave line exposed to direct sunlight – if you leave a spool on the dashboard of the car it will be ruined in a very short time. Line takes a lot of punishment and is constantly being worn away by the abrasive particles of sand and grit it collects from the water. Change it regularly, and burn the discarded nylon so that it cannot cause injury to wildlife.

Reel jamming

Q: My close-faced reel works fine until I wind in most of the line, at which stage it begins to screech and feel rough in operation. What could be the cause of this and the other rather stiff nature of some of my fixed spools?

A: Your closed-face reel is probably overfilled so when it is fully wound, the line is rubbing on the inside face of the pick-up pin housing. Overfilling is often the cause of line becoming tangled around the back of the spool, too. Try stripping off twenty metres or so.

The usual reason for stiffness in reels is not enough maintenance. Give them a good strip-down and clean and overhaul the workings, and pay particular attention to getting off any groundbait and dirt which has built up behind the spool housing. Clean the gears and give them a light oiling. And check spindles for pieces of nylon line that may have found a way inside and become wrapped around, and buried in the grease.

If you think the stiffness is just a case of the reel running dry of oil, check if there is an oil-screw at the rear of the body which you can remove, and run some oil inside.

After a hard season it pays to send reels back to the manufacturer because many provide excellent back-up services which cost very little to use, and this ensures everything is running at its best.

Loose joints

Q: My rod has worn loose at the joints and can be felt wobbling slightly. What can be done to tighten it?

A: If the joint is a spigot type and there is some exposed spigot showing when the rod is assembled, you can remove some material from the end of the female section so that more of the unused spigot can enter. Take off a little *less* than the exposed amount of spigot so that there is still clearance between the joints.

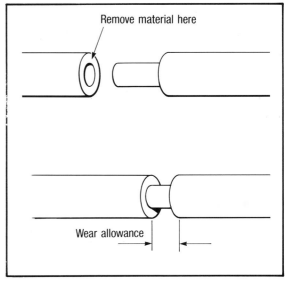

● *Loose spigot ferrules can be tightened by removing some material from the face of the female joint. A good-fitting ferrule should have a short section of the male spigot showing between the joints to act as a wear allowance*

You must remove the material carefully, binding the joint with sticky tape below where the cut is to be made. If you are going to saw it, use a very fine junior hacksaw and don't force anything – go gently, and don't try to break off the last few fibres. If you are only going to take off a small amount, it is best done with a fine file.

You can tighten up normal push-in or push-over joints a bit by treating them with candle wax. Rub the candle up and down the ferrule so it deposits a coating of wax and it will hold firmly.

In extreme cases or emergencies, if you jam a blade of grass between the joints it will hold them firmly. But never use anything too hard otherwise you will risk cracking them because of the uneven stress it will cause.

You can keep joints in good order by giving them a regular clean with a damp cloth. Otherwise sand, grit and mud will cause rapid wear and scratching which will then cause other little build-ups of grime, and eventually they will jam.

Locked sections

Q: How can the jammed sections of a carbon-fibre rod be parted?

A: Carbon fibre doesn't expand very much when heated so the old trick of holding a candle to them, which you could do with brass ferrules, doesn't work, and in fact will cause serious damage by melting the resins which bond the fibres together.

Get a friend to help and grasp the two stuck sections between you, so you each place one hand directly over the joint and the other just behind it. Begin by pulling straight – only if this fails should you use any twisting force. If your bankside efforts fail, try and carry the two sections home and leave them a couple of days in a warm room. Moisture may have caused a seal between the joints and it will dry off and the sections may come apart.

Stubborn joints will sometimes come apart if you tap them gently all over with a small piece of flat wood. But take care, the idea is only to set up small vibrations which may free the offending debris and nothing more.

Once you have got them free a good clean is in order otherwise the problem may occur again.

Dirty handle

Q: My rod handles are filthy. Groundbait has become crusted to them and started to go mouldy in places. What is the best way to clean off the dirt?

A: Cork handles can be scrubbed with a nail-brush and some warm, soapy water, but be sure to wash off *all* traces of soap and then allow the handle to dry completely before placing it back in your rod bag. You can give a cork handle that new feeling again by rubbing it all over with some fine glasspaper. But do this only when the cork is completely dry and don't use the treatment too often otherwise the diameter will suffer. And the easiest way to stop mould is to clean the handle as soon as possible after fishing.

You can wash foam, EVA handles with warm – not hot – water and a little soap but, again, you must wash them off with clean water and then let them dry naturally at room temperature.

Broken rods

Q: One of the female ferrules of my carbon match rod has cracked. Is it possible to repair this sort of damage?

A: Carbon and actually most man-made fibres can be repaired with some success, but really you must think of such work as a last-ditch effort. A far better option is if you try and get a replacement section from your tackle dealer. Many of the larger manufacturers operate a spares service – get your dealer's advice about how available they are.

If you want to try a repair, first clean the cracked section with a de-greaser such as methylated spirit, then allow it to dry. Next coat the mating male ferrule with a thin layer of Vaseline, and be sure to get a complete and even spread.

Make up some Araldite glue and smear it on the outside of the damaged joint, forcing it between the cracks if possible by opening them slightly with your fingernail. Remove any surplus glue that may find its way inside the ferrule and then insert the greased male – the grease is to prevent the glue sticking the two sections together, so it is important that you apply it thinly but without leaving any area unprotected.

Turn the male a few times to ensure a good fit, and then with it still in place build up a neat and even area of whipping which will cover the damaged part of the joint completely. And you must continue the whipping for a centimetre beyond each end of the longest crack. If there is any Araldite left, you can smear some into this whipping to give even more strength. Finally, twist the male section a few times and remove it. Leave the glue to cure completely before you varnish the whipping.

By whipping over the damage with the male joint in place, you reduce the risk of distortion considerably. It pays to use the slow-drying type of Araldite too, as this gives you more time to carry out all the operations before the two sections stick together.

Freeze up

Q: What can be done to prevent line freezing to rod-rings when float fishing?

A: Cheapest solution is to drop a few spots of glycerine onto each ring – this will keep them ice-free for long periods, but keep the bottle handy and apply as required. You can buy glycerine at any chemist, baker's shop or grocer (see colour photograph on p. 175).

Tackling up

Q: Often while tackling up I forget to open the bale arm of the fixed spool reel so that it is impossible to wind in line. Is there an easy way to eliminate this problem?

A: Only by doing it will you remember that you must always open the bale arm before threading line through the rod rings. But there is no need to untackle in order to put the fault right. All you need do is remove the spool of line and then open the bale arm. With it in this open position you can then replace the spool and close the bale arm. All is now tackled correctly and ready for the next stage.

You can keep line on spools tidy either by using the small tab situated on the side of some models or by slipping a wide elastic band over the line after use.

Leaky boots

Q: Waders are expensive yet mine never seem to last more than a season before starting to leak. What can be done to prolong their life?

A: Leaving your boots with the tops folded down is

the quickest way to cause cracking and eventually leaks.

After use you should wash your waders clean, and hang them soles uppermost in a cool, dry place. A proper wader rack is a good investment but a couple of wire coathangers will do the job – pass the boot's foot through and then press the wire down just enough to take the weight. Then hang the boot up away from direct sunlight or heat, and *never* try and dry boots quickly in front of a fire or radiator or any other direct heat source. Leaving them in the car boot is also a sure-fire way of ruining them quickly.

If you have insoles fitted you ought to remove them, so the inside of your boots can dry thoroughly, too.

Spade-end hooks

Q: Why is the spade end of a hook angled backwards away from the point side of the bend?

A: In fact not all spades slope backwards, some are left in line with the shank. The angle is to make sure

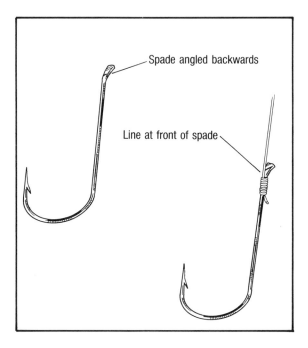

● *A spade-end hook has the spade angled away from the point to give clearance to the line, which should always come away from the shank on the point side*

that line is given plenty of clearance and can't be cut by the edge of the spade. If it is tied correctly, line should come away from the hook on the point side of the shank, that is to say in front of the spade so that the hook hangs straight and as far away from the spade edge as possible.

When you tie a spade-end hook, be sure to get the knot pushed right up to the base of the spade. If the spade is large it is worthwhile rubbing it down with an emery stone.

Line twisting

Q: I have a fast retrieve reel and find that it often makes my line twist into a spiral. Apart from slowing down the retrieve, is there anything more that can be done to prevent this trouble?

A: Pay special attention to getting all the shots on centrally, and in the case of double maggot baits always hook one on from the pointed end. On the retrieve, try and lift the tackle clear of the surface every so often during winding in. This little sort of bouncing motion will allow the kinks to unwind and will stop any spiralling from becoming serious.

COMFORT

Eye strain

Q: Although my eyesight is very good I seem to suffer from eye strain when float fishing – after an hour or so it becomes quite difficult to concentrate. Any suggestions?

A: What usually causes this sort of strain is glare. You can reduce the amount of light entering your eyes from overhead by wearing a cap with a long peak or an eyeshade (see colour photograph on p. 176). Even on days when the sky is overcast a shade has its advantages because it tends to help concentration by cutting out distractions from above.

Polarised glasses are good on very bright days and certainly a pair in the tackle box will be useful when you are trying to spot fish close to the surface or in shallow water. They also help to locate weed-beds and other snags which may be hidden from the naked eye.

If vision problems continue you should check that you are not colour-blind to certain float top shades – some people for example, find that very bright fire orange difficult to see.

Leaks

Q: My waterproofs are excellent, but I do find my arms and feet get wet when it rains because water finds its way down my wrists when I am casting, and inside my boots because it runs down my legs. Is there a simple way of solving the problem without buying a new outfit?

A: Rain does have a habit of getting into all sorts of places in spite of the very good modern waterproof materials you can buy nowadays. A jacket that has elasticated, knitted bands inside will protect your wrists best, and another very good and cheap way of stopping this annoying leak is by wearing an athlete's sweat band on each wrist – push the bands inside the cuffs and all should be well. If your sleeves are large you could seal them even more securely by slipping a strong elastic band over each one so that they are held down firmly against the sweatbands.

Always wear waterproof trousers *inside* the bottom of your jacket, and with the trouser bottoms *outside* of your boots. And a good hood with a storm flap at the collar is another essential. Take a fluffy towel – it is a fine thing to use as a scarf because it not only keeps out the wet but seals off the draughts, too!

Keeping warm

Q: Winter fishing has been miserable because I feel the cold so much. Are there any secrets to keeping warm in bad weather?

A: Float anglers – or for that matter, any sort of angler – will not fish efficiently if they are uncomfortable, but if you observe a few essentials and use a bit of commonsense you can fish right through the worst weather.

A good thermal shirt is a fine investment, but a true thermal only really works when worn next to the skin – the material from which it is made keeps the skin dry by 'wicking' away body moisture which would otherwise have a chilling effect. The thermal material also has good heat retention qualities. A considerable amount of body heat is lost from the head, so you should pay particular attention to keeping it covered – a woollen hat worn beneath a wind and waterproof hood is a good idea.

Protect your feet with a thermal 'moon boot' if possible, or otherwise wear several thin layers of socks and finally a thick sea-boot sock. A lining of clean, dry newspaper inside wellingtons and waders is the cheapest insulation available.

It is better to wear several thin layers of clothing rather than a single thick one, because a certain amount of air will be held between each layer which will act as extra insulation.

Finish off with a good waterproof, windproof suit – a one-piece provides fewer openings for draughts to find a way in; and protect yourself from wind-chill by using an umbrella whenever possible.

The traditional whisky flask is not in fact a good idea because blood will be drawn from the skin to the stomach to absorb the alcohol – once this happens you start to shiver and may suffer a real chilling. Far better to opt for a flask of hot soup.

Backache

Q: After carrying my tackle box I usually suffer from back-ache. Although the effects wear off after a short while, it is unpleasant while it lasts and maybe could lead to a serious problem. What is wrong?

A: Carrying a tackle box will put a bad twisting force on the spine unless you go about it correctly. Usual fault is the strap is too long, so the box is resting too low on the back. Shorten the strap, and wear it across the chest rather than on one shoulder so that the box sits squarely on your back just below the shoulder blades.

Try and balance your other tackle as well – you could wear the holdall with the strap across the chest from your other shoulder, and support it with your arm so that it points forwards. Your other free hand can take the bait and net bag, and this will make a nicely balanced load.

Check, too, from time to time that you are not carrying a lot of extra and unnecessary equipment which you are unlikely to use on that outing. And if you use a tackle trolley, take care not to twist your body by using only one hand to pull the load along. Either pull with both hands, or change hands regularly.

BAITS

Cooling bait

Q: On a number of summer visits to the water, bait has died while travelling by car to the waterside. What is the best way of keeping maggots cool during transit?

A: Use a coolbox intended for food and pack the bait boxes between some freezer packs. Otherwise take bait such as hempseed to the water in a frozen state and use this as the cooling agent.

Keep maggots in a fridge until the very last moment and be sure they have plenty of air space in the boxes you are going to use to transport them in. Shallow containers are best at all times.

Once the coolbox is packed and sealed, leave it that way until you arrive – there is no point in 'checking' en route because all you do is let out some of the cool air that was surrounding the boxes. If cooled to start with, and as long as the insulation is good, maggots will remain in prime condition for very long periods and there will certainly be enough air inside the coolbox to keep the semi-dormant bait alive for many hours.

A cheap alternative to a proper coolbox is to make one from thick pieces of polystyrene foam insulation material.

Beware of dark-coloured boxes and bags when you are at the waterside because these will not reflect the sun, and as a result a lot of heat will be generated inside them in a short time.

Should the worst happen and your maggots appear to be dead on arrival, empty them into as large a bowl or container as possible, and being careful to shade them, shake them up every few minutes – if you are lucky a fair number will revive. Discard the dead ones as they will often end up as floaters.

Taking worms abroad

Q: On an overseas fishing trip the Customs Officer refused to let me take worms into the country because they were packed in moss and soil. What are the rules, and can you suggest alternatives when taking worms abroad?

A: Some overseas Customs rules do ban any soil or plant life such as moss from being taken into certain countries, but worms will usually be allowed in if packed in some other material. Wet newspaper or carpet underfelt are both very good, and sacking or anything similar that will hold some moisture is fine. But just for good measure, it is best to let the worms spend a day or two working through some moss first in order to empty themselves of soil taken in during feeding.

Shred the newspaper into strips and give these a good soak, but take care not to get water in the box otherwise you could drown your worms.

Making groundbait

Q: I have been offered a good supply of stale bread but have no mechanical means of grinding it. Is there an easy way to produce groundbait without the need for a grinding machine?

A: A very quick and efficient way of making groundbait is by trampling it but first you must dry the bread thoroughly by baking it slowly in an oven or by storing it in a very dry and warm place like the airing cupboard. Once it is really dry you can grind it up by tipping some of it into something like an old bath and then trampling on it until you have reduced it to crumbs. These crumbs will vary in size and must be riddled – riddle off the whole batch. There will be some coarse crumb which won't pass through the riddle – put this back into the bath, add some more bread and repeat the process as often as required. No matter how often you trample it, there will always be some coarse crumb left over, and you use this as a sort of grinding medium for the new bread which you keep adding.

This 'grape-treading' technique is actually quite a fast way of producing groundbait and it will certainly give quicker results than a hand grinder.

Old food mixers or blenders can often be found in secondhand shops very cheaply and these are ideal for producing small batches of very fine crumb for use on waters such as canals. Even the trampling technique will break down some crumb to a fine dust. Separate it by using a kitchen sieve instead of a normal groundbait riddle.

All pure bread groundbait can be further enhanced by adding the suggested amount of one of the commercially produced additives such as Masterclass. Additives are also an easy means of producing groundbait in colours such as red and bronze.

FISH CARE AND IDENTIFICATION

Roach or rudd?

Q: How can roach be recognised from rudd?

A: Colour can be misleading, although as a general rule rudd have a slightly more golden shade to their flanks and deeper red fins than roach. The best means of identification is to look at the lips of the fish – on a rudd the bottom lip protrudes, while on a roach the lips are either level or with the upper one slightly protruding.

The rudd has a protruding bottom lip because it is a surface and mid-water feeder and the lower lip helps it intercept falling particles of food.

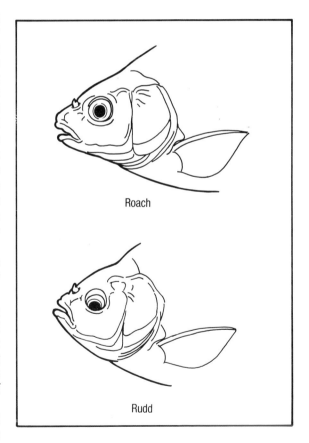

Roach

Rudd

● *A simple method of identifying roach from rudd is by the mouth. On a roach the bottom lip is slightly underslung, while the rudd's protrudes.*

Dace or bleak?

Q: My local river is populated by bleak, dace and chub. Are there any differences in the three species which make them easy to recognise?

A: Small chub are often mistaken for dace but a good, reliable quick check is to look at the anal fin – that's the one underneath the fish's body and

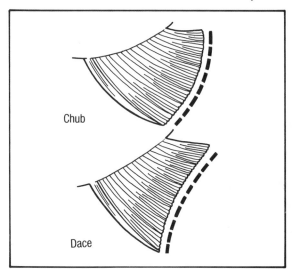

● *The anal fin of the chub is convex, while on the dace it is concave*

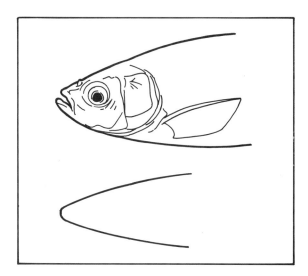

● *The bleak is slimmer than dace or chub and has a more pointed head when viewed from above*

immediately in front of the tail. On a chub it will have a rounded, convex edge while the dace has a concave form.

Bleak are a slimmer shape than chub or dace and the head and jaw is almost pointed when viewed from above. Chub and dace are more blunt at the head. A common give-away with bleak is that their bright silver scales will usually rub off on your hands very easily. Eye colour, too, tends to be a dark blue/green while chub and dace are more a bronze/brown.

Handling fish

Q: Is it a good idea to handle fish with a cloth and are there any British species that have poisonous spines?

A: Handling fish with a cloth is not a good idea, particularly if the cloth is dry. A dry cloth will remove some of the protective slime from the fish, and it will then be more prone to infection or parasitic attack. Hands are best, but just make sure they are wet – in the case of big fish, remove the hook while it is in the landing net but try and handle it as little as possible.

Many anglers worry about fish such as perch causing injury with their spikey dorsal fin (see colour photograph on p. 157). The fin is not poisonous and will not cause injury if it is held correctly, and in fact if you put the palm of your hand across the back of the fish and immediately over the fin, it cannot be erected. If the fin is already erect, you can fold it down quite simply by moving your hand from the head down towards the tail – do this in the opposite direction and you *may* impale yourself on a spine!

None of the freshwater species in Britain are poisonous, but there is a common sea fish called the weaver which has venomous spikes which can inflict serious wounds.

Returning the catch

Q: Sometimes a large fish will appear distressed when first released from a keepnet. What is the best thing to do to ensure the fish comes to no harm?

A: The important thing is that large fish should not be kept in small nets and even in a large one only for the minimum length of time. Always stake your nets out in deep water and never allow fish to slide down the full length of the net as this can damage their scales.

When you return a fish to the water, face it upstream and if possible in a slight flow – this will cause water to pass through the gills and assist its breathing. Support it gently by resting it in an upright position on the palms of your hands. Once it has recovered it will swim off strongly.

Bream and barbel often need some assistance in this manner, and take special care with barbel and carp that are placed in keepnets. Both species have stiff front rays to their dorsal fins and these can become caught in the mesh of your net.

With both large and small fish, it is best if you can hold a keepnet in the water with the opening submerged and allow them to swim out on their own. If you lift the bottom of the net slowly, this will steer them towards the opening.

Take care, too, not to put fish back where they may become trapped in thick blanket weed.

Moving fish

Q: A water I fish is full of small barbel, some of which could do well in another river near to my home. How should they be transported?

A: The short answer is, they shouldn't. It is illegal to move fish between Water Authority areas without a permit, and in any case taking fish away for the purposes of restocking would constitute a theft.

Clubs wishing to purchase fish or move them from one water to another must first seek permission from the Water Authorities concerned. The Authority into whose area the fish are to be delivered will have them inspected at source, and a health certificate will be issued.

Moving fish illegally is a stupid thing to do, and an action that can lead to many problems – it may even wipe out the other fish by exposing them to parasites or infections to which they have no natural resistance. Even fish that appear healthy and normal may be carrying disease dangerous to fish in other waters.

Introducing an alien species may also completely change the water's character. The barbel, for example, which many years ago were stocked into the River Severn by *Angling Times*, have since been blamed for the decline in the river's indigenous stocks of roach and chub.

Fish such as zander and catfish are among other species which have also caused major problems in otherwise prolific fisheries.

Acknowledgements

This book would not have been written but for the help and enthusiasm of Mac Campbell and Graham Gaches. Mac spent long and often cold hours on wet banksides, followed by late nights working in his darkroom, to produce many of the photographs for the pages which follow. A keen and experienced angler himself, Mac was always on hand to offer his own ideas and to lift my flagging spirit when things went wrong. The drawings are the work of Graham Gaches who transformed my rough sketches with great skill. The accuracy with which he draws is the result of natural talent and long experience gained while working as a full-time artist.

My sincere thanks are therefore extended to Mac and Graham, and to the many great anglers who have helped me so much over many years. Their unselfish attitude has made both the sport of angling and my own fishing hours so much the richer.

However, I dedicate this book to my parents, who encouraged my youthful attempts at angling, often at great expense both in time, money and patience. Without their understanding I might never have found what must be the greatest of all sports . . . angling.

ALLAN HAINES
Peterborough

Index

Index